SHAKESPEARE'S COMIC CHANGES

Shakespeare's Comic Changes

♦

The Time-Lapse Metaphor
as Plot Device

ROGER L. COX

The University of Georgia Press ♦ Athens and London

Paperback edition, 2011
© 1991 by the University of Georgia Press
Athens, Georgia 30602
www.ugapress.org
Designed by B. Williams & Associates
Set in Berkeley Old Style Medium by Tseng Information Systems
All rights reserved
Printed digitally in the United States of America

The Library of Congress has cataloged the hardcover edition
of this book as follows:
Library of Congress Cataloging-in-Publication Data
LCCN Permalink: http://lccn.loc.gov/90049014

Cox, Roger L.
    Shakespeare's comic changes : the time-lapse metaphor as plot
device / Roger L. Cox.
      xi, 205 p. ; 25 cm.
  ISBN: 0-8203-1308-4 (alk. paper)
  Includes bibliographical references and index.
  1. Shakespeare, William, 1564-1616—Comedies. 2. Shakespeare, William, 1564-1616—Characters. 3. Shakespeare, William, 1564-1616—Stories, plots, etc. 4. Characters and characteristics in literature. 5. Time in literature. 6. Metaphor. 7. Comedy. I. Title.
PR2981.C68   1991
822.3 20   90-49014

Paperback ISBN-13: 978-0-8203-3847-7
ISBN-10: 0-8203-3847-8

British Library Cataloging-in-Publication Data available

Cover illustration: Engraving by Richard Rhodes of Henry Fuseli's *Titania, Bottom and the Fairies*, 1793–94; courtesy of the British Museum.

To the memory of

my mother and father

The world view of particle physics is that of a world without "stuff," where what is = what happens, and where an unending tumultuous dance of creation, annihilation and transformation runs unabated within a framework of conservation laws and probability.

—Gary Zukav
The Dancing Wu Li Masters

CONTENTS

Acknowledgments   xi

1. Introduction   1

2. Metamorphosis and Other Transformations   16

3. Character-Change as Time-Lapse Metaphor   32

4. Farce and Beyond: Antipholus, Katherine, and Proteus   52

5. Romantic Comedy: Bottom, Shylock, and Oliver   70

6. History as Personal Reformation: Prince Hal, Harry Monmouth, and King Henry V   97

7. Transformation in Problem Comedy and Romance: Bertram, Angelo, and Leontes   122

8. Conclusion   144

Appendix 1. Comic Structure: Mistakes, Misfortunes, and Happy Endings   155

Appendix 2. Comic Character: The Invented Self   170

Notes   185

Index   199

ACKNOWLEDGMENTS

AMONG those who have been helpful to me in completing this book, I especially wish to thank Heyward Brock, Jerry Beasley, and William Frawley, who are my friends and colleagues at the University of Delaware. Knowledgeable in Shakespeare, literary history, and linguistics, they have provided both help and encouragement to me along the way. Nancy Grayson Holmes, editor at the University of Georgia Press, has likewise been very helpful in the final stages of the project.

The two essays reprinted here as appendixes first appeared, with slightly different titles, in the pages of *Thought* and *Soundings*. I am grateful to the editors of those journals for permission to reprint them here, since they represent my earliest attempts to answer some of the more difficult questions in connection with literary comedy, and they led me quite naturally to explore the unique nature of Shakespearean comedy.

SHAKESPEARE'S COMIC CHANGES

ONE

Introduction

◆

Ἐν ἀρχῇ ἦν ἡ μεταφορά.

THE most important question about the Shakespeare comedies, which encompasses many lesser ones about the individual plays, is whether or not they constitute a single group that we may refer to meaningfully as *Shakespearean comedy*. Most commentators think not, and some are quite emphatic in their denial.[1] Since about 1950, when the comedies first became the object of close scrutiny, critics have preferred either to deal with the plays individually or else to divide them into various categories such as festive comedies, romantic comedies, comedies of forgiveness, and romances. But the most successful of these attempts, by C. L. Barber and Robert G. Hunter, do not include more than half a dozen plays, and both critics find it necessary to cross over generic lines established either by the First Folio (*Henry IV* and *Cymbeline*) or by modern editions (*The Winter's Tale* and *The Tempest*) to connect those six.[2] Moreover, though Barber and Hunter each deal at length with six of the plays, no one play figures in both groups.

If it is true, as Hunter suggests in connection with his own grouping of the comedies of forgiveness, that "consideration of them as a group ought to illuminate each of them as a single work of art," then the same should be true of the Shakespeare comedies as a whole, including some plays of the other genres that resemble the comedies most strongly.[3] The difficulty comes of course in trying to specify a single device or characteristic that distinguishes all of those works not only from the other Shakespeare plays but from most other comedy as well. Alfred Harbage suggests that "if there is a unifying principle, it is a simple one. The plays *do* end happily, and in so doing seem to mark out a route to happiness."[4] And Kenneth Muir finds nothing in common among the comedies except the use of disguise.[5] Neither of these suggestions is very helpful, however, since nearly all comedies end happily; and disguise not only figures importantly in other kinds of comedy, it is also sometimes crucial in Shakespearean tragedy. *King Lear* is not less tragic because Kent and Edgar operate from behind disguises through much of the play.

But might there not be a connection, a family resemblance, among these plays other than a single, invariable device or characteristic? Ludwig Wittgenstein defines and elaborates the idea of family resemblance in relation to his concepts of numbers and games in a way that bears upon this question:

> We see a complicated network of similarities overlapping and criss-crossing: sometimes overall similarities, sometimes similarities of detail....
>
> I can think of no better expression to characterize these similarities than "family resemblances"; for the various resemblances between members of a family: build, features, colour of eyes, gait, temperament, etc. etc. overlap and criss-cross in the same way....
>
> And we extend our concept of number as in spinning a thread we twist fibre on fibre. And the strength of the thread does not reside in the fact that some one fibre runs through its whole length, but in the overlapping of many fibres.[6]

There is, I would argue, such a family resemblance among the Shakespeare comedies. The fiber that appears most frequently in the connecting thread is some form of the transformation comic plot, in which one or more of the characters change significantly, either willingly or upon compulsion, through education or through magic, effortlessly or with many "inward pinches"; and the happy ending comes about as a result of these changes. Disguise, or even simply a change of costume, sometimes signals a more important inward transformation; and this inward transformation is crucial to the outcome of the play.

There was of course ample precedent, both in folklore and in literature, for using the transformation plot—one thinks, for instance, of fairy tales, of Ovid's *Metamorphoses*, and of much medieval English literature. But Shakespeare's implementation of it in the drama is remarkable because his doing so involves the direct violation of an important classical rule. In the *Poetics*

Aristotle lists as the fourth requirement in connection with dramatic character that it be "consistent and the same throughout."[7] Likewise, Horace insists in the *Ars poetica* (first translated by Thomas Drant in 1567) that the dramatist should not represent a character as changing significantly within the course of a play. Here is the passage in Ben Jonson's translation:

> If something fresh, that never yet was had,
> Unto the Stage thou bringst, and dar'st create
> A meer new person, look he keep his state
> Unto the last, as when he first went forth,
> Still to be like himselfe, and hold his worth.[8]

A more modern version renders the last two lines as follows:

> Then see that to the very last it show
> Such as it was at first, consistent ever.[9]

According to Marvin Herrick, Aristotelian and Horatian criticism had become fused by the middle of the sixteenth century; and "this insistence upon self-consistency in tragic and comic characters, which had the authority of both Horace and Aristotle, led to highly conventionalized characterizations in both tragedy and comedy and is one of the distinguishing features of most neoclassical drama."[10]

Shakespeare refers to Aristotle only twice in all of his works, and the first of these references—by Tranio, in *The Taming of the Shrew*—might be taken within the context of Shakespeare's first transformation plot as an indication that the playwright was well aware of this particular restriction or prohibition:

> Let's be no stoics nor no stocks, I pray,
> Or so devote to Aristotle's checks
> As Ovid be an outcast quite abjured.[11]

Much later in the play Ovid is referred to or quoted as the author of the *Heroides* (III.i.28–29) and the *Ars amatoria* (IV.ii.8), but the Ovidian references that surround Tranio's statement here point to the *Metamorphoses*—Jupiter and Europa in this scene, and Venus and Adonis, Io, and Daphne in the one before (Induction ii). If, as seems likely, the reference in Tranio's speech is to Ovid as the author of change-stories, then the particular example of "Aristotle's checks" that has the greatest relevance is the requirement, reiterated by Horace in the *Ars poetica*—and perhaps pointed out to Shakespeare by Ben Jonson—that a character must not be allowed to change significantly in the course of a play. Even the title *The Taming of the Shrew* promises that the play will violate this Aristotelian rule, since the shrew can hardly be "tamed" if she remains "consistent and the same throughout."

According to the standard interpretation of this speech of Tranio's, it refers to the antithesis "between serious study, as typified by Aristotle, and preoccupation with lighter entertainment, as typified by Ovid."[12] The most obvious objection to the adequacy of this interpretation is that it requires a considerable leap of the imagination to equate the word *checks* with "serious study." Such an objection has long since been recognized as legitimate. According to Halliwell (1856), "it was Blackstone who first proposed to alter *checks* to *ethics*, a reading adopted by several modern editors, although it is clear that no such word can suit the metre."[13] The standard interpretation would of course be easier to defend as being entirely adequate if the text read *ethics* instead of *checks*; but unfortunately there seems to be no plausible reason for thinking that the word *checkes* (as it is spelled in the First Folio) involves any sort of mistake. The word *works* would fit the meter and would make clear that the entire reference was to Aristotle's writings in general; but the poet seems to have preferred the word *checks*.

My purpose is not to argue that the traditional interpretation should be rejected. As usual in Shakespeare, the meaning appears not to be univocal. My point is rather that such an interpretation by itself is not wholly adequate. The rest of the passage, which includes the words *sweet philosophy, logic, rhetoric, poesy,* and *metaphysics,* suggests that part of the reference is indeed to Aristotle's works in general; but the word *checks* (meaning "restraints, reproofs, rebukes") points in the direction of a specific contradiction between Aristotle and Ovid. The word itself suggests that there are certain practices to which Aristotle specifically objects but which are themselves a source of Ovid's charm. Critics sometimes prefer to emend the text, however, or to say, as does the Craig-Bevington edition, that such an emendation "has much to recommend it," rather than to admit the possibility that the "inappropriate" word may point to another level of meaning that would repay careful exploration.

The traditional interpretation of this passage is also open to at least one other objection. It apparently assumes that because the interpreter himself holds these two great classical authors in equally high regard, the playwright (Shakespeare)—though clearly not the speaker (Tranio)—does so too. Like "L'Allegro" and "Il Penseroso," the poet (Ovid) and the philosopher (Aristotle) represent, according to this view, strongly contrasting but perhaps equally attractive alternatives. Unfortunately, however, internal evidence for this assumption is entirely lacking. On the one hand, the Shakespeare plays simply teem with references to Ovid: the *Metamorphoses* is the only book ever brought onstage in any of the plays, where it is identified by a child who says, "My mother gave it me" (*Titus Andronicus* IV.i.43); and as late as *The Tempest,* whole lines are taken over, with very little change, from Golding's translation of the *Metamorphoses* (Prospero's speech, beginning V.i.33; cf. Golding 7.265ff.). On the other hand, Shakespeare refers to Aristotle only one other time in all of his plays, and that reference involves an anachronism of at least seven hundred years, and the substitution of "moral" for "political" philosophy, a mistake explained now by reference to contemporary translations of the passage thus awkwardly referred to (in *Troilus and Cressida* II.ii.166–67). In short, Ovid was a poet that Shakespeare apparently cherished from the time he was a child and from whom, according to one classicist, he learned 90 percent of all the mythology he knew, while Aristotle remained for him a forbidding figure ("Aristotle's checks") that he seems hardly to have known at all, except by name and reputation.[14] On the evidence of the plays themselves, one could argue that Tranio's juxtaposition of Ovid and Aristotle represents the contrast, not between "entertaining diversion" and "serious study," but between favorite poet and carping critic, though the latter is treated with all the respect and deference due to the man widely regarded as "the master of those who know."

As far as the Aristotelian-Horatian stricture about character-change is concerned, it by no means forbids what we usually refer to as character development. It merely applies to characterization what Aristotle says repeatedly about plot—that its development should conform to "what is possible as being probable or necessary."[15] It is surely both probable and necessary that human character, as represented in drama, should develop and mature in response to serious challenge. But that a character should supposedly go from one extreme to the other—from shrew to ideal wife (Kate), from shiftless youngster to chivalrous conqueror (Prince Hal), from murderous tyrant to fatherly recluse (Duke Frederick)—and always within the limits of a two- or three-hour play, is just as surely "impossible as being improbable and unnecessary," at least from a classical point of view. This fact of life and art provides the basis for Molière's farce *Le Bourgeois Gentilhomme.* It is patently absurd that a flat-footed bourgeois, however prosperous and successful, should undertake to make himself into a gentleman. He becomes instead, as Molière's audience could no doubt foresee, the butt of merciless satire and the object of ridicule. One of Shakespeare's special talents is his ability to dramatize character-changes that are grossly improbable but that nevertheless point the way for his audience, not toward an attitude of mockery and derision, but toward reconciliation and happiness.

We should observe too that the transformations associated with Shakespearean comic plots are not at all the same as the "recognition" (*anagnorisis*) and "reversal" (*peripeteia*) that Aristotle associated with tragic plots.¹⁶ Aristotelian recognition and reversal take place within the limits of a plot that conforms, as I have already indicated, to what is "probable and necessary." That is, they occur within a rational and realistic framework. Shakespearean comic transformations, on the other hand, are grossly irrational and unrealistic. They stand in relation to normally developing tragic characters as metaphor stands in relation to literal statement; they involve, not a gradual progression from one level of awareness to another, but a startling juxtaposition of radically different perspectives, a "leap" from one way of coping with the problems of human existence to another, nearly opposite way—such a leap as would lay the dramatic character open to the charge of inconsistency from an Aristotelian point of view.

A tragic character such as Hamlet may indeed lend itself to Aristotelian analysis. Once Hamlet recognizes that "the readiness is all," he is willing for the first time to "defy augury." At that point he reverses his judgment as to the appropriate way of dealing with his adversaries and goes to meet them on *their* terms rather than his own. As a result, he at last succeeds in removing what is "rotten in the state of Denmark," though he does so at enormous cost to himself and others. When Claudius uses the word *transformation* with reference to Hamlet earlier in the play, his speech is heavily charged with irony. Speaking to Rosencrantz and Guildenstern, he urges them to ingratiate themselves with the prince and to find out whatever they can about his state of mind:

> Something have you heard
> Of Hamlet's transformation—so call it,
> Sith nor th'exterior nor the inward man
> Resembles that it was. What it should be,
> More than his father's death, that thus hath put him
> So much from th'understanding of himself,
> I cannot dream of.
>
> (*Ham.* II.ii.4–10)

Such concern for his new stepson no doubt seems touching to Hamlet's old school friends, who of course do not realize that Claudius is simply trying to find out how much Hamlet knows or suspects about his father's murder. By using the word *transformation,* Claudius conveys the impression that he finds Hamlet's behavior utterly baffling and that he wants to do everything possible to relieve the young man's distress. That is to say, he uses the word *transformation* as a red herring, a means of getting people to think that he has not the slightest idea as to what may have wrought such an inexplicable change in the prince's attitude and disposition.

At any rate, neither what Claudius refers to as Hamlet's transformation nor what Aristotle classifies as recognition and reversal has much in common with Kate's "taming" or Bottom's "translation." Hamlet's sudden change of demeanor is perfectly understandable as the result of his discovery that his uncle, who is now king, has murdered his father and persuaded his mother to accept him as husband. Consequently, it makes sense to say of Hamlet, as of an actual person, that he is genuinely disturbed and depressed. It makes very little sense on the other hand to insist that Kate is (or is not) "really" changed or that Bottom is "in fact" metamorphosed or translated. And by the same token, it is obviously inappropriate to regard Kate's taming or Bottom's translation as instances of recognition and reversal. Shakespeare's two-faceted comic characters, like his two-faceted words, politely decline to be reduced to singleness or to be understood as progressing from one facet to another in some sort of orderly, rational fashion. Try as we may, we will have only limited success in coming to terms with Shakespearean comic plot and character if we insist upon regarding metaphoric juxtaposition as realistic progression. Kate the shrew and Kate the ideal wife, Bottom the actor and Bottom the ass-headed lover of Titania, Prince Hal and Henry V all involve—as does the metaphysical conceit—a yoking of opposites. Some wrenching is required, of course, to get both of these opposites into the same yoke, just as with puns, and just as with metaphysical conceits.

Thus by 1593, the date usually assigned to *The Taming of the Shrew*, Shakespeare had hit upon what was to become his favorite method for resolving comic conflict—transforming one or more of the principal characters. He uses this device over and over in plays that are otherwise radically different from each other, in *The Two Gentlemen of Verona, A Midsummer Night's Dream, The Merchant of Venice, Henry IV* (Parts 1 and 2), *As You Like It, Much Ado About Nothing, The Merry Wives of Windsor, All's Well That Ends Well, Measure for Measure, Cymbeline, The Winter's Tale,* and *The Tempest*. And if we include such plays as *King John* (Philip Faulconbridge) and *Henry V* (Henry himself), in which certain aspects of history are represented as comedy, then we may say that the transformation plot figures importantly in nearly half the Shakespeare plays, most of the rest being tragedies or else histories in the tragic mode. Only three of the comedies do not depend importantly upon transformation either to generate or to resolve their plots: *The Comedy of Errors*, generally thought to be the first of the comedies; *Love's Labor's Lost*, long regarded as the first of *all* the Shakespeare plays; and *Twelfth Night*, which depends, like *The Comedy of Errors*, upon twins and then upon the substitution of one twin for the other (Sebastian, Viola) to bring everything round right.[17]

These three nontransformational comedies are constructed on a different, though related, principle—that of doubling or even tripling. We see this principle at work in the transformational comedies too, but not to the same extent. As Puck observes when he says, "Two of both kinds makes up four" (*MND* III.ii.438), there are twice as many lovers in the main plot of *A Midsummer Night's Dream* as in the Pyramus and Thisbe subplot. But the complications and outcome of that plot depend primarily upon transformation. In *The Comedy of Errors,* however, the Plautine plot already involves one set of identical twins; and when Shakespeare adds another pair of such twins, he in effect "squares" the consequent confusion rather than simply doubling it. *Twelfth Night,* a far more sophisticated version of the twin-plot conception, involves a triangular love relationship (Viola-Orsino-Olivia), and no transformation even of the sort represented in Ovid's story of Iphis and Ianthe would accommodate the three lovers in any orthodox fashion. Therefore, Sebastian must be brought in, rather like a fourth player at bridge.[18]

Love's Labor's Lost is built upon threes rather than twos. The alliterative three-word title is appropriate for a play in which three young men (Berowne, Dumaine, Longaville) undertake to live for three years, sleeping only three hours a night, without the company of (three) young women. The concordance indicates that the word *three* occurs in this play more frequently than the words *mad* and *madness* do in *Hamlet.* The text literally teems with "three-piled hyperboles" (*LLL* V.ii.408), declarations of "threefold love" (V.ii.815), and references such as the one to "Cerberus, that three-headed canus" (V.ii.582). And just as the playwright squares the number of twins in *The Comedy of Errors,* he does likewise with a set of three in *Love's Labor's Lost,* though Costard is doubtful about the arithmetic:

> *Costard* O Lord, sir, they would know
>   Whether the three Worthies shall come in or no.
> *Berowne* What, are there but three?
> *Costard*   No, sir; but it is vara fine,
>   For every one pursents three.
> *Berowne*   And three times thrice is nine.
> *Costard* Not so, sir, under correction, sir, I hope, it is not so.
>   You cannot beg us, sir, I can assure you, sir; we know what we know:
>   I hope, sir, three times thrice, sir—
> *Berowne*   Is not nine?
> *Costard* Under correction, sir, we know whereuntil it doth amount.

Berowne   By Jove, I always took three threes for nine.
Costard   O Lord, sir, it were pity you should get your living by reck'ning, sir.

(*LLL* V.ii.486–97)

Finally of course all weddings are postponed for a year and a day, except that Armado declares that he has "vowed to Jaquenetta to hold the plough for her sweet love *three* year" (V.ii.873–74). The notes in most editions of this elegant and festive comedy inform us that *hold the plough* means "toil at husbandry" (*Pelican*) or "become a farmer" (*Riverside*), but neither editor seems to notice the similarity to Agrippa's remark about Cleopatra: "She made great Caesar lay his sword to bed; / He ploughed her, and she cropped" (*Ant.* II.ii.228–29). That is, she gave birth to Caesarion.

In short, all but three of the Shakespeare comedies either generate or resolve their plots by means of transformation; and those three are built instead upon doubling and tripling, upon the exploitation of similitude and/or arithmetic progression. And Shakespeare's interest in the transformation comic plot arises, I would argue, neither from his admiration for Ovid nor from any desire on his part to fly in the face of classical dramatic tradition. It is rather, I think, a by-product of his fascination with metaphor and with language itself. Character transformation is to human personality as the pun is to word meaning; and character-change requires the context of plot just as a pun requires the context of a sentence. Various mutually exclusive meanings are of course latent within a word even when it stands in isolation, but they do not call attention to themselves until they collide within the framework of a sentence. And metaphors, like puns, involve collisions and incongruities. As C. L. Barber suggests, "The action of metaphor is itself a process of transposing, a kind of metamorphosis."[19] When the metaphor is effective, the transposition does indeed produce a kind of metamorphosis—if not in the thing itself, then certainly in our way of regarding it.

Besides what he says about "family resemblances," Wittgenstein also provides insight into the function of metaphor in his *Philosophical Investigations*.[20] He discusses the psychological implications of "noticing an aspect" and of seeing something as something else ("seeing-as"). He uses the ambiguous duck-rabbit figure, borrowed from the psychologist Joseph Jastrow, to illustrate the process—part perception and part thought—by which we apprehend and interpret our environment. Marcus B. Hester and Virgil C. Aldrich have elaborated the significance of these observations for the analysis of metaphor.[21] Though I do not completely accept their interpretations, I agree that metaphor invites us to "notice an aspect" that we might otherwise miss and to see something as something different from what we would ordinarily take it to be. Wittgenstein represents very well the psychological process upon which the transformation comic plot depends when he puts these words into the mouth of a supposed interlocutor: "Imagine this changed like this, and you have this other thing."[22] Within the context of such a plot, the first "this" in Wittgenstein's sentence ("Imagine this") corresponds to the character as it appears in the early part of the play (*protasis*), the second ("changed like this") in the middle or transitional part (*epitasis*), the third ("this other thing") in the final part (*catastrophe*). In the early plays, other than *The Taming of the Shrew,* the pattern is not nearly so neat as this analysis would suggest, sometimes because the pattern is deliberately modified or embellished. In *The Two Gentlemen of Verona,* for instance, Proteus—in keeping with his name—changes not once but several times. Hence the suddenness of his last change, which some would attribute to Shakespeare's lack of skill at that point in his career or to his impatience with intractable story material.

In the transformation or "double-aspect" plot, heavily charged as it is with puns and metaphors, character-change functions as a special type of metaphor. For purposes of analysis I would propose the term *time-lapse metaphor.* By its very nature, successful characterization invites the audience to see a dramatic character *as* someone or something. (Hence the usefulness of stock characters, since they enable us to identify certain characters quickly as the clever servant, the raisonneur, or the pantaloon.) What the dramatist does in the transformation plot is to present the character first under one guise and then later, in violation of the classical rule, under another, quite different guise. Critics have tended to assume, at least in the early Shakespeare comedies, that one of these guises represented the "real" character and that the other was merely a *dis*guise: Katherine does not change "one tittle." "There is no real reformation" in Prince Hal. "Shylock is wrongfully compelled to forsake his religion."[23] That is to say, in *The Taming of the Shrew* and *The Merchant of Venice* we are told that the main character's first guise is authentic and the second one is spurious; and in *Henry IV* the situation is supposedly reversed—"The prince always knows what is right and prefers it; only appearances are against him."[24] But this procedure corresponds to explicating a pun by declaring one of its meanings to be irrelevant—by denying, quite simply, that it *is* a pun. To dislike Shakespeare's puns, as Dr. Johnson and Leo Tolstoy certainly did, is one thing; failure even to recognize them as puns would be quite another. And yet that is exactly what we do with the early double-faceted characterizations. Only in the later plays, when Shakespeare had fully mastered the time-lapse metaphor ("Those are pearls that were his eyes"), do critics willingly apply the terms *transformation, repentance,* and *conversion* to what happens in the play.

I have argued elsewhere that comedy becomes more "serious" when farcical structure is made to serve as the vehicle for more and more important subject matter, just as the game of poker becomes more and more serious when the stakes are raised from pennies (farce), to dollars (romantic comedy), to no-limit betting (romance), even though the rules of the game remain the same at each level. No-limit poker is every bit as serious as championship chess, but we should not mistake one game for the other simply because the players are equally serious. I have also argued that comic characterization involves the conflict between a "factual self," which any person shares with the rest of humanity, and an "invented self," which that same person creates in order to make a more favorable impression on other people (see appendixes). The argument traced in these chapters endeavors to elaborate and combine those two elements and to account for the manner in which time enters significantly into Shakespearean comic structure and characterization.

Like J. Alfred Prufrock, characters that are the center of interest in the Shakespeare comedies might (if they were sufficiently self-conscious to do so) take comfort in the fact that "There will be time, there will be time / To prepare [another] face to meet the faces that you meet." Most traditional comic characters work hard to keep *one* "prepared face" from slipping or disintegrating and revealing the unacceptable factual self underneath to the rest of the world; and most such characters finally end up losing the struggle and having to "face the music" in the form of "poetic justice." Shakespeare's transformational comedies, on the other hand, dramatize the process by means of which a comic character reluctantly exchanges one mask (or "invented self") for another. The first mask produces only alienation from society, but the second one enables the character to reenter society and presumably to live "happily ever after." Since both of these masks (or selves) are invented, it makes little sense to call one of them "real" and the other a disguise. It is exactly as if two characters onstage, identifiable only by their masks—one a braggart soldier and the other a clever servant—should exchange masks at some point. It would obviously be silly for us to argue at length as to which was the "real" clever servant and which the "real" braggart soldier.

This tendency to regard one guise as the "real" character and the other as a *dis*guise is common to playgoer and reader alike. Most of us operate on the assumption that "appearances change, but reality does not," and the disguise hypothesis enables us to reconcile the change-plot with that assumption. Nevertheless, when people discuss Shakespeare's transformation plots, someone usually asks, "Does the character *really* change?" Students sometimes ask the question in good faith in an effort to get information that will help in understanding the play. But just as often someone will pose the question in rhetorical fashion in order to point out that of course we would be foolish, in the face of Shakespearean irony, to suppose anything of the sort: "Ah! But does the character really *change?*" Either way, the question must be dealt with seriously since in the first case the person who asks supposes that the question is meaningful and relevant, and in the second case the person obviously regards the question, with its implied negative answer, as the clincher of his or her argument. In any event, we can hardly avoid the question because it appears to be so simple and straightforward, and because the legitimacy of the play's ending would seem to depend upon the answer.

It is of course absurd to suppose that an imaginary character "really" does anything. For this reason the implied answer to the rhetorical version of the question is indeed no; but the question and its answer only appear to clear up the problem of character-change because they involve unconscious equivocation. Simply because a nonexistent character cannot, by definition, be regarded as changing within the framework of ordinary human experience, it does not follow that we should regard such a character as incapable of change (or inversion) within the framework of a play. No one supposes that imaginary characters actually eat or drink; but if the playwright represents them as doing so within a play, we should have no difficulty accepting the representation. The glutton, after all, is a stock character out of New Comedy, and most of us are inclined to think that someone who sees or reads such a play and then asks, "Ah! But does this supposed glutton *really eat?*" has somehow missed the point. When we look at the question carefully, we see that it throws no light whatever on the play; it merely reveals a fundamental confusion on the part of the questioner.

If the word *really* is misleading in dealing with the transformation comic plot, so too is the implied "either/or" structure of the question. In this respect it is akin to Miranda's questions in the first act of *The Tempest*:

> What foul play had we that we came from thence?
> Or blessèd was't we did?
>
> (I.ii.60–61)

But Prospero's response quickly sets matters straight:

> Both, both, my girl!
> By foul play, as thou say'st, were we heaved thence,
> But blessedly holp hither.
>
> (I.ii.61–63)

In transformation plots, the characters in question *both* retain their identity *and* change significantly. The emphasis is equally upon continuity, the retention of certain characteristic elements, and upon change, the emergence of new and significantly different ones.

An analogy from physics may help to clarify the point. Anyone who has played with a clear prism knows that when a beam of white light passes through it, the white light is refracted into the various colors of the spectrum and the direction of the beam is changed. The questions one might ask about the beam of light are similar to those raised by character-change in the transformation plot. Is the light that emerges from the far side of the prism the same light that enters the near side? Yes—if the light is blocked at its source, the beam disappears on both sides of the prism; they must then be the same light. Is the light significantly changed when it passes through the prism? Yes—in both color and direction. In short, the answer to both questions is yes. It is the same light that enters the prism and that exits from it, but it is significantly changed as a result of passing through the prism. In one sense, the two are identical; in another sense they are radically different. And neither of the two statements cancels out or even conflicts with the other. The mistake we often make in commenting upon characterization within a transformation plot is in supposing that the two observations are in the relationship of contradictories. When we detect that a dramatic character is in some ways the same at the end of the play as at the beginning, we conclude (deductively, it would seem) that the character is not significantly changed, that there is no "real" transformation. But such a conclusion is simply a non sequitur; the plot is analogous to a prism, and the character to a beam of light that passes through it.

Such a plot modifies traditional comic form in a very important way. The happy ending of comedy has been associated almost from the beginning with some conception of moral appropriateness; the double plot, with "an opposite issue for the good and the bad personages," says Aristotle in the *Poetics*, "belongs rather to Comedy" than to tragedy.[25] But poetic justice is consistent with a happy ending only if the antisocial behavior of the "bad personages" is not so villainous as to require death as the appropriate penalty and if the offending person is not one with whom the audience, for reasons other than the offense itself, has good reason to empathize. Thus, any traditional comedy that deals with important social issues and that reflects an awareness that even the best people may sometimes be guilty of gross offenses against their fellow human beings must either sacrifice the happy ending, in which case it probably ceases to be a comedy, or else the playwright must abandon the idea of strict moral appropriateness. By implementing the transformation comic plot, by enabling "bad personages" to change into "good" ones, Shakespeare makes it possible to deal in comedy with some of the most important social problems and to involve his protagonists meaningfully with those problems not only as victims but also as offenders. But he can do so only by substituting wish fulfillment for moral appropriateness as the key to the happy ending.[26]

This substitution accounts in large measure for the mellowness and warmth of Shakespearean comedy as compared with the plays of Jonson and Molière, the meaning and structure of which depend upon a moral and satiric point of view. Malvolio, whose exit line "I'll be revenged on the whole pack of you!" strikes us as harsh and ridiculous, is perhaps unique among Shakespearean comic figures; and it is significant that he appears in *Twelfth Night,* the only one of the mature Shakespeare comedies that makes no use of the transformation plot. In *As You Like It,* on the other hand, Jaques certainly thinks in terms of "merit" and "deserving"; but even he confesses in his final lines that "Out of these convertites / There is much matter to be heard and learned" (V.iv.178–79). And in *The Tempest* Caliban, who is surely a less winsome character than either Malvolio or Jaques, takes his leave promising to "be wise hereafter, / And seek for grace" (V.i.295–96). It may be true, as Northrop Frye suggests in "The Argument of Comedy," that "comedy is designed not to condemn evil, but to ridicule a lack of self-knowledge."[27] It would perhaps be more accurate, however, to say that satire is designed to condemn evils, traditional comedy to ridicule a lack of self-knowledge, and Shakespearean comedy to represent the process by which self-knowledge is actually achieved—if and when it can be achieved without irreparable loss, with "not so much perdition as an hair." The manipulator figure, so characteristic of Shakespearean comedy, is of course necessary to prevent such loss in serious comedy unless the author intervenes with some sort of deus ex machina, as Molière does at the end of *Tartuffe.*

The satirist, who condemns evils, or the writer of traditional comedy, who ridicules a lack of self-knowledge, consciously or unconsciously assumes a posture of moral superiority; and the laughter engendered is essentially Hobbesian, the expression of at least mild derision and contempt. Except in the three comedies that make no use of the transformation plot, such laughter is inconsistent with the overall tone of Shakespearean comedy; and when it is forthcoming, it is soon undercut by one of the other characters in the play, as when Duke Senior chides Jaques:

> Most mischievous foul sin, in chiding sin.
> For thou thyself hast been a libertine,
> As sensual as the brutish sting itself.
>
> (*AYL* II.vii.64–66)

One may say that whenever a moralizing statement by one of the characters in a Shakespearean comedy seems to be consistent with the meaning of the play as a whole, the function of such a statement is to point out the folly of moralizing, to expose the hypocrisy implicit in judging our fellow humans harshly, and to show that in ridiculing we become ridiculous. In a sense, all of Shakespearean comedy moves in the direction of *The Tempest* and culminates in Prospero's final words, addressed directly to the audience: "As you from crimes would pardoned be, / Let your indulgence set me free" (Epilogue 19–20). Such an attitude both springs from self-knowledge on the part of the writer and encourages self-knowledge in the hearer or reader; and the transformation plot is a nearly perfect vehicle for its dramatic implementation.

Northrop Frye concludes "The Argument of Comedy" by saying that "for Shakespeare, the subject matter of poetry is not life, or nature, or reality, or revelation, or anything else that the philosopher builds on, but poetry itself, a verbal universe." This is why the transformation comic plot is best understood as time-lapse metaphor. It is also true, however, that language and poetry, unlike music, refer explicitly to human experience; and the language of comedy returns over and over again, as Socrates suggests in Plato's *Philebus*, to self-knowledge or the lack of it.[28] With the possible exception of Terence's play *The Brothers*, traditional comedy represents the human personality as being essentially static in this respect. It remained for Shakespeare to trace, in comic drama, the process by which most people actually achieve some degree of self-knowledge. And he represents it not simply as realistic progression, nor as recognition and reversal, but as sudden and improbable transformation.[29]

TWO

Metamorphosis and Other Transformations

◆

> In nova fert animus mutatas dicere formas
> corpora: di, coeptis (nam vos mutastis et illas)
> adspirate meis primaque ab origine mundi
> ad mea perpetuum deducite tempora carmen.

SHAKESPEAREAN comic plots reflect an interest in three principal types of change: Ovidian metamorphosis, moral and intellectual growth, and religious awakening. Because it is largely external, Ovidian metamorphosis appeals primarily to the imagination rather than to the intellect, and it provides a nearly inexhaustible supply of poetic image and story. Moral and intellectual growth on the part of individual comic characters reflects Shakespeare's concern with the substance of comedy, which has to do with self-knowledge or the lack of it; and Shakespeare is nearly unique among comic dramatists in representing what happens when a comic character actually achieves some degree of self-knowledge. The transformation takes on a religious aspect, however, when self-examination leads to repentance, which then evokes forgiveness on the part of others; and the frame of reference shifts from moral and legal judgment to gracious acceptance and a new beginning. This emphasis upon character-change is entirely consistent with a similar emphasis in language and diction—both involve the exploitation of multiple possibilities, of word meanings in the one case and of human personality traits in the other. The overall result of this combination is a kind of comedy which is remarkably humane and mellow as compared with traditional comedy, largely because the latter relies heavily upon consistent characterization, unambiguous diction, and morally appropriate endings.

The three types of change correspond approximately to the three main stages in the development of Shakespearean comedy—farce, romantic comedy, and romance. The Ovidian element is most prominent in the farcical plays: references to Ovid abound in *The Taming of the Shrew*; almost the whole fifth act of *A Midsummer Night's Dream* is given over to a hilarious version of "Pyramus and Thisbe"; and *The Merry Wives of Windsor* culminates in a parody of the Actaeon story. Young men initially lacking in self-knowledge but eventually "educated" by their female counterparts emerge as untraditional heroes in the romantic comedies—Orlando in *As You Like It*, Claudio in *Much Ado About Nothing*, and Bertram in *All's Well That Ends Well*. The religious element, prefigured in *The Merchant of Venice*, comes to prominence in *Measure for Measure*, *The Winter's Tale*, and *The Tempest*. There is of course considerable overlapping. The religious aspect begins to appear as early as *The Two Gentlemen of Verona*, and the Ovidian influence is still clearly evident in *The Tempest*. Likewise, *A Midsummer Night's Dream* is well on its way to being a romantic comedy, while *Much Ado*, *All's Well*, and *Measure for Measure* can justifiably be grouped with *The Winter's Tale* and *The Tempest* as comedies of forgiveness. Nevertheless, the three main stages of development in Shakespearean comedy are reasonably clear; so too, I think, are the types of transformation associated with those three kinds of comedy.

Most simply defined, a literary metamorphosis is the story of a "magical or miraculous transformation into a new shape."[1] In Dryden's translation, the first line of Ovid's *Metamorphoses* reflects part of this definition: "Of bodies chang'd to various forms, I sing." The next two lines, containing the conventional invocation, account for the magical or miraculous element by attributing these changes to the gods themselves: "Ye Gods, from whom these miracles did spring, / Inspire my numbers with coelestial heat."[2] As we read further in Ovid, we discover that the changes he describes are not strictly limited to those of form or shape but include changes of color, of sex, and of other things as well. Indeed, what is probably one of the oldest surviving examples of metamorphosis (in the *Iliad* 2.308 ff.) represents the transformation of a living snake into stone, presumably without any change in shape. This particular snake, under the watchful eyes of the Greeks, had devoured eight baby sparrows and their mother:

> After he had eaten the sparrow herself with her children
> the god who had shown the snake forth made him a monument,
> striking him stone, the son of devious-devising Kronos,
> and we standing about marvelled at the thing that had been done.[3]

The prophet Kalchas then interprets the event allegorically, saying that the nine sparrows correspond to the nine years that the Greeks have fought against the Trojans, "and in the tenth year we shall take the city of the wide ways."

Two characteristics of Ovidian metamorphosis are thus referred to in the definition itself: the change is purely external, and it involves the supernatural. A third characteristic, which some critics have been reluctant to recognize, is no less significant than the others: the change-story is often either explicitly sexual or else has strongly erotic overtones. Probably the oldest subject for transformation stories is the one that Ovid treats first, the creation of the world out of chaos; and even so chaste a writer as John Milton does not suppress the sexual overtones of that archetypal transformation when he invokes the aid of the Holy Spirit:

> And chiefly Thou O Spirit, that dost prefer
> Before all Temples th' upright heart and pure,
> Instruct me, for Thou know'st; Thou from the first
> Wast present, and with mighty wings outspread
> Dove-like satst brooding on the vast Abyss
> And mad'st it pregnant.[4]

It may be that sexual reproduction provides the most realistic analogy for the "miraculous" element in transformation stories, or perhaps sexual union best represents the coming together of opposites into a single entity. At any rate, transformation stories often refer to sex—directly, as when Iphis is changed from a girl into a boy in order to marry Ianthe, or indirectly, as when the mulberry is changed from white to red as a result of Pyramus's bloody suicide when he thinks that a lion has killed his beloved Thisbe. In a good many of Ovid's stories, the transformation has the specific function of providing the means for gods to achieve their amorous purposes with small risk of discovery, as with Jupiter and Io; of making sexual union impossible, as when Syrinx is delivered from the embraces of Pan by being changed into reeds; or even, in certain cases, of making such union possible and practical, as when Tiresias is changed from a male into a female and then, seven years later, back into a male in order to qualify him to settle the argument between Jupiter and Juno as to which sex derives the greater pleasure from love. As far as Shakespeare is concerned, the erotic nature of these stories is apparently part of what makes them appealing; Gilbert Highet puts the matter simply and accurately when he says that "most of the *Metamorphoses* is concerned with sex and the supernatural, both of which interested Shakespeare."[5]

To say that Ovidian change is largely external is not to deny the significance of the change-stories. It is, on the contrary, an attempt to specify part of their meaning. Quite often the point of the story is that whatever outward change a particular character may undergo, his or her essential character is unaffected. Indeed, the newly acquired form or appearance sometimes represents that underlying temperament more clearly and accurately than the original appearance had done. Midas, having demonstrated that he was a fool and an ass first by requesting the golden touch and then by preferring Pan's music to Apollo's, is rewarded by having his own ears changed into ass's ears; and he is at pains to conceal them under a turban for the rest of his life. As G. Karl Galinsky observes in *Ovid's "Metamorphoses": An Introduction to the Basic Aspects,* Ovidian transformations "often are not capricious but turn out to be very meaningful because they set in relief the true and lasting character of the persons involved. The physical characteristics of the personages are subject to change, but their quintessential substance lives on."[6] The laurel tree into which Daphne is transformed is no more willing to receive Apollo's kisses than the human Daphne had been:

> The tree still panted in th' unfinish'd part:
> Not wholly vegetive, and heav'd her heart.
> He fixt his lips upon the trembling rind;
> It swerv'd aside, and his embrace declin'd.[7]

Galinsky traces this feature of the *Metamorphoses* to the philosophy of Posidonius, to that of the Pythagoreans, and ultimately to Heraclitus, who asserted that "man's character was his fate."[8]

Within the context of Ovidian metamorphosis one may claim, as critics often do of characters in the early and middle Shakespeare comedies, that Daphne is not "one whit" changed from what she had originally been; but it seems an odd thing to say under the circumstances. The only identifiable "character" that Daphne has in Ovid's story is expressed in her determination to resist the advances of Apollo, and this resistance is no less apparent in the tree than in the girl. But to insist upon this continuity without a corresponding emphasis upon the utterly changed appearance leaves the reader in serious doubt as to whether the critic who stresses that point attaches any real significance to the difference between a tree and a human being. Such insistence seems in fact to deny the value, and even the point, of Ovid's artistic representation and to reduce the story to a single unambiguous meaning which has the distinct advantage of being equally applicable to nearly all of the metamorphoses. The inadequacy of this approach is, or at least should be, almost self-evident: it seeks the primary meaning of the change-story in whatever element is left unaffected by the change that gives the story its special interest and appeal. It is rather like urging the reader of

Pinocchio to ignore the tendency of Pinocchio's nose to get longer when he tells a lie and advising him to attend to the story's realistic elements instead.

The second characteristic of Ovidian metamorphosis is that it involves the supernatural. The changes, our poet tells us, result from the action of a god: "Ye Gods, from whom these miracles did spring." Ovid's attitude toward the gods is complex and ironic, but it would take a highly ingenious, or rather naive, interpreter to argue that Ovid's constant reference to the gods expresses a recognizably religious attitude. Commentators are fairly consistent on this point. L. P. Wilkinson says of Ovid's gods, "Their chief motives are lust (especially in the males) and revenge for slights (especially in the females)." John M. Fyler, in *Chaucer and Ovid,* echoes Wilkinson and is even more emphatic: "The gods are Hellenistic jokes, not the cosmic forces of the *Aeneid;* their motives for causing metamorphoses are almost always comic or petty."[9] In short, Ovid's gods are anything but a symbolic representation of the poet's "ultimate concern"; they are instead a highly conventional and artificial way of explaining events for which there can be no realistic or rational explanation.

Ovid's gods serve at least one other important function—they provide what is often referred to as "comic distance." That is, they play a role akin to that of the animals in a beast fable. Domestic squabbles between gods are inherently amusing; those between human beings are more often tragic, pathetic, or merely boring to witness. Philandering husbands and jealous wives may furnish the raw material for "drama" or for New Comedy, but they create a realistic atmosphere that is foreign to the playful tone of the *Metamorphoses*. In "The Nun's Priest's Tale," Pertelote's imperious question to Chantecleer, "Have ye no mannes herte, and han a berd?" is inherently funny because the question is addressed to a rooster.[10] By the same token, much of Juno's anger and petty scheming are amusing because they are directed against the chief of the Olympian gods. He in turn is ridiculous because, though preeminent among immortals, he must contend, if not with leaky bathroom fixtures and obstinate front-yard crabgrass, then certainly with a quarrelsome and jealous woman, who is not only his wife but also his sister. This Olympian male adolescent must use all of his nearly inexhaustible resources to stay even half a step ahead of his eternally watchful sister-wife.

Ovid carries this device for obtaining comic distance one step further than does the beast fabulist. In "The Nun's Priest's Tale" the animals are the only significant characters in the plot; the human characters are little more than bewildered onlookers. Ovid makes the human and the nonhuman characters partners in the action, with results that are sometimes disastrous for the humans. In book 3, Juno's patience, worn thin by a long series of Jupiter's escapades, finally comes to an end when she discovers that Semele is pregnant by him. Decreeing that "the guilty wretch [Semele] shall die," she prompts Semele to test her lover's identity by insisting that he make love to her "in all the pomp of his divinity." Semele complies and persuades Jupiter to grant her a single wish, little realizing what the fulfillment of that wish will involve. Though the amorous god has his thunderbolt specially prepared with "less flame and fury in its make" and though he does everything he can to reduce the impact of his dazzling approach, poor Semele gets burned to a crisp in his passionate embrace. The encounter, as described in Addison's translation, is brief and fiery:

> The mortal dame, too feeble to engage
> The lightning's flashes, and the thunder's rage,
> Consum'd amidst the glories she desir'd,
> And in the terrible embrace expir'd.[11]

But Jupiter, resourceful as ever, is able to perform an emergency Caesarean section, transplant the embryo to his own thigh, and bring the baby (Bacchus) to full term.

The passage quoted most frequently as evidence of Ovid's attitude toward the gods appears in the *Ars amatoria* (1.637ff.): "Expedit esse deos et, ut expedit, esse putemus. . . ." Wilkinson paraphrases the entire passage in this fashion: "It is expedient there should be gods, and this being so, let us suppose they exist. For the good of society we should keep up the traditional religious ceremonies, and use the gods to enforce the commandments: 'Thou shalt live innocently, for the gods are not remote or indifferent' (What use would the aloof Epicurean gods be as safeguards for society?); 'Thou shalt pay back what is entrusted to thee'; 'Honour thy father and thy mother'; 'Thou shalt not defraud'; 'Thou shalt do no murder.'" The attitude expressed in these lines is, to be sure, casual rather than pious, and mildly moral rather than fervently religious; but some of that flavor comes, not from Ovid, but from Wilkinson's paraphrase. Wilkinson says, for instance, that "to take 'numen adest' as a statement of the poet's own view would be absurd: it is meant to be in inverted commas."[12] This may or may not be true—I for one can only judge what Ovid *meant* to say by what he *did* say—but to render *numen adest* ("Divinity is present") as "the gods are not remote or indifferent" is like translating the student's *adsum* response to the roll call as "I am not absent." That is, it "loses something in translation"; and the translator's claim that it is supposed to lose something in translation must indeed be taken with a grain of salt. When he goes so far as to insert his own argument into the paraphrase by means of the hit-and-run parenthetical question "What use would the aloof Epicurean gods be as safeguards for society?" Wilkinson is not translating or even paraphrasing, but rewriting. What we are dealing with here seems to illustrate the Italian adage, *Traduttore, traditore,* "Translator, betrayer."

I am not arguing, as Fränkel does, that Ovid is best understood as saying of the gods, "Let us rather continue to worship them with modest piety, in the fond, if forlorn, hope that they reward those who wrong no one," or as LaFaye does when he says that Ovid "croit à l'existence des dieux et à la necessité du culte."[13] They are going as far in one direction as Wilkinson does in the other. The attitude that Ovid displays is neither that of the lukewarm believer nor that of the derisive skeptic—he simply does not appear to think or feel as strongly about the matter as either of these views would suggest. For the most part, it seems much more accurate to say that his attitude toward the gods is consistently playful. He responds to them and to the tales of their exploits as modern Italians frequently react to any story that they suspect of being apocryphal: *Se non è vero, è ben trovato,* "If it isn't true, it's well contrived." Readers have long responded in this way to Ovid's *Metamorphoses,* and it seems unlikely that they would have done so if such a response were not closely akin to the attitude that underlies the whole poem. The question of belief never really arises; neither Ovid's faith nor the factuality of his stories is ever at issue for the reader who finds the *Metamorphoses* a source of continuing delight.

Besides its emphasis upon externals and its tendency to explain miraculous change as being the result of intervention by one or more of the gods, Ovidian metamorphosis tends to be preoccupied with the erotic element in human experience. The analysis of this characteristic has led commentators away from literary questions about Ovid's *Metamorphoses* and toward life questions about human psychology, social behavior, and the like. Wilkinson deals briefly with the subject under the heading "Grotesqueness, Humour, Wit," and his approach indicates the direction which the discussion has usually taken:

> Is there some fascination, subtler than meets the eye, in the idea of metamorphosis which haunts the folklore of almost all nations? . . . Anything weird, of course, appeals to the part of us which enjoys fear that is unaccompanied by danger, the feelings we titillate by reading ghost stories. But Fränkel, who cites an imaginative experience of childhood recounted by André Gide, may possibly be right in suggesting that there is ultimately something sexual about them. If so, however, the springs are deep in the well of the subconscious. With what mod-

est restraint Ovid, so often referred to in tones that suggest he was salacious, describes the changing of Iphis from a girl into a boy![14]

Galinsky continues the discussion in much the same vein and adds a note of warning about the dangers of psychologizing Ovid: "Citing a childhood reminiscence of André Gide, both Fränkel and L. P. Wilkinson also suggest that there may be 'a sensual element in the metamorphosis theme.' Fränkel has been judicious enough not to press the point, and the *Metamorphoses* as a whole do not have to be rescued from a psychoanalytical Procrustes couch. . . . We must keep in mind that it would be a fundamental misinterpretation to look upon the *Metamorphoses* as a psychological textbook."[15] Thus, just as discussion of the gods in Ovid has wandered off into questions about religious faith and Ovid's own belief or the lack of it, so the obvious sexuality of the change-stories has been more or less consigned to the realm of psychology and thereby dismissed as irrelevant to a discussion of the *Metamorphoses* as literature.

As I have already suggested, if one wants a nonliterary explanation for the sexual element that seems to be inherent in metamorphosis, one need not go beyond the obvious fact that sex, which involves both the union of opposites and the "miracle" of conception and birth, provides a real-life analogy for what happens in the change-stories. And there are perfectly good literary reasons both for Ovid's manner of representing the gods and for his preoccupation with sex as the basic subject matter in the *Metamorphoses*. An unsympathetic reader may regard Ovid's masterpiece as superficial, irreverent, and blatantly erotic. But a reasonable answer to this triple charge might run as follows: First, Ovid is above all a literary artist, and like any other artist, his primary concern is with externals that make a direct appeal to the senses; his main interest, therefore, is in the tangible, the audible, and the visible. Second, his representation of the gods is governed by literary, rather than religious, considerations; the gods provide an acceptable explanation for the miraculous changes, and they establish the comic perspective or "distance" which is indispensable to the artistic effect of the stories. Third, Ovid is preoccupied with sex for the same reason that all comic writers are: it is the basic subject matter of the genre in which they are working. He is in fact remarkably restrained and delicate; one need only compare him with Aristophanes or Rabelais to acquit him of any charge that his writing is lewd or even unseemly.

Before leaving our discussion of Ovidian metamorphosis we should note that the most important structural element in these stories is their tendency to overlap or envelop each other. The most obvious feature of Ovid's poem as a whole is that the entire fifteen books form an endless chain; one story leads into another without pause, and even the arbitrary division into books is not allowed to break the chain. Often a story begun at the end of one book is finished at the start of the next. The tales are self-propagating, as it were; and the only way to have a beginning and an ending is to impose some semblance of chronological order by beginning with the creation of the world and continuing up to the writer's present time. But it would be a mistake to assume that this observation applies only to the relationships among the stories and not to each of them individually. Some of the stories involve a series of transformations: Midas is first granted his wish for the golden touch; when that proves unsatisfactory, it is taken away, and he is given a pair of ass's ears instead. Most people are familiar with the first part of the story; Chaucer retells the second part in "The Wife of Bath's Tale," and students are sometimes at a loss to know whether Chaucer's interpolated story refers to "the same Midas" as the one who had the golden touch.

Perhaps the best analogy for this structural element is the echo or the mirror, which has its dramatic counterpart in the play within a play. At its best, this device produces an effect that is both haunting and puzzling. Moreover, the device tends to direct the observer's attention away from itself and to send the would-be interpreter off in pursuit of the answers to life questions which are echoed or mirrored, but not answered, in the story itself. The overlapping and interlocking stories of Echo and Narcissus illustrate this feature of Ovidian metamorphosis—echoing sound and reflected image are central to the two stories.[16] The stories themselves are so intertwined that they can hardly be told separately, and it is in connection with Narcissus that Galinsky issues his warning about the dangers of psychologizing the *Metamorphoses*. These two stories are no less intertwined than the two snakes that Tiresias separates, not once, but twice; and both stories are enveloped and contained within Tiresias's own story, which is told in connection with a dispute, between the king and queen of the gods, on the subject of sex. This mirroring and echoing seems in fact to be the most important single feature of the metamorphosis stories, more important than the metamorphosis itself, which is often relegated (as in the story of Narcissus) to a position of minor importance. It may be true, as Gilbert Highet has suggested, that "most of the *Metamorphoses* is concerned with sex and the supernatural, both of which interested Shakespeare"; but it seems equally clear that the parallelism or reflexive structure of Ovid's stories likewise fascinated the author of *Hamlet* and *King Lear*, of *The Taming of the Shrew* and *A Midsummer Night's Dream*.

A SECOND type of transformation in the Shakespeare comedies, most obvious in the plays of the middle period such as *As You Like It*, is a moral change in one or more of the main characters. Unlike the Ovidian metamorphosis of the earlier plays (which is perhaps most closely approximated in Bottom's "translation" into an ass), this change (1) is internal rather than external, and (2) it represents a given character's own intellectual and moral progress. Furthermore, such a change culminates in the development of a mature and workable relationship between lovers; that is, (3) romantic love emerges as an authentic value in these comedies. Though it still has its origins in love at first sight, romantic love goes far beyond the simple physical attraction or the desire for a large dowry which provides an entirely sufficient motivation for lovers in the early comedies. According to Peter G. Phialas, the romantic comedies (from *The Two Gentlemen of Verona* to *Twelfth Night*) involve "the achieving by the chief characters, whose attitudes are thus comically reduced, of a change or growth; and the emergence, stated or implied, of an ideal attitude, 'ideal' here meaning the best that can be hoped for in the world we know." In the later plays of this group, says Phialas, "that ideal attitude is represented throughout in the temperament of the heroine."[17]

This gradual change in an imagined character, though it may seem commonplace to a twentieth-century reader, appears far less frequently in pre-Shakespearean literature than either sudden external change—which we find in Ovid, in ballads such as "Kemp Owyne," and in the folklore of most nations—or religious awakening, which we encounter repeatedly in the Bible, in medieval drama, and in confessional writings of all sorts. There are, I think, three main reasons why we have so few examples of such character change in imaginative literature, especially the drama, before Shakespeare. First, because the change is almost entirely internal, it is difficult to represent in nonallegorical art, which makes its primary appeal to the senses rather than to the intellect. Second, Aristotle and Horace, whose influence can hardly be overestimated, specifically forbade the representation of radical change in a dramatic character of the sort that involves a complete reorientation, rather than a normal (that is, "probable and necessary") development. And third, the gradualness of such a change, if it is to be realistically represented, requires a lengthy, step-by-step exposition of the kind that we have come to associate with the novel rather than with the drama.

The novel, of course, did not really come into its own until the eighteenth century, and the Bildungsroman, whose special function it was to represent such a change in the protagonist, did not appear on the scene until the publication of *Wilhelm Meisters Lehrjahre* in 1795–96. Many of the novels on which most of us grew up—*David Copperfield, Great Expectations, The Way of All Flesh, Sons and Lovers*, and a host of others—are directly descended from *Wilhelm Meister*.[18] When we turn later in life to a close reading of the Shakespeare comedies, this element seems entirely familiar. Interwoven as it is in Shakespeare with the more spectacular Ovidian changes and the more traditional religious conversions, this growth in self-knowledge seems to us rather ordinary and perhaps even "realistic" in comparison with certain other features of Shakespearean drama.

Regardless of whether Shakespeare was following the example of earlier writers in representing such moral and intellectual changes or whether he was striking out in a new direction, we may be certain that down through the history of comic theory, from Plato to Northrop Frye, there has been general agreement that a lack of self-knowledge on the part of one or more of the characters is fundamental to comedy. In Plato's *Philebus*, Socrates and Protarchus discuss the "mixed feeling of pain and pleasure" which the spectators at a tragedy or "even at a comedy" sometimes experience. This discussion leads Socrates to discourse on "the nature of the ridiculous," which he identifies as "a certain kind of badness." It is, says Socrates, "that part of badness in general which is opposite to the state of which the inscription at Delphi speaks." When Protarchus asks, "You mean 'Know thyself,' Socrates?" he responds, "I do. And the opposite of that, in the inscription's language, would plainly be 'Do *not* know thyself.'"[19] Frye's assertion that "comedy is designed not to condemn evil, but to ridicule a lack of self-knowledge" makes the same point; one need only glance at the comedies of Ben Jonson and Molière, both of whom were writing comedy within the classical tradition, to see the justice of these observations.

What Socrates says also helps us to understand the basis for the classical objection ("check") to radical change in dramatic characters. "Ridiculous" characters, who "do not know themselves," are clearly fools; and characters who *do* know themselves are, just as clearly, wise. To represent both character types in a single personage is therefore equivalent to asserting mutually contradictory statements. If one is true, then the other must be false. From a purely logical point of view, the dramatist would be attempting to represent something that both is and is not itself, "mixing apples and oranges," as we are inclined to say when we think that someone is becoming hopelessly confused. We are perfectly willing to concede that both apples and oranges go through a ripening process (develop normally), but we strongly object when someone calls the same piece of fruit first an apple and then later an orange (changes its identity).

Shakespeare certainly demonstrates an awareness of the close connection between comedy and a lack of self-knowledge on the part of comic characters. He occasionally makes that connection explicit, as, for instance, in Rosalind's exhortation to Phebe, "Mistress, know yourself" (*AYL* III.v.57), and in the second lord's question about the extent of Parolles' self-knowledge: "Is it possible he should know what he is, and be that he is?" (*AWW* IV.i.43–44). But unlike writers in the classical tradition, Shakespeare is not content simply to "ridicule a lack of self-knowledge." The characters who dominate and control the action of these plays (Rosalind, Viola, and Helena) possess considerable self-knowledge, and their function is not only to expose the shortcomings of other characters but also to educate them and make them suitable marriage partners by the end of the play. That is, holding a particular character's lack of self-knowledge up to ridicule often functions in Shakespearean comedy not as an end in itself but as a necessary first step toward that character's achieving some degree of self-knowledge under the guidance of another character who dominates the action and movement of the play and propels both the individual character and the play as a whole toward the happy ending.

This second type of transformation, reflecting an increase in self-knowledge, gained not (as in the tragedies) at the cost of irreparable loss and immense suffering, is most clearly represented in the middle comedies. A good deal of study has been devoted to this aspect of the plays, especially by those critics who approach the Shakespeare comedies by means of character analysis. It is sufficient for our purposes to observe that such transformation, more realistic than Ovidian metamorphosis and more common in human experience than religious conversion or awakening, is perfectly consistent with both. In a sense it simply involves the application of the metamorphic process to a matter with which comedy had apparently been preoccupied almost since its inception—self-knowledge and/or the lack of it. Classical comedy, in spite of Aristotle and Horace, occasionally suggests such a change in comic character. Menander's *Grouch*, the oldest surviving example of New Comedy, represents the protagonist as softening his attitude near the end of the play; and Terence's *Brothers* shows characters exchanging attitudes and positions as do Kate and Bianca in *The Taming of the Shrew*. For the most part, however, dramatists working within the classical tradition were "so devote to Aristotle's checks" that Ovid did indeed become "an outcast quite abjured," at least as far as the representation of significant change in a dramatic character was concerned. But Shakespeare, obviously enamored of shifts and changes, substitutions and transformations, is a consistent writer; and it would seem odd if his fondness for transformation had not extended to the intellectual and moral side of human experience as represented in the drama.

THE third type of transformation, foreshadowed in the denouement of *The Two Gentlemen of Verona*, illustrated in *As You Like It*, and fully developed in *The Tempest,* has its literary origins in biblical narrative, medieval drama, and confessional writings. Like the moral change, it is internal rather than external; like the Ovidian, it involves the supernatural, though in this case the reference is to God rather than gods. Lastly, unlike either of the first two types of change, it culminates in repentance and forgiveness rather than in sexual attraction and romantic love. It of course does not exclude or simply replace the sexual and romantic elements, but it goes beyond them and completes them either within the same plot, as in *Much Ado About Nothing,* or in a separate and parallel action, as in *The Tempest.* The Shakespeare plays are, to be sure, secular representations rather than specifically religious ones; but there can be little doubt that the nature of the experience involved in this third type of change is basically religious—it makes use of the traditional religious vocabulary ("mercy," "grace," "repentance," "conversion," and the like); and the plays contain an abundance of biblical references and allusions.

The prototype of the conversion story is that of Paul's conversion on the road to Damascus, recorded in the ninth chapter of Acts. The conversion story itself occupies about three fourths of the chapter (vv. 1–31). There is then a one-line pause in the text of the Revised Standard Version (RSV), and the rest of the chapter (vv. 32–43) consists of two brief stories about Peter—his curing a paralytic named Aeneas and his raising a woman called Tabitha from the dead. At first it seems odd that these two brief episodes, which apparently have nothing to do with the conversion of Paul, should be juxtaposed with that story and included in the same chapter. But certain motifs connect these episodes with the conversion story. The most obvious recurring element is revealed in the words spoken first to the cripple and then to the dead woman: "'Aeneas, Jesus Christ heals you; rise and make your bed.' And immediately he rose" (Acts 9.34). Then again, Peter says, "'Tabitha, rise.' And she opened her eyes, and when she saw Peter she sat up" (9.40). The voice that speaks to Saul (Paul's name before his conversion) is that of the risen Christ: "Rise and enter the city"; and we are told that "Saul rose from the ground" (9.8). Later, when the scales fall from his eyes, Saul "rose and was baptized" (9.18). Another, subtler connection between Saul and Tabitha (or Dorcas) comes by means of an image. Saul's acquiescence in the stoning of Stephen is delicately worded: "Then they cast [Stephen] out of the city and stoned him; and the witnesses laid down their garments at the feet of a young man named Saul" (Acts 7.58). Only later, at the beginning of the next chapter, is his relationship to the events made explicit: "And Saul was consenting to his death" (8.1). When Peter enters the room where the body of Dorcas (Tabitha) is laid out, we are told that "the widows stood beside him weeping, and showing coats and garments which Dorcas made while she was with them" (9.39). Then Peter is represented as "consenting to her resurrection."

More significant confirmation of the relationship between these two episodes and the conversion of Paul is to be found in the ninth chapter of Matthew's gospel. The chapter opens (vv. 1–8) with the story of Christ's healing a paralytic, with the words "Rise, take up your bed and go home" (Matt. 9.6). A little later (vv. 18–26) we read that a ruler comes to Jesus, saying, "My daughter has just died." Jesus goes with him, doing other miracles along the way, and when they arrive, "He went in and took her by the hand, and the girl arose." Between these two miracle stories, which are perhaps the "originals" of the ones associated with Peter in Acts 9, Matthew modestly and briefly records his own conversion or ordination: "As Jesus passed on from there, he saw a man called Matthew sitting at the tax office; and he said to him, 'Follow me.' And he rose and followed him" (Matt. 9.9). Apparently Matthew considered that within the context of these two miracle stories, his own transformation from tax collector to servant of Christ needed no explanation whatever beyond these few lines of simple prose narrative.

As they appear in Matthew, the two miracle stories serve as a kind of "envelope" for the brief story of Matthew's own conversion; in Acts, two nearly identical stories are added as postscripts to the more detailed representation of Paul's astonishing transformation. As the author of Acts, Luke makes them more than just postscripts, however. They follow quite naturally in the wake of Paul's temporary blindness and of the "scales" that fall from his eyes. The stories of Aeneas and Tabitha, juxtaposed with the narrative of Paul's conversion, serve to externalize Paul's change, to render outward and visible what would otherwise be inward and unseen. They become figurative elements in Paul's own story: he was blind, and now he sees; he was lame, and now he walks; he was dead, and now he lives. Later, as Christ's ambassador to the Gentiles, Paul would wrestle with the question of what such transformation means and how it is achieved, particularly as these questions relate to the experience of non-Jews: Must a Gentile be converted to Judaism before becoming a Christian? Paul's answer, when it comes, is unequivocal: "For neither circumcision counts for anything, nor uncircumcision, but a new creation" (Gal. 6.15, RSV). In other words, outward signs mean very little according to St. Paul; indeed, they mean nothing at all, in and of themselves. What really matters is the inward change, the complete reorientation of the individual's life and values—"a new creature," in the language of the King James Version.

For religious awakening, then, as for Ovidian metamorphosis, Shakespeare had perfectly good models in the literature with which he was familiar. Interestingly, the most conspicuous feature of both types of transformation as represented in earlier literature is parallelism, an element that apparently fascinated Shakespeare as much as the transformation itself. What we observe as we progress through the Shakespeare comedies is not simply the gradual development of his skill in handling plot, or the maturing of his capacity to represent human character, or even his growth as a poet. What we see also is the no less important change in his interest in changes, the transformation of his concern with transformation. Beginning with Ovidian metamorphosis, he goes on to the representation of moral and intellectual change, and finally to religious transformation. He does not abandon the first when he proceeds to the second or third, however. His lifelong interest in Ovid and farce is still apparent in *The Tempest,* and his awakening interest in the social significance of repentance and forgiveness is evident in the denouement of *The Two Gentlemen of Verona.* He quickly moves away from the morally appropriate ending characteristic of New Comedy toward a denouement in which judgment is perfectly clear, but harsh penalty is suspended—not because information is forthcoming which clears up the problem, as in *The Comedy of Errors,* but because the other characters recognize and accept as authentic the change that has taken place in one of their fellows, as in *The Tempest.*

For the interpretation of Shakespearean comedy, the most important question arising from these transformations may be stated as follows: How seriously are we to take the changes of attitude and character that are often indispensable to the happy ending of a Shakespeare comedy? Fortunately, the answer is not especially difficult: We regard the character-changes in any particular play just as seriously as we regard the play, as a whole, in which they occur. This answer is less a recommendation to the audience of the plays than an observation about most people's actual response to them. The problem (and, I would say, the error of interpretation) arises when we make the highly questionable assumption that the structure and conventions of a play that we do not take very seriously must be fundamentally different from those of another play that we regard as being more serious and meaningful. Larry Champion, for instance, reserves the term *comedies of transformation* for *The Winter's Tale* and *The Tempest.* He must therefore argue—apparently retrospectively—that the title *The Taming of the Shrew* is purely and simply ironic, that the characters in this play are "creatures who arouse humor directly from action, not from hypocrisy or transformation." According to Champion, "Petruchio is the same pompous and egocentric ass at the end of the play . . . that he was at the beginning. . . . Nor has Kate changed one tittle!"[20] It would be one thing to claim that the transformation process that Shakespeare represents so convincingly in *The Winter's Tale* and *The Tempest* is in *The Taming of the Shrew* grossly exaggerated or simply ineffective. It is quite another thing, however, to assert categorically that in the earlier comedy the transformation referred to in the title and insisted upon in the play itself simply is not there. Such a view is roughly equivalent to claiming that there are no "real" mistakes of identity in *The Comedy of Errors* and no "actual" bed trick in *All's Well That Ends Well* or *Measure for Measure*.

At the end of the second induction to *The Taming of the Shrew* we are offered two contrasting definitions of comedy, the first by Christopher Sly and the second by the Page, who pretends to be the "transformed" Sly's wife. Sly asks whether a "commonty" is not "a Christmas gambol or a tumbling trick"; and the Page replies negatively, contending that it is "more pleasing stuff." It is, says the Page, "a kind of history" (Ind. ii.126–38). In the various Shakespeare comedies, the emphasis alternates between the two elements to which these definitions refer—festivity and carefully structured plot. C. L. Barber has analyzed the first, Northrop Frye and Robert Hunter the second. Within the context of *The Taming of the Shrew,* the Page is quite right; the play in which he appears (if only by way of introduction) acquaints us with Shakespeare's neatly plotted comedy, just as *Love's Labor's Lost* gives us what is probably the first example of his primarily festive comedy. In the later plays, the emphasis may be upon the festive, as in *As You Like It* and *Twelfth Night,* or upon carefully constructed plot, as in *All's Well That Ends Well* and *Measure for Measure*. Occasionally the two are almost perfectly balanced and blended, as in *A Midsummer Night's Dream,* or else juxtaposed in an alternating pattern, as in *Henry IV*. What needs to be emphasized, however, is that transformation is common to both. Though it is more obvious in the more elaborately plotted comedies because of its more conspicuous function there, it is explicit in both types and almost always makes possible and leads into the happy ending.

❧ THREE ❧

Character-Change as Time-Lapse Metaphor

◆

Those are pearls that were his eyes.

PHILOSOPHICAL reexamination of metaphor began, perhaps by coincidence, at about the same time as serious critical study of the Shakespeare comedies. Max Black's influential essay entitled "Metaphor" appeared in 1955 though it had been anticipated, at least in some respects, by I. A. Richards's writings in the 1920s and 1930s.[1] Similarly, C. L. Barber's book *Shakespeare's Festive Comedy* was published in 1959, preceded by, among others, H. B. Charlton's *Shakespearian Comedy* in 1938 and Northrop Frye's essay "The Argument of Comedy" in 1948.[2] Because Richards was not a professional philosopher, his arguments had no great impact on the philosophical community, which was then dominated by logical positivism. After the appearance of Black's essay, however, philosophers began to inquire much more seriously into the nature and function of metaphor; and the outpouring of essays on metaphor, like that on Shakespearean comedy, dates from the 1950s and 1960s.

The two lines of inquiry come together, of course, in any consideration of Shakespearean imagery. Caroline Spurgeon's book *Shakespeare's Imagery and What It Tells Us* (1935) was perhaps the first to focus on an aspect of the Shakespeare plays which the New Critics took up and pursued, though with a different emphasis, in the 1940s and 1950s. But the conception of metaphor and simile that pervaded orthodox thinking on the subject continued to be essentially Aristotelian, derived primarily from the *Poetics* and the *Rhetoric* and, except for I. A. Richards, elaborated only slightly by medieval and modern theorists. Mark Johnson has summarized that conception as follows: "A metaphor is an elliptical simile useful for stylistic, rhetorical, and didactic purposes, but which can be translated into a literal paraphrase without any loss of cognitive content."[3] The extent to which this conception has dominated our view of Shakespearean metaphor is reflected in one of the standard handbooks on Shakespeare, which asserts that "the badge of metaphoric language is that it must always be translated in the imagination" and that "all metaphors are 'fallacious.'" But this same handbook tells us that Shakespeare's aphorisms, which are "reminders of truths already known," call for an entirely different response: "We should not, however, reduce them to their primitive form, but take them as they are. They do not contradict traditional wisdom, but they often refine upon it, alter its emphasis, and give it new force and beauty."[4]

Such an attitude toward Shakespearean aphorisms seems eminently sensible. It is self-evident that Edgar's statement in *King Lear* "But then the mind much sufferance doth o'erskip / When grief hath mates, and bearing fellowship" has more value, or at least a different value, than the old saw "misery loves company." But why then must Shakespearean metaphors "always be translated in the imagination" or reduced to "their primitive form" of literal language? There can be only one meaningful answer to that question, and it is this: Because our conception of metaphor tells us that they "must be so translated." But might it not be that Shakespeare's metaphors, no less than his aphorisms, have a relation to traditional wisdom that we can best describe by saying that they "often refine upon it, alter its emphasis, and give it new force and beauty"? The claim that metaphors "must always be translated in the imagination" is simply a special application of the assertion that poetry must always be translated into prose in order to be made intelligible, and such a view is radically inconsistent with the contention that the works of Shakespeare have a special value that is irretrievably lost when they are simply paraphrased.

Because my own concern is purely practical, I do not propose to set forth a complete theory of metaphor but only to clarify several points that may be of help in understanding Shakespeare's transformation comic plots. Among these points are (1) the relationship between metaphor and simile, (2) the relationship between metaphor and literal statement, (3) the manner in which time may enter into metaphor, and (4) the manner in which metaphor generates metaphor. In the *Poetics* Aristotle acknowledges, in the sections on diction, that a mastery of metaphor is indispensable to the poet: "But the greatest thing by far is to be a master of metaphor. It is the one thing that cannot be learnt from others; and it is also a sign of genius." In the sections on plot, however, he asserts that "the poet must be more the poet of his stories or Plots than of his verses, inasmuch as he is a poet by virtue of the imitative element in his work, and it is actions that he imitates."[5] Because Aristotle's conception of metaphor was limited to the poet's diction and verses, he did not perceive the connection between metaphor and plot, even though "the greatest thing by far is to be a master of metaphor," and at the same time "the poet must be more the poet of his stories or Plots than of his verses."

Although its significance for the plots of the Shakespeare comedies will not be apparent until later, let us consider first the relationship between metaphor and simile. Aristotle's statement on the subject appears not in the *Poetics* but in the *Rhetoric*:

> The Simile is also a metaphor; the difference is but slight. When the poet says of Achilles that he
>   Leapt on the foe as a lion,
> this is a simile; when he says of him 'the lion leapt,' it is a metaphor—here, since both are courageous, he has transferred to Achilles the name of 'lion.' . . . [Similes] are to be employed just as metaphors are employed, since they are really the same thing except for the difference mentioned."[6]

Hence arises the theory that a metaphor is simply an "elliptical" or "compressed" simile; they are essentially the same thing, except that in metaphor the word *like* or *as* is omitted.

But close examination reveals that such is simply not the case—the view of metaphor as "elliptical simile" rests on what is at best a half-truth and at worst a badly mistaken conception. It should be apparent, for instance, that in English *any simile implicitly contradicts its corresponding metaphor.*[7] The statement "Kate is a shrew" is obviously metaphoric, whatever theory we may use to interpret its meaning. Its corresponding simile, "Kate is *like* a shrew," means something different, however, and its full meaning may be written out as follows: "(Kate is *not* a shrew, but in at least one way) Kate is *like* a shrew." Unless what is contained in the parenthesis is distinctly implied by what is outside the parenthesis, the simile itself makes no sense at all. When someone says that "a shrew is a shrew," the person may pass for a poet or at least for a parodist (cf. "A rose is a rose . . ."); but when someone says that "a shrew is *like* a shrew," listeners may look at each other as if to ask silently, How long has this person been this way? In logical terms, the first statement is a tautology; the second is sheer nonsense because it implies that a particular thing simultaneously is and is not itself.

To regard metaphor as elliptical or compressed simile is thus equivalent to claiming that an affirmative statement is merely an elliptical negative statement. "Kate is a shrew," in this analysis, is just an abbreviated way of saying "Kate is *not* a shrew." It is obvious, of course, that typographically the only difference between the two statements is that one of them contains three letters that the other does not; but to contend that the two sentences "are really the same thing except for the difference mentioned" can only (if the contention is taken seriously) lead to enormous confusion. It is far more accurate to say that what a metaphor boldly asserts, a simile suggests in timid and hesitating fashion while granting that the claim expressed in the corresponding metaphor is simply false. Rather than regarding metaphor as "elliptical simile," we should regard simile as "eviscerated metaphor."

One may also specify the relationship between metaphor and simile in grammatical terms: in English, the function of metaphor is nominative; that of simile is adjectival or adverbial. The statement "Kate is a shrew" implies that the second noun may be substituted for the first, as in Aristotle's example from the *Rhetoric,* "The lion (Achilles) leapt." The statement "Kate is *like* a shrew," on the other hand, makes use of a prepositional phrase that functions as an adjective; and the meaning of that statement is exactly equivalent to "Kate is shrewish." Syntactically, one may substitute an adjective for a noun only when both are predicative, but the two meanings are then significantly different: "Kate is a shrew" versus "Kate is shrewish." The first assertion is much stronger than the second for the obvious reason that a noun actually *is* something, whereas an adjective merely describes something in terms of something else; and if a picture is worth a thousand words, then a familiar concrete noun is worth a thousand adjectives, including those that are cognate with the noun in question.

Even when an adverbial modifier retains the noun itself within the phrase (as in "as a lion," which is equivalent to "leoninely"), the case of that noun (lion), in English, though not in Greek, is objective rather than nominative. *Webster's Third New International Dictionary* (1971) identifies *as,* meaning "after the manner of: the same as: LIKE," as being a preposition; according to *The American Heritage Dictionary* (1971), "when *as* is a preposition (sense of being in the role of) it is invariably followed by a noun or pronoun in the objective case." In Greek, on the other hand, the word corresponding to *as* in Aristotle's example is not a preposition but a particle (ὡς); and it is followed by a noun in the nominative case (ὡς δὲ λέων ἐπόρουσεν). Thus Aristotle would have observed no grammatical distinction between the two examples and would quite reasonably have dismissed the particle as being structurally insignificant, to the great confusion of English speakers who read him in translation and unconsciously assume that Greek and English grammar are parallel in this respect, when clearly they are not.

The relationship between metaphor and literal statement is likewise the subject of considerable confusion. Traditional theory, as summarized by Mark Johnson, indicates that metaphor can be (and some would say *must* be) translated into literal language, and that this "translation" can be made "without any loss of cognitive content." Such a claim implies that metaphor and literal statement are separate and distinct, presumably analogous to two separate languages, even if (as with French and English) the two languages possess some of the same vocabulary and rules of grammar. But analysis of the matter almost forces one to conclude that *the distinction between metaphor and literal statement is not at all clear, and any line of demarcation between them is utterly impossible to establish.*[8] Consider the following case. Ludwig Wittgenstein says in his *Notebooks,* "My *whole* task consists in explaining the nature of sentences." In the *Tractatus Logico-Philosophicus* he twice asserts that "a proposition is a picture of reality" (Der Satz ist ein Bild der Wirklichkeit.) The question then arises whether this statement, carefully constructed by a major language philosopher of the twentieth century to "explain the nature of sentences," is a literal statement or a metaphor; and that question is complicated by the fact that Wittgenstein's word *Bild* (image, figure, or picture) is closely akin to εἰκών (likeness, image), Aristotle's word for "simile." The commentator in *The Encyclopedia of Philosophy* says categorically that "the picture theory of propositions . . . is the central idea of the *Tractatus*"; but his commentary does not really answer our question: "Wittgenstein's explanation consists in the striking idea that a sentence is a *picture.* He meant that it is *literally* a picture, not merely *like* a picture in certain respects."[9] The distinction made here is the one between literal statement ("*literally*") and simile ("not merely *like* a picture"); and we can make that distinction for ourselves since Wittgenstein's sentence does not contain the word *like* or *as.* To insist upon this self-evident distinction only has the effect of lumping literal statement and metaphor together as opposed to simile, which, though it is not very helpful, at least tends to confirm our earlier distinction between metaphor and simile.

Consider also the statement "Matter (or mass) is dormant energy." The sentence is obviously self-contradictory, since if energy is inert or "sleeping," then it is not recognizable as energy. Before Albert Einstein formulated the special theory of relativity with its astonishing corollary $E = mc^2$, the statement would probably have been regarded as a fanciful idea, utterly at odds with the laws of the physical universe. Can we get around the difficulty, then, by saying that the sentence "Matter is dormant energy" was a metaphor until 1905, a theory until 1945, and a literal statement after that? Obviously that stratagem will not really take care of the difficulty, because neither the statement itself nor the laws of the physical universe have changed during that period; only our conception of them has changed. Clearly something is wrong, however, when students in university classrooms are routinely instructed to regard the category of statements which includes "Matter is dormant energy" as inherently fallacious when scientists unanimously accept that same statement, or at least its mathematical equivalent, as expressing an authentic insight into the nature of the universe.

The relationship between metaphor and literal statement is not analogous to that between two languages. Rather, they are two ends of a continuum, and most metaphors—all but the most striking and powerful of them—are as close to the middle of that continuum as they are to the end which we might label "pure metaphor." Moreover, the same sentence may, in certain cases, function both as metaphor and as literal statement; and the obviousness or self-evident truth of the literal statement may serve to establish or reinforce the metaphoric meaning. In such cases, the metaphoric meaning may be entirely consistent with traditional wisdom, but the metaphor itself serves to "refine upon it, alter its emphasis, and give it new force and beauty." Take for instance John Donne's familiar metaphor, "No man is an island." The literal meaning of the sentence is obvious and indisputable, and the metaphoric meaning is certainly consistent with traditional wisdom. The metaphoric meaning must of course be *apprehended* in the imagination, and imagination does indeed "apprehend / More than cool reason ever comprehends." But surely it need not be "translated"—we gain no more by reducing this metaphor to "All men are brothers" than we do by reducing Edgar's statement in *King Lear* to "Misery loves company."

"No man is an island" is an example of what has been called "twice-true metaphor," though I think it would be more accurate to regard it as "twice-true statement," since the sentence is true once as literal statement and once as metaphoric statement, not twice as metaphor.[10] Wittgenstein's sentence "A proposition is a picture of reality" is, I think, a statement of this same type; but since the metaphoric meaning is nearer to the middle of the continuum than in the case of "No man is an island," the metaphoric and literal meanings are much closer together, and therefore more difficult to sort out, than in Donne's metaphor. Because "proposition" and "picture" seem to us to be entirely separate categories (cf. "matter" and "energy"), to join them by means of the verb *is* produces what strikes us as a metaphor. And the statement's literal meaning is based upon the following chain of reasoning: " 'I understand a sentence without having had its sense explained to me.' . . . This can appear to one as a remarkable fact. If it is a fact, the only possible explanation would be that a sentence *shows* its sense. It shows how things are if it is true. . . . This is exactly what a picture does. A sentence composed of old words is able to communicate a new state of affairs by virtue of being a picture of it."[11] Thus, the metaphoric and literal meanings of Wittgenstein's sentence overlap and support each other.

Apart from vocabulary or diction, the metaphoric strength of "No man is an island" depends mainly upon two variables: (1) the remoteness or oppositeness of the subject and predicate terms joined by *is* (the "yoking of opposites," as Dr. Johnson characterized the metaphysical conceit) and (2) the grammatical or logical structure of the sentence itself (in this case, a universal negative statement). The universal negative is the only one of four structures usable in a categorical syllogism in which the subject and the predicate terms are both distributed—the statement, that is, tells us something about *all* men and something about *all* islands. Any corresponding affirmative statement may be (1) a tautology ("A rose is a rose"); or it may be (2) an exact definition ("A square, in Euclidean geometry, is an equilateral quadrangle in which all of the angles are right angles"). But the most useful affirmative statement is (3) the universal affirmative, in which the subject term may be described as a subset of the predicate term ("All dogs are animals"). The metaphor with which Donne follows "No man is an island" is of this third sort: "Every man is a piece of the continent, a part of the main." The subject and predicate terms are no less remote from each other than in the first metaphor, but the universal affirmative form of the statement has, of course, an undistributed predicate. We are still told something about all men ("every man") but *not* about all land masses, nor even all parts of them ("a piece of the continent, a part of the main"). Donne remedies this weakness to a certain extent by supplying two predicates, but the weaker structure produces a slightly weaker metaphor despite the multiplication of examples.

Most metaphoric statements are not, however, equivalent to universal affirmative ones. The principal basis for asserting that "all metaphors are fallacious" lies in the assumption that because metaphor involves the identification of two things that are not identical, some absurdity or incongruity is inherent in every metaphor. But to make the statement "Kate is a shrew" equivalent to a universal affirmative, one would have to restate it as follows: "Kate is a shrew (and nothing but a shrew)." Not even the boldest metaphor one is likely to encounter in literature makes such a sweeping claim. The only identification asserted by most metaphors may be written out in this fashion: "(At least one characteristic of) Kate is (the same as at least one characteristic of) a shrew." This formula is equivalent to the particular affirmative statement "Some A are (some) B." That is to say, most metaphors are simply affirmative statements in which neither the subject nor the predicate term is distributed—the weakest, incidentally, of the four structures usable in a syllogism—and by no stretch of the imagination can one legitimately claim that such a statement implies complete identification of its subject and predicate terms. If one were so bold as to make such a claim, it could only be regarded as the conclusion of an inductive argument; and as such it would be an example of extremely hasty generalization. The most that one can say with accuracy is that metaphor, by its very nature, leads the reader or hearer to overestimate the degree of identification between its subject and predicate terms.

We are now in a position to explain more fully the assertion that metaphoric and literal statements are two ends of a continuum and that most metaphors are closer to the middle of that continuum than to the end of it which we might label "pure metaphor." The other end (purely literal statement) consists of statements that tend to be either definitions or else statements in which the subject term is a subset of the predicate term. Metaphoric statements, on the other hand, are those in which the subject and predicate terms are apparently distinct and remote from each other—sometimes startlingly so—and this remoteness is bridged by the structure of the statement, which may take the form of a universal negative but more often that of an affirmative statement that creates the impression of being universal either because its subject is singular (and therefore suggests that it is a "class of only one member") or else because it is plural (and therefore suggests that the crucial word *all* is operative though absent). The manner in which a statement may be manipulated toward one end or the other of the continuum is demonstrable in the case of "twice-true statements." Wittgenstein's enigmatic statement about propositions can be made more metaphoric by compressing it to "Sentences are pictures." Conversely, it may be made more literal by expanding it in the direction of exact definition: "All true propositions are pictures of reality as we conceive it because they *show* their meaning even to one who may not have encountered that meaning before, and this is exactly what pictures do."

These statements about the relationship between metaphor and literal statement may justify at least one generalization. I have said that the two kinds of statement are two ends of a continuum and that in their purest form meaningful literal statements tend to be either definitions or else specifications of relationship, while metaphoric statements tend to associate or connect things that we ordinarily think of as distinct and separate. If so, we may say that *in general, literal statement analyzes whereas metaphor synthesizes.* It would appear that Immanuel Kant, who originated the distinction between analytic and synthetic judgments, assigned greater significance to the latter than to the former. According to *The Encyclopedia of Philosophy*, within the Kantian framework "synthetic judgments are informative; they tell us something about the subject by connecting or synthesizing two different concepts under which the subject is subsumed. Analytic judgments are uninformative; they serve merely to elucidate or analyze the concept under which the subject falls." At any rate, Willard Quine has argued that "even if a distinction could be drawn between analytic and synthetic statements or between logical and factual truth, it is impossible to draw a sharp boundary between them."[12] This conclusion corresponds to my earlier assertion about the relationship between literal statement and metaphor, that any line of demarcation between them is impossible to establish.

The third point in connection with metaphor that requires clarification is the manner in which time may enter into metaphor. Obviously, most metaphors depict a kind of "frozen moment," whatever the tense of the linking verb used in the metaphoric statement; and philosophical analysis has therefore confined itself primarily to timeless metaphor. Aristotle's example in the *Rhetoric*, "the lion (Achilles) leapt," though it involves the use of a past-tense verb, is no more "timeful" than "Kate is a shrew." Whether the tense is past or present, no time is represented significantly as passing within the framework of the statement. Time enters into metaphor when two simple (that is, timeless) statements are first compressed by omitting the verb between subject and predicate in each case and are then joined by a linking verb that indicates not being, but becoming. In *The Taming of the Shrew*, we learn in Act I that "Kate is a shrew"; in Act V we are both told and shown that "Kate is an ideal wife." The main plot of the play may be summarized in one time-lapse metaphor: "Kate the shrew becomes Kate the ideal wife."

Of the two statements that go into the making of the time-lapse (or compound) metaphor, one ("Kate is a shrew") is at least recognizably metaphoric, since the categories referred to in the subject and predicate terms are distinct and remote from each other. The other statement ("Kate is an ideal wife") is indistinguishable from literal statement—it is apparently of the type in which the subject term is a subset of the predicate term, and this predicate term lacks any clear definition. But for that purpose the playwright may adopt whatever definition is close at hand, and the late sixteenth-century conception of the good wife is outlined, with appropriately farcical elaboration and overstatement, in Kate's final speech. Because Shakespeare's representation of Kate as shrew strikes us at first as realistic rather than metaphoric, most of us tend to accept it as a particular kind of antisocial behavior that is set forth at the beginning of the play, like Bertram's insufferable snobbism in *All's Well* or Leontes' furious jealousy in *The Winter's Tale*.

Some feminist critics, however, following the lead of George Bernard Shaw, find the characterization of Kate offensive from beginning to end.[13] But this refusal to accept one of the play's givens is an ideological, not a literary, objection; it is like condemning Virgil's *Aeneid* as imperialistic warmongering, regardless of whether or not, as Tennyson claimed, the poet tells his story in "the stateliest measure / ever molded by the lips of man." From a purely ideological standpoint, things go from bad to worse in *The Taming of the Shrew* when Kate does an about-face, apparently caving in to the social pressures of her times. One might say, in feminist terms, that what the play represents is this: "Kate the honest shrew becomes Kate the lying wife." But such a statement is simply another version of the no-transformation view—the word *honest* is equivalent to "real," and *lying* is equivalent to "disguised." Kate herself, we are told once more, "has not changed one whit"; "there is no *real* reformation." And in this view neither Kate's final speech, nor her father's assertion that "she is changed as she had never been," nor the play's title can be regarded as a reliable indicator of what is going on at the heart of this farcical plot.

Perhaps the most beautiful and powerful of Shakespeare's time-lapse metaphors occurs in *The Tempest,* in Ariel's second song to Ferdinand, the "dirge" that begins "Full fathom five thy father lies" (I.ii.397–405). The first three lines of the song are progressively metaphoric, and part of the effect depends upon the difference between what Ferdinand knows and what the audience knows. Because Ferdinand does not know whether his father is dead or alive, he presumably regards the first line as literal statement; and he is in no position to judge its factuality. The audience, however, has Prospero's assurance (confided earlier to Miranda)

> that there is no soul—
> No, not so much perdition as an hair
> Betid to any creature in the vessel.
> (I.ii.29–31)

We therefore conclude, though perhaps unconsciously, (1) that the statement is not literally true and so its primary meaning must be metaphoric and (2) that the play's time frame is beginning to dissolve, or at least to shift.[14] Since we know only that Alonso is safe, not what is happening to him (or indeed what may already have happened), the line's present-tense verb *lies* leaves us in the dark as to Alonso's "present" metaphoric condition, just as Ferdinand is in the dark as to his father's "present" literal condition. As it turns out, Alonso himself confirms that the song's metaphoric meaning applies to events that occur later in the play's time frame. Believing that Ferdinand has drowned, he says,

> Therefore my son i' th' ooze is bedded; and
> I'll seek him deeper than e'er plummet sounded
> And with him there lie mudded.
> (III.iii.100–102)

Thus, even two acts later the verb *lies* shifts to the future tense ("I'll . . . lie"). In short, the verb in the line "Full fathom five thy father lies" serves as what might be called a "predictive present tense" in the metaphoric meaning of the line, which of course is lost upon Ferdinand but, one would hope, not upon the audience.

The song's second line, "Of his bones are coral made," is recognizable as a time-lapse metaphor, though its structure is different from any that we have encountered before. There is of course a certain awkwardness, at least to modern ears, in the wording of the line. The Elizabethans were, as we know, less strict in the matter of spelling and subject-verb agreement than moderns are—the *OED* cites this sentence from Hakluyt's *Voyages:* "The currals does grow in the manner of stalkes upon the rockes on the bottome, and waxe hard and red." But even so, the word *coral* would seem to be a special case since even now the plural with an *s* is used routinely in referring to the animals themselves ("corals") but not to their skeletal remains ("coral reefs," or "pieces of coral"). The statement itself is a passive-voice construction, "B are made of A," which is approximately equivalent in meaning to "A become B." This in turn is a time-lapse metaphor consisting of two statements, one literal ("those were his bones") and one metaphoric ("his bones are coral"). As in any metaphor, the subject and predicate terms are in a sense remote from each other (bones, coral); and as in any time-lapse metaphor, the grammatical structure links the two terms by means of a construction that suggests, however faintly, the passage of time. The verb form in this line also has the effect of blurring even further the time reference of the tense system; even if it is metaphorically true that "Of his bones are coral made," the present-tense passive-voice verb gives no indication whatever as to when this process takes, took, or will take place.

The line that follows, "Those are pearls that were his eyes," brings the time-lapse metaphor to perfection. There is not the slightest hint of awkwardness about the wording, and the meaning is crystal clear. It is as if the expression the writer is only striving for in the previous line suddenly emerges in all its force and beauty. The remoteness between subject and predicate terms (eyes, pearls) is considerably greater than in the previous metaphor, since pieces of coral are, in a vaguely literal sense, the "bones" of coral polyps. The statement, consisting of one main and one dependent clause, is again the conflation of two statements, one literal ("those were his eyes") and the other metaphoric ("his eyes are pearls"). And the structure of the statement suggests the passage of time not by the bland word *becomes* (as in "Reason *becomes* the marshal to my will," MND II.ii.120), nor by the slightly awkward passive voice (as in "Of his bones are coral made"), but by the subtle though unmistakable shift from present tense in the main clause to past tense in the dependent one: "Those *are* pearls that *were* his eyes."

The second and third lines of the song bring the rest of the tense sequence into agreement with the "predictive present tense" of the first line. The difference between *were* and *are* is indistinguishable from the difference between *are* and *will be* except in relation to the listener's own present time, which in the traumatic experience of tempest and shipwreck becomes dissolved into a continuing "today." The significance of the time-lapse metaphor is concentrated not in the difference between "then" and "now," but in the distinction between "before" and "after" regardless of its relation to an elusive present, which is constantly slipping away and becoming the past. The song thus emphasizes the distinction between "before" and "after" (rather than that between "then" and "now") by changing the reference of the tenses. The "actual" future is represented by the present tense, and the "actual" present by the past: "Those are (i.e., will be) pearls that were (i.e., are) his eyes."

The sentence that follows these time-lapse metaphors has the character of literal statement, and it depicts in general terms the remarkable or even mysterious transformation of which the preceding metaphors are particular examples:

> Nothing of him that doth fade
> But doth suffer a sea-change
> Into something rich and strange.

Partly because coral and pearls presumably retain their beauty and luster much longer than human bones and eyes do, the statement suggests (but does not actually say) that the "rich and strange" thing that Alonso has become (or soon *will* become) is more enduring than the original Alonso, who consists (or *did* consist) primarily of things that "fade." The word *suffer*, whose primary meaning here is "undergo," likewise suggests (but again does not actually say) that the process is not (or will not be) an easy one. Coral and pearls of course come from the sea; but in calling the entire transformation a "sea-change," the writer brings into sharp focus what is (or will become) the most important strand of imagery in the whole play:

> Their understanding
> Begins to swell, and the approaching tide
> Will shortly fill the reasonable shore,
> That now lies foul and muddy.
> (V.i.79–82)

One can only suppose that it is "the approaching tide" of metaphor and imagination that will shortly fill (or has already filled) "the reasonable shore" of thought and judgment, that otherwise lies (or will lie) "foul and muddy." Indeed, one cannot help marveling at the power of metaphor not only to compress ideas and conceptions but to compress the passage of time as well. Even the word *tempest*, which furnishes the title for the play, means "time" no less than "storm." The play's insistence upon the shortness of time (as in "The time 'twixt six and now / Must by us both be spent most preciously," I.ii.240–41) is only the most external and obvious manifestation of its concern with that subject.

Before turning to a final consideration of the relationship between character change and time-lapse metaphor, let us examine one more point in connection with metaphor itself—the manner in which metaphor generates metaphor. That it does so very prolifically is observable, quite apart from the Shakespeare plays, in the evolution of Christian thought and doctrine. The central belief of Christianity is reflected in the doctrine of the Incarnation, which affirms "that the eternal Son of God took human flesh from His human mother and that the historical Christ is at once fully God and fully man."[15] This doctrine may be stated more compactly in the form of a time-lapse metaphor: "In Christ, God the infinite and unknowable becomes man the finite and knowable." Such a powerful metaphor has of course generated all sorts of supporting metaphors, such as that of the Resurrection ("after three days, Christ the dead man becomes Christ the living God") and the doctrine of Transubstantiation ("in the Eucharist, the bread and wine become the Body and Blood of Christ"). John, the most metaphoric of the gospels, sets the example for such language: "Jesus answered them, 'Destroy this temple, and in three days I will raise it up.' The Jews then said, 'It has taken forty-six years to build this temple, and will you raise it up in three days?' But he spoke of the temple of his body. When therefore he was raised from the dead, his disciples remembered that he had said this; and they believed the scripture and the word which Jesus had spoken." (John 2.19–22, RSV). Christology may thus be more or less accurately described as the "unpacking of a metaphor"—perhaps the most powerful metaphor in human history. And this central metaphor seems restlessly to seek expression in other, closely related metaphors.[16]

Tradition has it that the same author wrote the fourth gospel and the book of Revelation. Whether or not that is true, this final and most richly metaphoric section of the New Testament provides examples of time-lapse metaphor in which *both* statements that go into the making of the compound metaphor are themselves metaphoric: "For the Lamb in the midst of the throne will be their shepherd" (Rev. 7.17, RSV). In order for the statement to be of any significance at all, the reader must understand that "Christ is the Lamb of God" (John 1.29, 36). Also implied in the metaphor is the gospel assertion, "I [Christ] am the good shepherd" (John 10.11). Any attempt to combine the two metaphors by means of a present-tense verb that indicates being rather than becoming results in a contradictory and therefore nonsensical statement: "The lamb is the shepherd." But a present-tense verb of becoming or a future-tense verb of being removes the difficulty: "The lamb becomes the shepherd," or (in fact) "The Lamb will be their shepherd." Interestingly, the doubly metaphoric character of the statement resides not simply in the oppositeness or separateness of the categories referred to in the subject and predicate terms ("Christ is lamb," and "Christ is shepherd") but in the *reversal* or *interchange* of roles within the same metaphoric category (lamb, shepherd), which implies the passage of time, since simultaneity implies only contradiction. Thus, "The lamb will be their shepherd"; and the meaningfulness of the statement depends upon the reader's understanding that Christ is both "lamb" and "shepherd," though not simultaneously.

Simile, by comparison with such metaphor and double metaphor, seems not to possess this astonishing fecundity and richness of meaning; it is thus more adequately described as being "useful for stylistic, rhetorical, and didactic purposes" than is metaphor. The synoptic gospels of course make considerable use of simile, primarily in parables, which either employ actual similes (e.g., "The kingdom of heaven is like a grain of mustard seed") or else are constructed in such a way as to require point-by-point analogical interpretation (e.g., the Parable of the Sower). The highly metaphoric gospel of John, however, contains no parables at all, and the disciples apparently had misgivings about their use.[17] According to Matthew, "the disciples came and said to him, 'Why do you speak to them in parables?' And he answered them, 'To you it has been given to know the secrets of the kingdom of heaven, but to them it has not been given. . . . This is why I speak to them in parables, because seeing they do not see, and hearing they do not hear, nor do they understand'" (Matt. 13.10–13). Then follow several parables, those of the weeds of the field, the pearl of great price, and various others. In effect, Jesus tells them, "Metaphor is too rich for their stomachs; I therefore start them with the pabulum of similitude—it provides at least some nourishment, and it is watered down enough for them to digest."[18] As I suggested earlier, simile is eviscerated metaphor; it therefore lacks the strength to generate its own kind in the manner of metaphor. Whenever metaphor appears significantly either in poetry or in discourse, it often entrains a whole series of other metaphors almost spontaneously. But once a simile, however elaborate it may be, has run its course, it seems to sputter and quit like an engine that stubbornly refuses to keep going.

WITHIN the framework of the Shakespeare comedies, character-change involves the dramatization of a time-lapse metaphor. At the beginning of the play we see one or more of the characters in a particular light. We begin, to use Wittgenstein's phrase, by "noticing an aspect" of the character; and we end by "noticing a different aspect." To borrow another of Wittgenstein's insights, the playwright offers this invitation to his audience, "Imagine this changed like this, and you have this other thing." Except for the element of progression (an identifiable "before" and "after"), the effect of character-change in Shakespearean comedy is comparable to our experience with ambiguous drawings such as the duck-rabbit figure that Wittgenstein borrows from Jastrow or the beautiful-young-woman-ugly-old-hag picture that psychologists and consultants are fond of showing to their students and clients.[19] In the duck-rabbit sketch, the long loops extending from the circular "head" are the duck's bill when we see it one way and the rabbit's ears when we see it the other way. Most people tend to see the figure alternately as duck and rabbit; some see it only as one or the other; and a very few cannot see it as either one. (Wittgenstein calls this latter difficulty "aspect-blindness" and suggests that it may be comparable to color-blindness or to tone-deafness.) How then are we to respond to the art critic with perfectly good credentials who informs us, in an authoritative voice, "The figure is *really* a duck (because that's what I saw when I first looked at it); and this rabbit business is merely a trick on the part of the draftsman to fool the unperceptive"?

Unfortunately, there are at least two important elements in our cultural tradition that dispose us to regard Shakespearean character-change in this fashion. One is the Aristotelian-Horatian emphasis upon character consistency in drama, reflected clearly in most neoclassical plays. Such an emphasis is perhaps a corollary of the insistence upon clear and unambiguous diction, and it should not be surprising that the same Dr. Johnson who regarded Bertram, in *All's Well That Ends Well*, as being arbitrarily "dismissed to happiness" cordially disliked Shakespeare's puns. The other influence descends to us not from Aristotle but from Plato and is reflected in the traditional wisdom which assures us that appearances change but reality does not and that human nature never changes. But the assertion that reality does not change depends entirely of course upon how we define reality; and modern physics seems to be moving toward a view of reality that is more nearly consistent with the pre-Socratic conception of reality as constant flux than with Plato's theory of forms. As for the view that human nature never changes, one would think that Charles Darwin had dealt that conception a devastating blow; and even if he did not, history is full of examples to show that whether or not human nature is slow to change, individual people sometimes change quite suddenly and unpredictably.

The characters in the Shakespeare comedies do not change *because* they operate within the framework of a comic plot; indeed, such changes are utterly foreign to traditional comedy, whose main features include consistent characterization, unambiguous diction, and a morally appropriate ending. On the contrary, the Shakespeare comedies, which rely heavily upon character shifts and changes, puns and double entendres, and wish-fulfilling endings, resemble traditional comedy almost by coincidence. Their atmosphere is often, though by no means always, light and amusing, even in the "darkest" of the comedies; and their endings are "happy," not because the characters get what they deserve, but because by the end of the play they express their willingness to accept a kind of grace—or, like Caliban, they suggest that they will actively seek it. The characters do not change in order to make the play "turn out like a comedy"; rather, the characters change—just as word meanings change in the lines those characters speak—and the play's overall form bears a resemblance to traditional comedy because the "happy ending" that grace brings in its wake is more deeply satisfying than the ending produced by moral justification. Such an ending is also much more closely allied with genuine self-knowledge; and self-knowledge or the lack of it, as Socrates perceived very clearly before Plato and Aristotle muddied the waters, is at the heart of comedy.

Character-change in the Shakespeare comedies serves as a kind of barometer to indicate the extent to which the character's self-knowledge increases. And our response to those changes when they occur is often a measure of our own self-knowledge or the lack of it. Just as those who like to think of their own use of language as being clear and unambiguous may groan or even hold their noses when they encounter a really good pun, those who regard the human personality as being unified and simple tend to smile condescendingly when they see Kate represented not as shrew but as ideal wife, or to be outraged when they see Shylock displayed not as Jacob the clever supplanter but as Laban the outwitted and deserted old father. Others, however, may burst out laughing when they hear the same pun, or grin rather broadly when they see and hear the "new" Kate, or smile a bit grimly when they see and hear the "new" Shylock, especially if they have a little money and a daughter or two. Our laughter, as some philosopher has probably observed, becomes more muted as the joke strikes closer to home. It should be obvious that what happens to Shylock is certainly not morally appropriate; and in this way the play endeavors to *show,* as well as to *say,* that "in the course of justice none of us / Should see salvation." In terms of the biblical source, justification by faith supersedes justification by works of the law. In terms of the play, those who "give and hazard all" and who "stand for sacrifice" end more happily than those who "stand here for law" and who demand to know "What judgment shall I dread, doing no wrong?"

Shakespeare's character-changes thus exploit the richness of human personality, just as his puns exploit word meanings and his metaphors exploit combinations of images and ideas. But all puns and most metaphors are essentially static and timeless—single collisions, as it were, rather than chain reactions. We can ignore Shakespeare's "bad puns" ("Bootless home ... and in foul weather too") and his "mixed metaphors" ("to take arms against a sea of troubles"); but we have to cope, one way or another, with his time-lapse metaphors. We either have to explain them away ("there is no real reformation"), or else we have to brace ourselves and take the full force of their impact. "Those are pearls that were his eyes" is so beautiful and so powerful that commentators do not feel constrained to warn us that of course eyes do not become pearls or that we should somehow translate such a statement in our imagination into something that is consistent with traditional wisdom. "The spirit gone, man is garbage" probably catches the meaning a little better and certainly makes a more direct appeal to the modern mind; but then again, it is only another time-lapse metaphor. It would appear to be extremely difficult to convey the same meaning and emotion in purely literal language; and even if one could, the statement would surely lack the simplicity, brevity, and impact of Shakespeare's (or even Heller's) metaphor.

Lastly, we should consider how time-lapse metaphor becomes the basis for plot in the Shakespeare transformation comedies. Most simply described, the plot itself consists of a series of episodes in which the playwright, usually by means of the manipulator figure (e.g., Petruchio, Portia, Rosalind), gives the main characters a dose of their own medicine. That is, the manipulator explores what happens when one character is treated as he or she routinely treats others. There is of course no better remedy for cynicism, no better prescription for achieving self-knowledge, than to put offenders in the place of their victims and to show them, both by statement and by example, the implications of their own attitudes and behavior. For the sake of brevity, we will take our illustrations from the first and the last of the transformation comedies, *The Taming of the Shrew* and *The Tempest*.

I have already said that we may summarize the main plot of *The Taming of the Shrew* more or less adequately in the statement "Kate the shrew becomes Kate the ideal wife." Petruchio outlines his method for "taming" Kate in the speech (one hesitates to call it a soliloquy) at the end of Act IV, scene i, that begins "Thus have I politicly begun my reign" and ends with the invitation "He that knows better how to tame a shrow, / Now let him speak: 'tis charity to show." Because they are on the periphery of the plot, certain minor characters are able to comment upon the action more directly and more objectively than anyone else. Shortly before Petruchio's exposition of his own method, Curtis, one of Petruchio's servants, responds to Grumio's description of their master's behavior with the words "By this reck'ning he is more shrew than she" (IV.i.74). And Peter, who is so insignificant that his name does not even appear in the cast of characters, says, "He kills her in her own humor" (IV.i.167). In short, the method for taming Kate is to treat her no less shrewishly than she habitually treats others; and the main plot consists of scenes in which Petruchio does exactly that. Kate ends, of course, by abandoning her shrewish ways and embracing her new role as wife no less energetically than she had formerly embraced her role as shrew.

Likewise, in *The Tempest*, Alonso, who had been a willing conspirator against Prospero in the episode that Prospero describes to Miranda in Act I, scene ii, becomes the intended victim in a corresponding episode on the island itself, when Sebastian and Antonio plot against him in a fashion that closely parallels the earlier episode. A third version of the conspiracy, in which Caliban, Stephano, and Trinculo plot to kill Prospero, serves as a reductio ad absurdum in relation to the central episode, much as the Inductions serve that purpose in *The Taming of the Shrew*. As a result of both his victimization and the apparent loss of his son, a "sea-change" overtakes Alonso, who enters the play as an unrepentant conspirator and who leaves it asking, and receiving, Prospero's forgiveness. Their reconciliation is symbolized in the marriage of Ferdinand and Miranda, whose courtship constitutes a subplot separate from, but ultimately linked with, the main plot. Gonzalo summarizes the events of the play in language that is both literal and metaphoric:

> in one voyage
> Did Claribel her husband find at Tunis,
> And Ferdinand her brother found a wife

> Where he himself was lost; Prospero his dukedom
> In a poor isle; and all of us ourselves
> When no man was his own.
>
> (V.i.208–13)

As in *The Taming of the Shrew,* the main instrument for "reforming" Alonso in *The Tempest* is to treat him as he had earlier treated someone else. Gonzalo suggests, when he says "all of us [found] ourselves," that the significance of the experience is by no means limited to Alonso; and Prospero's epilogue expresses the hope that the members of the audience have shared in that experience and will put its meaning into practice themselves.

Such analysis does not of course do justice to either the language or the plots of the plays in question. But it does, I hope, help to establish the relationship between the literal and the metaphoric, the manner in which time may enter into metaphor, and the fundamentally metaphoric nature of the plots. Most critics tend to regard the plots, especially in the earlier plays, as being equivalent to a series of dubious literal statements rather than as one bold metaphor, a time-lapse metaphor that invites us to see the character first in one way and then later in another, quite different way. Our training equips us to evaluate literal statements on the basis of reason and to "translate" simple (timeless) metaphors into literal statements. Consequently, when we encounter the more complex time-lapse metaphor, which stubbornly resists such "translation," we try to cope with it by cutting it in two and accepting the part that is consistent with present-day common sense while rejecting the other part (whether literal or metaphoric) because it is inconsistent either with common sense or with the part we have already accepted, or both.

Following this procedure, we accept Kate as shrew (simple metaphor), but we tend to reject Kate as ideal wife (simple literal statement) because that view of her is inconsistent both with the earlier, already accepted view of her as shrew and with the present-day view of what constitutes an ideal wife. Similarly, we regard as "real" the (sixteen-year-old) Prince Hal who vanquishes Hotspur at the battle of Shrewsbury even though there is no historical evidence to support such a view, because that view is consistent with his character as Henry V, the historical victor at the battle of Agincourt; and we reject the view of Hal as dissipated prince both because it is inconsistent with the later Henry V and because Hal predicts his later heroic behavior as early as Act I, scene ii, of *Henry IV, Part 1.* Thus, "there is no real reformation; the prince always knows what is right and prefers it; only appearances are against him."[20] And in dealing with both plays, we seem to be considerably more comfortable once we have explained away the time-lapse metaphor, just as Dr. Johnson was more comfortable with Shakespeare when he could ignore those awful puns, which he regarded as the poet's "fatal Cleopatra."[21]

Character-change in the Shakespeare comedies does indeed cause something of a credibility strain in the mind of the viewer or reader but probably no more so than love at first sight, which characterizes those same plays all the way from *The Comedy of Errors* straight through to *The Tempest*. But why should one reader be regarded as naive for rejecting Lucentio's claim (*Shrew* I.i.143–55) to having fallen in love at the first good sight, while another is regarded as sophisticated for rejecting Kate's claim (V.ii.141–84) to having changed her attitude at the first good opportunity? Both objections are made on precisely the same grounds—namely, that such sudden shifts are patently unrealistic. Near the end of Chaucer's "Wife of Bath's Tale," the old hag suggests to her unwilling husband that she might remedy whatever is troubling him within three days ("er it were dayes thre") if she were so inclined. As the story nears its happy ending, she proposes tomorrow morning as the deadline ("And but I be to-morn"); but when even that seems too long for her impatient young husband to wait, she simply tells him to lift up the curtain that separates them ("Cast up the curtyn"). He does as he is told, and his heart is bathed in bliss when he sees his beautiful young bride. No objection to the ending on the basis of realism, however cogently argued, can spoil Chaucer's story. Fortunately much the same is true of the Shakespeare comedies.

ҩ FOUR ҩ

Farce and Beyond

Antipholus, Katherine, and Proteus

◆

For she is changed as she had never been.

THE dates of the earliest Shakespeare plays are by no means certain, but modern editors tend to regard *The Comedy of Errors*, *The Taming of the Shrew*, and *The Two Gentlemen of Verona* as the first of the comedies. These three plays clearly indicate both the young dramatist's starting point within the genre of comedy and the direction in which he was to develop throughout his career as a comic writer. *The Comedy of Errors* reveals his dependence upon classical sources, his fondness for farcical situations, and his preoccupation with mirror images. The mirroring is of course hardly subtle, but it is the device upon which the entire play rests. *The Taming of the Shrew* reflects his discovery and first significant use, for comic purposes, of the transformation plot and of the framing device. The siblings of this play, far from being identical twins, are polar opposites who ultimately exchange roles; and the main play is itself represented as a play within a play. *The Two Gentlemen of Verona*, often regarded as "Shakespeare's earliest attempt at romantic comedy," continues the love-transformation theme, juxtaposes it with the parallel (and sometimes conflicting) theme of friendship, and achieves its comic resolution by means of one character's repentance and another's forgiveness.[1] Although none of the three plays is a masterpiece, considered as a group they display the main structural features of Shakespearean comedy and prefigure the later stages of its development.

The principal difference between the first two comedies arises directly from the difference between simile and metaphor. As I have already indicated, the plot for *The Taming of the Shrew* may be summarized in the time-lapse metaphor Kate the shrew becomes Kate the ideal wife. *The Comedy of Errors,* on the other hand, is built upon a simile that Shakespeare borrowed from Plautus, who may in turn have borrowed it from Menander, or Philemon, or Diphilus: "(Antipholus of Syracuse is *not* Antipholus of Ephesus, but in almost every way) Antipholus of Syracuse is *like* Antipholus of Ephesus." The errors which constitute the plot of the play result from the failure of the other characters to recognize that Antipholus of Syracuse is not Antipholus of Ephesus; and these errors continue unabated until the end of the play, when the twins appear together onstage and are properly sorted out. Besides the mistakes of identity upon which the plot depends, the errors mentioned in the title also include mistaken hypotheses advanced by the twins themselves to account for their own bewildering confusion. Such hypotheses, however interesting they may be out of context, serve in the play only as sources of amusement, because the audience knows from the beginning that they are utterly inappropriate as explanations for the events represented onstage.

The limitations of *The Comedy of Errors* are rooted in the fact that although metaphor generates metaphor prolifically, simile does not generate simile in any comparable fashion. The only such proliferation in this play comes about as a result of the first simile's dividing itself, like an amoeba, into two similes of identical cognitive content: "Antipholus of Syracuse is like Antipholus of Ephesus" gives rise, by a process of binary fission, to "Dromio of Syracuse is like Dromio of Ephesus." One could repeat the process any number of times, but it would only yield more similes that were parallel, equal, and equivalent. None of them would serve as supporting similes that could embellish or extend the structure of the play by creating the basis for an interesting subplot that would supplement, rather than simply repeat, the main plot. In *The Merchant of Venice* Shylock is asked why he had brought up and retold with obvious relish the story of Jacob's ewes and rams: "Was this inserted to make interest good? / Or is your gold and silver ewes and rams?" Shylock replies, "I cannot tell; I make it breed as fast" (I.iii.90–92). Shakespeare is able to make his metaphors "breed as fast" as Jacob's ewes and rams; but his similes, like everyone else's, can only reproduce themselves by a kind of mitosis.

The transformation motif is as prominent in *The Comedy of Errors* as in any of Shakespeare's later comedies, but only as a tentative—and mistaken—explanation for the confusion, not as part of the mechanics of the plot. Antipholus of Syracuse, finding himself a stranger in Ephesus, soon announces his suspicion that the city's reputation is well deserved:

> They say this town is full of cozenage:
> As, nimble jugglers that deceive the eye,
> Dark-working sorcerers that change the mind,
> Soul-killing witches that deform the body,
> Disguisèd cheaters, prating mountebanks,
> And many such-like liberties of sin.
> (I.ii.97–102)

Not long thereafter, Dromio of Syracuse comes to a similar conclusion and envisions the possibility that he may fall victim, as Falstaff does a decade or so later in the Forest of Windsor, to some very hostile spirits:

> This is the fairy land. O spite of spites,
> We talk with goblins, owls, and sprites!
> If we obey them not, this will ensue:
> They'll suck our breath, or pinch us black and blue.
> (II.ii.188–91)

Perhaps out of modesty, he suggests that he has suffered a fate more closely akin to the one that Bottom will undergo in the forest outside of Athens:

> Dromio S.   I am transformèd, master, am I not?
> Antipholus S.   I think thou art, in mind, and so am I.
> Dromio S.   Nay, master, both in mind and in my shape.
> Antipholus S.   Thou hast thine own form.
> Dromio S.   No, I am an ape.
> Luciana   If thou art changed to aught, 'tis to an ass.
> Dromio S.   'Tis true; she rides me and I long for grass.
> 'Tis so, I am an ass; else it could never be
> But I should know her as well as she knows me.
> (II.ii.194–201)

Such "transformation," which in plot terms neither significantly "changes the mind" nor effectively "deforms the body," might be described as "pre-Ovidian." It works no meaningful change in anyone or anything; it is attributed not to the gods, but to witches, conjurers, and mountebanks; and its relationship to love (either *eros* or *caritas*) is doubtful at best.

The literary vehicle for transformation is metaphor, which involves synthesis. Because any simile implicitly denies its corresponding metaphor, it affirms separation and distinction while asserting one or more points of resemblance. Similarity-versus-difference figures in both metaphor and simile: the greater the similarity between subject and predicate terms of a metaphor, the closer it will come to literal statement (because it approaches tautology); and the greater the similarity between the two terms of a simile, the more likely it is that one of them will be mistaken for the other (because it approaches the assertion that one is an identical copy of the other). Identical twins exploit this possibility to the fullest, and *The Comedy of Errors* is the classic literary example. But even the strongest speech in the play is weakened by what might be called the "simile-implication"—the realization, at least by the audience, that the immediate problem arises entirely from similarity of appearance. In what comes closer than anything else in the play to an impassioned speech, Antipholus of Syracuse pleads with Luciana:

> Against my soul's pure truth why labor you
> To make it wander in an unknown field?
> Are you a god? Would you create me new?
> Transform me then, and to your power I'll yield.
> But if that I am I, then well I know
> Your weeping sister is no wife of mine,
> Nor to her bed no homage do I owe.
>   (III.ii.37–43)

The audience knows full well (and Antipholus of Syracuse strongly suspects) that the answer to the questions "Are you a god? Would you create me new?" is an unequivocal no. Therefore the line "Transform me then, and to your power I'll yield" does not represent a genuine possibility even within the limited framework of the play. On the contrary, the "real" situation is reflected in the *if* clause—"But if that I am I"—which rests on what the audience has known from the beginning, namely that Antipholus of Syracuse is *not* Antipholus of Ephesus, however much he may look like him.

Moreover, time in no way enters into the simile on which the play is based. The two Antipholuses are now, always were, and always will be indistinguishable from each other. Time figures in the play only as the framework on which the errors and their consequences may be displayed. The audience is reminded at intervals that a certain amount of time has passed; but that fact would have no importance if Egeon, the father of the two Antipholuses, were not under sentence of death. And the audience, knowing that the play is entitled *The Comedy of Errors*, will not be unduly concerned about the supposed threat to Egeon. Certainly it would be misguided to argue that Shakespeare, in the first of his comedies, is careful to observe the "unities." If he appears to do so, it is only because the play he is following is itself classical and the simile upon which everything rests would have difficulty supporting a time frame that extends beyond a single day. Within the limits of such a play, there could not be any more adequate way to distinguish between two separate days in Ephesus than there is for distinguishing between the two Antipholuses themselves. And unfortunately, although the two Antipholuses may be brought onstage alternately to create a certain amount of controlled confusion, there is no convenient way of alternating between today and tomorrow within the time frame; and there would not be much point in it either since the two days, unlike the two Antipholuses, could hardly be dismayed at being mistaken for each other.

These statements are intended as analysis and not as a judgment of the play. *The Comedy of Errors* is, I think, an extremely amusing farce, as successful in its way as anything else that Shakespeare wrote. To produce a thoroughly entertaining five-act play upon nothing more substantial than a borrowed simile and another simile cloned from the first one is no small achievement.[2] I cannot agree, however, with Northrop Frye, who finds in the play "a metamorphic structure, a descent into illusion and an emergence into recognition." Nor can I agree with William Carroll, who asserts that "in several ways, *The Comedy of Errors* and *Twelfth Night*—Shakespeare's two most Plautine comedies—represent his deepest explorations into metamorphosis." It is necessary, I think, to read *The Comedy of Errors* retrospectively from the vantage point of the later comedies in order to discover a romance structure or a philosophical meaning in the play. Synthesis is indispensable to metamorphosis (or any other kind of transformation), and a plot based upon twins precludes the possibility of meaningful synthesis. Carroll observes that Shakespeare "seems, in short, to have rejected the basic assumption that identical twins are identical. For dramatic purposes, the most important fact about identical twins is that they are and must be finally different."[3] But the word *identical* has two distinct meanings: one and the same, as in "the identical person," and exactly alike, as in "an identical copy." The crucial point about twins, who may indeed be absolutely identical and indistinguishable, is not that they "are and must be finally different," but that they are "forever separate and distinct." They are certainly identical copies, but they are not and never can be one and the same. Nor can there ever be a fusion of the two as there might be, for instance, in marriage.

WHEN we turn to *The Taming of the Shrew*, we find a play built not upon simile but upon metaphor; and the central metaphor generates others that become the basis for the subplot and for the Inductions. The metaphor itself is not a particularly strong one, because the first element (Kate the shrew) is hackneyed and the second (Kate the ideal wife) is open to objection from the standpoint of definition. Nevertheless, it is sufficiently strong to create considerable disagreement between those who regard the plot as metaphor and those who regard it as literal representation. The first group, for whom the main plot justifies "the willing suspension of disbelief," takes the title at face value and accepts the play as a dramatization of the taming of the shrew. The second group, for whom the cognitive content of the plot is to be understood as literal statement, asserts that the statement which the play makes is simply false—that no one in the play changes significantly, least of all Kate herself, who has merely "teamed up with her husband in order to display her temperament more efficiently."[4] The dispute, in other words, is between those who distinguish in plot terms between weak metaphor and improbable literal statement on the one hand, and those who implicitly deny the validity of any such distinction on the other. The dispute continues, with only brief intervals of agreement as we progress through the Shakespeare comedies, until the metaphors become so strong that it becomes impossible to avoid regarding the plots as metaphoric.

Even in *The Taming of the Shrew,* however, the play's central metaphor is strong in comparison with simile if we may judge by its capacity to generate supporting metaphors. Because the secondary metaphor is weaker than the primary one (as the subplot is weaker than the main plot), the playwright resorts to multiple examples, as does John Donne when he follows up "No man is an island" with "every man is a piece of the continent, a part of the main." And so we find *four* characters in the subplot "later posing as" someone else. At Lucentio's instigation, Tranio trades hat and cloak with his master; and in a moment "Tranio is changed into Lucentio" (I.i.233). Not content merely to exchange roles with his servant, Lucentio creates a new role for himself as the fictitious schoolmaster, Cambio, in order to "undertake the teaching of the maid" Bianca. (As a noun, the Italian word *cambio* means "change, shift, exchange." As a verb, it is the first-person present indicative of *cambiare,* "I change.") The Pedant, or "authentic" schoolmaster, assumes the role of Lucentio's father Vincentio, whom he resembles "as much as an apple doth an oyster" (IV.ii.101); and Hortensio, suitor to Bianca, poses as Litio, another fictitious schoolmaster. We need alter or change only slightly the dramatis-personae description of Lucentio, and expand it a bit, to articulate the principal form of the play's secondary metaphor: Lucentio the lover of Bianca becomes Cambio the supposed teacher of Bianca. One of the ways in which plot and subplot are bound together is that Kate and Bianca, like Lucentio and Tranio, exchange roles: as Kate displays "her new-built virtue and obedience," the formerly submissive Bianca makes her appearance as one of "these headstrong women," who must be schooled to obey.

The play's tertiary metaphor provides the basis for the Inductions: Sly the drunken tinker becomes Sly the supposed nobleman. This version of the transformation motif, which is third in order of importance but first in order of presentation, puts the whole thing on the level of a practical joke. The dramatic method seems clear enough: the playwright begins with the weakest metaphor, the one in response to which no one, except of course Sly himself, is expected to "suspend disbelief." He then proceeds to the next stronger metaphor, the subplot in which four characters deliberately assume false identities in order to win the already desirable Bianca in marriage. He then goes to the main plot, in which Petruchio's strategy, which has some elements in common with that of the practical joker in the Induction and the lovers in the subplot, ultimately makes the shrewish Katherine willing to assume the identity of an ideal wife. The plot and subplot culminate simultaneously in the marriage banquet at the end of the play, and it would obviously be poor strategy to return to the Sly episode merely in the interest of symmetry. The "frame" is therefore incomplete, as it must be unless the playwright chooses to reduce the play's final effect to the level of its weakest metaphor.[5]

The three metaphors correspond roughly to three stages in the development of human consciousness: innocence, experience, and maturity. Sly, the perennial innocent, remains impervious to experience, partly because of his own obtuseness and partly because the lord and his servants are merely playing a joke on him. Bianca, whose "schoolmasters" are simply imposters posing as competent instructors in an effort to gain their own ends, likewise remains an innocent, more visibly so at the end of the play than at the beginning. Kate, however, begins as an innocent, then struggles with experience through much of the play, and finally emerges from it considerably chastened and mellowed. Because stage three often presents much the same appearance as stage one (as the reformed alcoholic often looks and acts like the innocent nondrinker), the casual observer may easily mistake the one for the other. This, in addition to matters already discussed in earlier chapters, is another reason why readers sometimes assert that Kate does not "really change" in the course of the play.

In no other Shakespeare play is there greater emphasis upon costume, disguise, role switching, and role reversal than in *The Taming of the Shrew*. Two of the most boisterously funny parts of the play are built upon costume and costume making—the outrageous get-up in which Petruchio makes his appearance at the wedding (III.ii) and the haberdasher-tailor episode (IV.iii). Petruchio's own garb is characterized by Baptista as a "shame to your estate, / An eyesore to our solemn festival" (III.ii.96–97) and by Tranio as "these unreverent robes." But after the rejection of the frustrated tailor,

Kate's "honest mean habiliments" provide the opportunity for Petruchio to moralize on the relation between costume and character:

> Our purses shall be proud, our garments poor,
> For 'tis the mind that makes the body rich;
> And as the sun breaks through the darkest clouds,
> So honor peereth in the meanest habit.
> What, is the jay more precious than the lark
> Because his feathers are more beautiful?
> Or is the adder better than the eel
> Because his painted skin contents the eye?
> O no, good Kate; neither art thou the worse
> For this poor furniture and mean array.
> (IV.iii.168–77)

Costume thus serves in the play as a metaphor for outward and visible elements, which are often unreliable indicators of worth. The distinction that Petruchio insists upon here is not so much the difference between "seeming" and "being" or between "appearance" and "reality," as it is between those parts of one's being which are of primary importance and those which are not. The body, after all, is certainly a part of one's being; but, as Petruchio reminds Kate, "Tis the mind that makes the body rich" (cf. Sonnet 146). Consequently, Kate is none the worse "for this poor furniture and mean array."

Petruchio's method as tamer is to hold a mirror up to Kate, and by so doing "he kills her in her own humor" (IV.i.167). Since the play is a farce, the mirror is of course a fun-house mirror, and the distorting elements are exaggeration and irony. Any impartial observer, not comprehending Petruchio's motive as articulated at the end of Act IV, scene i, might conclude as Curtis does that "he is more shrew than she" (IV.i.73). His judgment on her dress is implicit in the fantastical garb he dons for the wedding and in the episode with the costumers. Having held the mirror up to her in this fashion, he goes on to provide the verbal commentary in the speech just quoted—though she may be as plain looking as the lark or the eel, she is indeed as fine as the bluejay or the adder (neither of which is held in universal esteem). The dialogue and stage business having to do with costume relate finally to temperament and courtesy; by building up Kate's estimation of herself, by convincing her that she is a splendid person despite how she looks in "this poor furniture and mean array," Petruchio induces her to choose another costume, as it were, which she models for us very elegantly in her long final speech.

The subplot, which exploits costume and disguise brilliantly in the interest of role change and role reversal, supports the main plot beautifully in this respect. When Bianca unmasks Lucentio to her father with the words "Cambio is changed into Lucentio," Lucentio hastens to explain:

> Love wrought these miracles. Bianca's love
> Made me exchange my state with Tranio
> While he did bear my countenance in the town,
> And happily I have arrivèd at the last
> Unto the wishèd haven of my bliss.
> (V.i.112–16)

The line "Love wrought these miracles" can be counted upon to evoke laughter in almost any production of the play, and this laughter results mainly from Lucentio's use of the word *miracles*. The meaning of the word certainly undergoes some comic distortion, but that distortion is no greater than the distortion of the word *love* in the same line. Within the subplot, the meaning of *love* is equivalent to "love at first sight," as defined in an exchange between Tranio and Lucentio near the beginning of the play:

> Tranio   I pray, sir, tell me, is it possible
> That love should of a sudden take such hold?
> Lucentio   O Tranio, till I found it to be true
> I never thought it possible or likely.
> But see, while idly I stood looking on,
> I found the effect of love-in-idleness
> And now in plainness do confess to thee,
> That art to me as secret and as dear
> As Anna to the Queen of Carthage was,
> Tranio, I burn, I pine, I perish, Tranio,
> If I achieve not this young modest girl.
> (I.i.143–53)

The word *miracles* is at least as appropriate for the irrational and improbable events of the subplot as the word *love* is for the motivation behind them, since such "love" is merely a comic convention, as artificial in its way as the "miracles" that it produces. *Love* has long since become a comic cliché; *miracles*, however, produces an effect that is fresh and surprising. The difference between the two words in this context is quite simply the difference between a "living" metaphor and a "dead" one.

In short, the miracles to which Lucentio refers are at least as authentic as the love which wrought them. Both are conventions of Shakespearean comedy, and both refer (though perhaps remotely) to something genuine in human experience. Anyone who comments on the subplot by saying that Lucentio does not really love Bianca is clearly refusing to accept one of the givens of the play, and much the same is true of skepticism about Lucentio's miracles and Kate's transformation. These elements differ from their counterparts in other Shakespeare comedies primarily in this respect: *The Taming of the Shrew* is a parody of the typical transformation plot, and therefore everything about it is done with tongue in cheek. Petruchio's declaration that, offered a large enough dowry, he will marry *any* woman, "Be she as foul as was Florentius' love" (I.ii.67), invites the audience to set the play they are watching against a background provided by such transformation tales as the Loathly Lady story. And, as usual in the Shakespeare comedies, references to Ovid's *Metamorphoses* abound. In the Induction, the disguised lord and his servingmen propose to bring Sly pictures of Io and Daphne—the one changed into a heifer and the other into a laurel tree—in an effort to convince the lowborn and drunken Sly that he is "a lord and nothing but a lord" and that he has "a lady far more beautiful / Than any woman in this waning age" (Ind. ii.52–61). Later we encounter references to Europa as "the daughter of Agenor," for whom "great Jove" transformed himself into a bull (I.i.165–67), and to Helen of Troy as "Fair Leda's daughter," as if to remind us of her origin in the encounter between Leda and Jove, who had assumed the form of a swan for his amorous visit (I.ii.239).

The reformed Kate is the caricature of an ideal wife just as, earlier, she had been the caricature of a shrew. Likewise, Lucentio is the caricature of a passionate lover, and Petruchio is the caricature of an all-powerful transformation worker. Petruchio is neither conjurer nor magician nor saint; his only credentials are displayed by Tranio, who claims in response to Bianca's question that there is indeed a "taming school" where

> Petruchio is the master,
> That teacheth tricks eleven and twenty long
> To tame a shrew and charm her chattering tongue.
> (IV.ii.56–58)

The Inductions outstrip the larger play in this regard—they are a parody of a parody. The transformation is fraudulent and everyone knows it. The love element lacks both mystery and romance, as we see when Sly urges the disguised Page, "Madam, undress you and come now to bed" (Ind. ii.115). Finally, the transformer is simply a nobleman playing a trick upon a poor churl. If some commentators have thought it necessary to point out that Kate's final speech is both "exaggerated" and "susceptible of an ironic interpretation," it may be because they do not recognize the play as a parody, in which exaggeration and irony are two of the chief ingredients. To call Kate's final speech "exaggerated and ironic" is therefore rather like calling Falstaff "obese," as if the casual observer might not have noticed that he tended to be rather plump.

Because *The Taming of the Shrew* is the first of the comedies to be built upon a time-lapse metaphor, it is also the first to take on meaningful ambiguity, an element that is almost entirely lacking in *The Comedy of Errors*. What little ambiguity that play possesses is confined to the minds of the twins themselves as they explore one hypothesis after another (deliberate deception, madness, dreaming) in an effort to sort out their own confusion. The audience never really shares in that confusion; it merely sits back and, from a detached and superior position, enjoys watching the twins muddle through the difficulties whose cause remains unknown to the twins themselves until the end of the play. Not one of the twins possesses any more character than is necessary for his role in the plot, and the plot itself is hardly what one would call thought-provoking. In *The Taming of the Shrew*, however, we begin to experience some uncertainty as to how we are to respond to the characters and what we are to make of them, not only as we watch their antics onstage but even afterward as we reflect on them in the study.

The Comedy of Errors contains many references to transformation, but they strike the reader or audience as pointless because they do not figure importantly in the action nor do they serve as meaningful commentary upon complex and interesting characters. In *The Taming of the Shrew,* the title itself leads us to expect at least one transformation, and the plot certainly fulfills that expectation. In *The Two Gentlemen of Verona,* the title creates no such expectation—it gives very little indication as to the thematic content and almost none as to the structure of the play. But the names of the main characters do. Indeed, the names in this play turn out to be almost as significant as the names in allegory, though the play itself is certainly not allegorical.

Jonathan Goldberg, in *Voice Terminal Echo,* makes much of the names, as well he might: "What's in a name? For Silvia, it is her destiny (already written in the *silva* tradition) and her destination (both in *The Two Gentlemen of Verona* and the texts it generates). In a word, her name is a genealogy, and in the play in which she appears, her generation is the generation of the letter—literally and figuratively." The male characters' names are likewise significant: "Not merely the swain of pastoral romance, Valentine's name means lover." And most important of all, "Proteus's name directs us to what might be designated the master text that determines character in *The Two Gentlemen of Verona,* Ovid's *Metamorphoses.*⁶ From a literary character called Proteus we should expect any number of shifts and changes, and Shakespeare's Proteus turns out to be aptly named. In the *Odyssey,* Menelaus describes to Telemachus his encounter with the elusive deity:

> We with a cry sprang up and rushed upon him, locking him
> in our arms, but the Old Man did not forget the subtlety
> of his arts. First he turned into a great bearded lion,
> and then to a serpent, then to a leopard, then to a great boar,
> and he turned into fluid water, to a tree with towering branches,
> but we held stiffly on to him with enduring spirit.⁷

But because Shakespeare's knowledge of Homer was extremely limited—Chapman's translation of the *Odyssey* did not appear until 1616—it seems likely that his acquaintance with Proteus came from his reading of Ovid.

In the *Metamorphoses* there is a brief but significant reference to Proteus in book 8, just after the story of Baucis and Philemon, whose "thatched roof" Jaques refers to in *As You Like It* (III.iii.7–8). The passage in Golding's translation runs as follows:

> He hilld his peace, and bothe the thing and he that did it tell
> Did move them all, but *Theseus* most. Whom being mynded well
> To heere of wondrous things, the brooke of *Calydon* thus bespake.
> There are O valiant knyght sum folke that had the powre too take
> Straunge shape for once, and all their lyves continewed in the same,
> And othersum to sundrie shapes have power themselves to frame,
> As thou O *Protew* dwelling in the sea that cleepes the land.
> For now a yoonker, now a boare, anon a Lyon, and
> Streyght way thou didst become a Snake, and by and by a Bull,
> That people were afrayd of thee too see thy horned skull.
> And oftentymes thou seemde a stone, and now and then a tree,
> And counterfetting water sheere thou seemedst oft to bee
> A River: and another whyle contrarie thereuntoo
> Thou wart a fyre.⁸

Proteus, it would seem, had the power not only to change his shape at will but even to take one shape and then, almost simultaneously, another that was "contrarie thereuntoo." In *The Two Gentlemen of Verona,* such protean change serves as a metaphor for the human inconstancy produced by "the chameleon Love" (II.i.158), which has an apparently endless capacity to "alter" (II.iv.125) and to "deform" (II.i.59) its hapless victims. These transformations figure importantly in both dialogue and plot.

Proteus confirms the appropriateness of his name at the first opportunity. Before the first scene is half over, he rhapsodizes, "Thou, Julia, thou hast metamorphosed me" (I.i.66). The name Proteus is Homeric, and the vocabulary ("metamorphosed") is Ovidian; both name and vocabulary suggest that more transformations will be forthcoming. But the structure of this play is more complex than that of *The Taming of the Shrew* in at least two ways. First of all, *The Two Gentlemen of Verona* is built not upon a single compound metaphor but upon a whole series or chain of them: Proteus the faithful friend of Valentine becomes Proteus the passionate lover of Julia; Proteus the passionate lover of Julia becomes Proteus the still more passionate lover of Silvia; and so forth. The metaphoric nature of these statements is less obvious than is the case with "Kate the shrew becomes Kate the ideal wife" because neither of the simple statements that go into the making of the compound metaphor is itself metaphoric—"Proteus is the faithful friend of Valentine" is plainly literal as compared with "Kate is a shrew." There is, however, an element of contradiction between "faithful friend of A" and "passionate lover of B" which is comparable to the contradiction between "shrew" and "ideal wife." According to Berners A. W. Jackson, "What we have, in fact, is a conflict between the claims of two conventions; the plot contains not only a love story, where love must be all, but a love story combined with a type of story where the whole point is to show that love is not all."[9] Likewise, the contradiction between "lover of B" and "lover of C" arises not from the literal meaning of the terms, but from the fact that loving C necessitates casting off B. As with Demetrius and Lysander in *A Midsummer Night's Dream,* it never enters the young man's head to love both women at the same time.

As we observed in connection with John Donne's metaphors, a metaphor in which both the subject term and the predicate term are distributed ("No man is an island") is stronger than one in which either term is undistributed ("every man is a piece of the continent"). As we also observed, the writer may remedy this weakness to a certain extent by multiplying examples ("a piece of the continent, a part of the main"). By the same token, the writer may remedy the comparative weakness of a compound metaphor in which neither of the main elements is itself metaphoric ("Proteus the faithful friend of Valentine becomes Proteus the passionate lover of Julia") by extending it into a chain of compound metaphors of the same sort. In such a chain, the predicate term of each metaphor becomes the subject term of the next one. Thus, the plot for *The Taming of the Shrew* is based upon one compound metaphor, whereas the plot for *The Two Gentlemen of Verona* rests upon a chain of similar but weaker metaphors.

The second element that contributes to making the plot of *The Two Gentlemen of Verona* more complex than that of *The Taming of the Shrew* is that the condition or identity specified in the subject term of each compound metaphor reflects a genuine social or philosophic value, and its abandonment therefore amounts to a betrayal. In *The Taming of the Shrew* it is quite clear that most of the characters attach no great value to shrewishness. Consequently, Katherine's abandonment of that character delights nearly all of them. But what happens when loving one girl necessitates neglecting a friend? And worse, what happens when loving a second girl necessitates abandoning the first one—especially when the second girl happens to be the neglected (and now betrayed) friend's fiancée? In this respect, *The Two Gentlemen of Verona* looks forward to the problem plays as much as it does, in other ways, to the high romantic comedies.

As we have already observed, the play's plot represents a fusion of two different stories, a love story derived from Montemayor's *Diana* and a friendship story like that of Titus and Gisippus, from Elyot's *The Governor*. In order to combine the stories, Shakespeare must obviously make at least one of the characters common to both stories. Actually, both Proteus and Silvia figure in the two triangles, but no wrenching is required in making Silvia do double duty. There is considerable wrenching, however, when the friend-lover character shifts from one role to the other. Shakespeare renders the changeability palatable by associating the character with the mythical figure of Proteus, and he adds an element of psychological realism by portraying Proteus as being amazed and distressed by his own inconstancy. The speeches in which he articulates this distress are among the most memorable in the play:

> To leave my Julia, shall I be forsworn;
> To love fair Silvia, shall I be forsworn;
> To wrong my friend, I shall be much forsworn;
> And ev'n that pow'r which gave me first my oath
> Provokes me to this threefold perjury.
> Love bade me swear, and Love bids me forswear.
> (II.vi.1–6)

Proteus is probably the first of Shakespeare's lovers to make use of equivocation to rationalize his own fickleness:

> Unheedful vows may heedfully be broken,
> And he wants wit that wants resolvèd will
> To learn his wit t'exchange the bad for better.

. . . .

>   Julia I lose and Valentine I lose.
>   If I keep them, I needs must lose myself;
>   If I lose them, thus find I by their loss:
>   For Valentine, myself; for Julia, Silvia.
>   I to myself am dearer than a friend,
>   . . . .
>   I cannot now prove constant to myself
>   Without some treachery used to Valentine.
>   (II.vi.11–32)

This capacity for rationalization, though we may find it amusing in a Falstaff, strikes us as somewhat sinister in a lover or friend.

The crux of the plot and the thing that even more people object to than to Kate's final speech in *The Taming of the Shrew* is of course Proteus's attempted rape of Silvia, the interruption by Valentine, and the rapid-fire repentance, forgiveness, and disposition of the female characters in what would seem to be rather crass fashion. The critic can only offer a hypothesis as to how the scene is *supposed* to work; each member of the audience will decide for himself or herself whether it actually *does* work. The crucial passage is short enough to reproduce almost in its entirety. When Proteus threatens Silvia, "I'll force thee yield to my desire," Valentine springs forth from his hiding place and denounces his false friend in roundest terms:

> *Valentine*   Naught but mine eye
>   Could have persuaded me. Now I dare not say
>   I have one friend alive; thou wouldst disprove me.
>   Who should be trusted, when one's right hand
>   Is perjurèd to the bosom? Proteus,
>   I am sorry I must never trust thee more,
>   But count the world a stranger for thy sake.
>   The private wound is deepest. O time most accurst,
>   'Mongst all foes that a friend should be the worst!
> *Proteus*   My shame and guilt confounds me.
>   Forgive me, Valentine. If hearty sorrow
>   Be a sufficient ransom for offense,
>   I tender't here. I do as truly suffer
>   As e'er I did commit.
> *Valentine*   Then I am paid,
>   And once again I do receive thee honest.
>   Who by repentance is not satisfied

> Is nor of heaven nor earth, for these are pleased.
> By penitence th'Eternal's wrath's appeased;
> And, that my love may appear plain and free,
> All that was mine in Silvia I give thee.
>
> (V.iv.64–83)

The modern reader probably cannot help thinking that Valentine must already have been on the lookout for a way to be rid of Silvia, but such a view is both uncharitable and inappropriate.

The episode's dramatic success depends upon at least three different matters: a final twist in the Proteus myth, an element in the nature of comedy, and a religious attitude presumably shared by author and audience. Robert G. Hunter has demonstrated Shakespeare's reliance upon a shared belief in the social efficacy of repentance and forgiveness, and I refer the reader to his treatment of this third point.[10] As for the first one, according to the *Oxford Classical Dictionary* Proteus "has the power to take all manner of shapes, but if held till he resumes the true one, will answer questions." Whether Valentine actually lays hands upon Proteus is not indicated in the text, but there can be little doubt that he apprehends him or catches him in the act. Valentine's only question ("Who should be trusted, when one's right hand / Is perjured to the bosom?") is of course rhetorical, but Proteus, by his reply to Valentine, provides an answer of sorts. The main point, however, is that in some sense Proteus does "resume his true shape" by managing to combine two aspects of himself as friend of Valentine and as lover of Julia; in doing so he not only reconciles conflicting conventions in the two stories on which the plot is built and brings them to a satisfactory conclusion but rounds out his own representation of the Proteus story as well. As often happens in comedy, the final twist of the story enables us to have it both ways—Proteus gives every indication that he will be both friend to Valentine and lover to Julia, just as the hag in "The Wife of Bath's Tale" promises, at story's end, that she will be "bothe fair and good," both beautiful and faithful.

The second point, which has to do with the nature of comedy itself, involves the brevity of the episode and the suddenness with which the plot is resolved. In both the superiority and the incongruity theories of laughter, suddenness is a crucial element. Thomas Hobbes, who is generally credited with originating the moral or superiority theory, asserted that laughter results from a feeling of "sudden glory" when the ego is inflated by the pleasure we take either in our own momentary success or in someone else's ridiculous failure. With a similar emphasis upon suddenness, Immanuel Kant, who first articulated the incongruity theory, suggested that laughter has its source in "the sudden transformation of a strained expectation into nothing."[11] The sudden collapse of Proteus's projected rape certainly strikes the audience, Renaissance or modern, as ridiculous; and the equally sudden repentance and forgiveness strike us in much the same way. In short, the treatment of these events is deliberately comic; but that does not mean that there is anything funny about rape, or repentance, or forgiveness in and of themselves. Just as love at first sight is the comic version of romantic affection, so repentance at first blush and forgiveness at first request are the comic representations of those quite serious actions.

Because the ridiculous has so important a role in comedy, we may express the comic effect of this episode in *The Two Gentlemen of Verona* by means of a near tautology: the things that make it ridiculous are the very things that make it comic. And much the same is true of Valentine's encounter with "certain outlaws" in the forest near Mantua, Shakespeare's first version of the green world that is to figure so importantly in later comedies. To be sure, this forest is the setting for Proteus's final transformation, but the play does very little to suggest a cause-and-effect relationship between setting and transformation. At the beginning of this same scene Valentine muses on the pastoral setting in a way that faintly suggests Duke Senior's speech that introduces us to the forest of Arden:

> How use doth breed a habit in a man!
> This shadowy desert, unfrequented woods,
> I better brook than flourishing peopled towns.
> Here can I sit alone, unseen of any,
> And to the nightingale's complaining notes
> Tune my distresses and record my woes.
> (*TGV* V.iv.1–6)

It is presumably from behind a bush of some sort that Valentine emerges to foil Proteus's assault upon Sylvia; but one hardly gets the impression that this forest, like Arden, has "books in the running brooks, / Sermons in stones, and good in everything" (*AYL* II.i.16–17).

Considered as a group, these first three plays display in preliminary form the most important characteristics of mature Shakespearean comedy. The possibilities arising from the dramatization of a time-lapse metaphor soon replace the limitations of a plot based upon mere similarity of appearance; and consequently a genuine ambiguity concerning human motivation and action takes the place of simple confusion. The richness and fecundity of metaphor also makes possible, in *The Taming of the Shrew*, an interesting and meaningful subplot, which the simile-based *Comedy of Errors* lacks. *The Two Gentlemen of Verona* presses the time-lapse metaphor even further, representing a main character as changing repeatedly and finally returning to a modified form of his original condition. To a certain extent, this circularity of form has the effect of undoing the changes represented in each of the time-lapse metaphors upon which the play is built; and as a result, there is considerably less difference between the Proteus of Act V and the Proteus of Act I than between the Kate of Act V and the Kate of Act I. In later plays, Shakespeare makes use of the chain metaphor to trace stages in the development of characters without returning them to their original condition. The later technique will combine plot features of *The Taming of the Shrew* and *The Two Gentlemen of Verona*. The character's condition at the end of the play may be very different from what it had been at the beginning, as with Kate; but the process will sometimes be traced in steps or stages, as with Proteus.

The other characteristics of later Shakespearean comedy are likewise present in one or more of the first three plays. Reflexive structure—stories within stories and plays within plays—is important in *The Taming of the Shrew*, though its integration into the play as a whole is less successful than in later plays. And *The Two Gentlemen of Verona* represents an ingenious attempt to synthesize two quite different stories from separate sources. The contrast between two different settings also appears in embryonic form in at least two of the plays. But the difference between Sly's Warwickshire and Kate's Padua is not kept before the audience in any meaningful way, and the forest outside of Mantua strikes us as almost a parody of Shakespeare's later "green worlds." The poetry of all three plays is recognizably Shakespearean, but there is very little of the lyrical quality that is so abundant in the next few plays, nor is there any suggestion of the subtlety of rhythm created by the incongruity of sentence length and line length that characterizes the poetry of the later plays. All in all, the three comedies are interesting not only in themselves but also for the light they throw on the ones that follow and for the insight they provide into the methods that are to yield more fascinating results beginning with *A Midsummer Night's Dream*, in which skillfully constructed transformation plot, purposefully contrasted settings, and magnificent poetry come together for the first time.

FIVE

Romantic Comedy

Bottom, Shylock, and Oliver

> 'Twas I. But 'tis not I. I do not shame
> To tell you what I was, since my conversion
> So sweetly tastes, being the thing I am.

IN *A Midsummer Night's Dream*, *The Merchant of Venice*, and *As You Like It*, the transformation plot continues to be of primary importance; and its effect is most easily observed in the character-changes that take place as the plot progresses. In addition to the plot, which we may regard as a kind of constant, three variables begin to have greater impact upon the structure of the play than had been the case in the first three comedies: strongly contrasted settings, a benevolent and effective manipulator figure, and self-consciousness (or the lack of it) on the part of the characters who change. As we saw in *The Comedy of Errors*, which makes no use of the transformation plot, there was only the one urban setting; there was no manipulator figure in the play itself—all manipulation was done by the playwright himself from outside the structure of the play—and the characters were extremely self-conscious about changes they thought were taking place within themselves but were rooted in mistakes of identity, resulting from similarity of appearance. In the other two early comedies, the three variables begin to emerge, but their impact upon the structure of the plays is limited.

The forest outside Athens is indeed, to borrow Chaucer's phrase, "fulfild of fayerye"; Belmont, at some distance from Venice, is flooded with moonlight and music; and Arden is represented as a combination of Sherwood Forest, the antique world, and Eden before the Fall. And in all three plays this second world contrasts starkly with a court or urban setting in which autocratic rule or the power of money is dominant. In *A Midsummer Night's Dream*, the manipulator role is divided between Theseus and Oberon, both of whom falter at times; but it is assumed more confidently first by Portia, in *The Merchant of Venice*, and then by Rosalind, in *As You Like It*. Self-consciousness on the part of characters who change is delightfully nonexistent in *A Midsummer Night's Dream*; it must be inferred from speeches by Shylock and others in *The Merchant of Venice*; and it is perfectly explicit in Oliver's character and speeches in *As You Like It*. All of these elements, which have been analyzed at considerable length in the vast body of Shakespeare criticism, are fused in the poetry of the plays; and this poetry far surpasses anything to be found in the first three comedies.

Because Shakespearean transformation plots are essentially metaphoric, the author's mastery of metaphor is reflected in the plots of these plays just as clearly as in the poetry; and it is with plot that we are primarily concerned. But since the metaphoric nature of the plot is most easily observed in the changes that various characters undergo, we will continue to focus upon certain central characters—not as realistic representations of human beings, but as indicators of plot movement and development. Such characters are sometimes, though by no means always, the protagonists; but they do tend to be the ones that persist in our memory long after intricate details of the plots have become blurred in our minds. Both Bottom, in *A Midsummer Night's Dream*, and Shylock, in *The Merchant of Venice*, come very close to stealing the show despite being "minor" characters as far as the main plot is concerned. Oliver, in *As You Like It*, does not captivate our interest to the same extent as Bottom and Shylock; but his role is equally important for understanding the play in which he appears.

As much as any of the Shakespeare comedies—and more than the earliest of them—*A Midsummer Night's Dream* illustrates and reveals the double vision that characterizes the Shakespeare plays in general; both characters and author seem to "see these things with parted eye, / When everything seems double" (IV.i.188–89). The play within the play is both "tedious" and "brief," both "merry and tragical" (V.i.56–58). Like Caliban in *The Tempest*, Bottom is "a most delicate monster" (*Tmp.* II.ii.88–89); and the entire play is both a transitory "illusion" and "something of great constancy," its theme both "weak and idle" on the one hand and powerfully expressive of "strong imagination" on the other. The play is thus susceptible of analysis from nearly opposite points of view, as Norman Rabkin has shown *Henry V* to be.[1] To take just one example, Marjorie Garber observes in commenting upon the snake in Hermia's dream that "the snake, long a representative of violation and betrayal in scripture and in emblem books, is also a familiar Freudian image for male sexuality."[2] Such doubleness makes terms like "elegant and subtle" or "gross and palpable" equally appropriate in describing the play; but neither pair of adjectives, used separately, tells the whole story.

Some recent critics have emphasized the gross and palpable at the expense of the elegant and subtle, which used to figure more prominently in descriptions of *A Midsummer Night's Dream*. William Carroll, for instance, asserts that "Bottom and Titania apparently consummate *their* 'marriage' offstage, comically grotesque though it sounds."[3] Such an emphasis is not so much mistaken as it is partial and incomplete, especially when it goes so far as to reject or exclude alternative suppositions. Lovely lady enamored of priapic quadruped was of course a favorite subject in what used to be called "blue movies"; but one of Shakespeare's synthesizing skills is precisely his ability to combine the gross and palpable with the elegant and subtle. Consider, for instance, the lines

> To-morrow night, when Phoebe doth behold
> Her silver visage in the wat'ry glass,
> Decking with liquid pearl the bladed grass
> (A time that lovers' flights doth still conceal).
> (I.i.209–12)

These lines certainly evoke the tender night presided over by chaste Phoebe, who sees her own reflection "in the wat'ry glass" and sympathetically conceals amorous elopements ("lovers' flights") from the prying eyes of hostile courtiers. But they also evoke the shadowy image of coitus interruptus alfresco, "liquid pearl" falling upon "bladed grass" as a consequence of at least one lover's rapturous "flight," the amorous activity itself concealed by the friendly darkness of the same summer night.

As far as the "offstage consummation" is concerned, I tend to be cautious about assuming what may or may not happen offstage except insofar as such an assumption is required in order to make sense of the text. To a certain extent these imaginings are an integral part of any individual's personal response to the work of art, as Keats implies when the speaker in the "Ode on a Grecian Urn" raises the question

> What little town by river or sea shore,
> Or mountain-built with peaceful citadel,
> Is emptied of this folk, this pious morn?

Here more than one possibility is contemplated, and there is no suggestion that one is more probable than another. William Carroll, however, clearly states that he "disagrees" with David Young's conclusion, in *Some-*

thing of Great Constancy, that "the 'marriage' [of Bottom and Titania] is probably never consummated."⁴ Such matters, as Sir Thomas Browne observes, though they are "puzzling questions, are not beyond all conjecture." They do, however, fall into the same category as Mona Lisa's legs—she presumably had a pair, but what they may have looked like is anyone's guess. There is certainly no historical evidence that La Gioconda was a double amputee; and the plumpness of her face suggests that she, like the mistresses imagined by Browning's bishop, may indeed have had "great smooth marbly limbs." But when all is said and done, we have to admit that such conjectures about Mona Lisa's legs tell us more about the mindset of the individual viewer than about the portrait itself or the creative process behind it.⁵

Less is known about the sources for *A Midsummer Night's Dream* than about the sources for most of the other Shakespeare plays. What little is known for certain can be summarized briefly: "No source known for the main plot; for [the subplot,] the Pyramus and Thisbe story, [in] Ovid, *Metamorphoses* (tr. Golding, 1567), Bk. IV."⁶ The main plot may be regarded, however, as an elaboration of the Pyramus and Thisbe story itself. As Peter Phialas suggests, "The archetypal 'Pyramus and Thisbe' fable is roughly reproduced in the love story of Hermia and Lysander."⁷ In Ovid, the lovers hope to marry but are kept apart by tyrannical parents; they therefore flee through city gates to a rendezvous, where they encounter unforeseen difficulties. In Golding's version of the story, Ovid's lovers

> covenanted to get
> Away from such as watched them, and in the Evening late
> To steale out of their fathers house and eke the Citie gate.
> (4.104–6)

In *A Midsummer Night's Dream*, Lysander and Hermia likewise propose to elope:

> To-morrow night, when Phoebe doth behold
> Her silver visage in the wat'ry glass,
> . . . .
> Through Athens gates have we devised to steal.
> (I.i.209–13)

According to Golding's narrator, Pyramus arrives late for the appointment and is terrified when he sees a lion's footprint in the sand: "But when also the bloudie cloke he saw / All rent and torne, one night (he sayd) shall lovers two confounde." (4.132–33). Correspondingly, when Lysander and Hermia arrive in the forest, closely followed by Demetrius and Helena, the audience soon learns, as Puck sets to work, that "one night shall lovers *four* confound." The meaning of *confound* shifts, of course, from "ruin" or "destroy" in Golding to "mix up" or "mingle indistinguishably" in Shakespeare.[8]

To this germ of a story Shakespeare applies three familiar principles of comic development: doubling, mistakes, and reversals. The first of these (doubling) he had already put to good use in *The Comedy of Errors*, in which each twin doubles his brother and the second set of twins doubles the first set. Here, he increases the number of lovers from two to four; as Puck says, "Two of both kinds makes up four" (*MND* III.ii.438). The second principle (mistakes) comes into this play, as it had into *The Comedy of Errors*, as a result of similarity of appearance. Puck's reliance upon "Athenian garments" is of course inadequate for distinguishing between Lysander and Demetrius, and his mistake leads to an unintended mix-up or reorientation of the four lovers, which Oberon describes as "Some true-love turned, and not a false turned true" (III.ii.91). The third principle (reversal) figures most importantly in connection with the metamorphosis; the cause-and-effect relationship between story and metamorphosed plant is neatly reversed from what it is in Ovid. Shakespeare "transplants" Ovid's mulberry, which had changed color as a *result* of the lovers' being confounded, transforms it to the love-in-idleness, "Before milk-white, now purple with love's wound" (II.i.167), and makes it the *cause* for the lovers' confusion in *A Midsummer Night's Dream*.[9] To these three should be added a fourth and much more unusual technique, the creation of an artificial being—the man-ass Bottom (and its parody, the man-lion Snug), on the pattern of the griffon (II.i.232), which in Greek mythology had the body of a lion and the head of a bird, or the centaur (V.i.44), which had the head, arms, and trunk of a man and the body and legs of a horse.

The first two techniques are common enough in farcical comedy; but the third and fourth are sufficiently unusual to call for an exposition of sorts in the play itself. For this exposition Shakespeare borrows again from Golding's Ovid. In book 1, Apollo pursues the reluctant Daphne and addresses her as follows:

> Stay Nymph: the Lambes so flee ye Wolves, the Stags ye Lions so:
> With flittring fethers sielie Doves so from the Gossehauke flie,
> And every creature from his foe. Love is the cause that I
> Do followe thee.
>
> (1.611–14)

During the first scene in the forest, Helena, pursuing Demetrius, speaks to him in similar but inverted fashion:

> Run when you will. The story shall be changed:
> Apollo flies and Daphne holds the chase,
> The dove pursues the griffon, the mild hind
> Makes speed to catch the tiger—bootless speed,
> When cowardice pursues, and valor flies.
> (MND II.i.230–34)

The principle of inversion or reversal seems clear enough: Apollo says "Stay," whereas Helena says "Run"; Ovid's stags flee from his lions, whereas Shakespeare's mild hind pursues his tiger. The words "The story shall be changed" are plainly literal, though the structure of the statement closely resembles that of a time-lapse metaphor. And the roles of the sexes are reversed to match the reversal of predator and prey—"Apollo flies and Daphne holds the chase." But the most surprising change that Shakespeare makes in adapting the lines from Golding is to substitute the mythological griffon for the naturalistic goshawk—"The dove pursues the griffon." Like the griffon, which is a composite of two natural creatures, Bottom becomes a composite of man and ass, both of which exist in nature; but the composite itself never has and never will exist except within the confines of artistic representation. "With flittering feathers" the "silly dove" Titania pursues the "griffon" Bottom, promising to "purge his mortal grossness." Bottom, with ass's nole firmly fixed upon his head, is a living pun—the synthesis of two entirely separate species.

Much has been written about Bottom; in *Shakespeare's Comedies of Play*, J. Dennis Huston goes so far as to make him the focal point and "hero" of the play.[10] The general tendency is to see him in the context of Ovidian metamorphosis, and this seems reasonable enough since the play contains so many other Ovidian elements.[11] Moreover, the most probable date for the play is 1595, the year which, according to Hallett Smith, "saw the height of the Ovidian fad." William Carroll asserts that Bottom's translation is "the only onstage physical man-to-beast transformation in all of Shakespeare's plays" and goes on to say that because Bottom is an ass to begin with, "his literal metamorphosis *into an ass* is not surprising."[12] But all of this may have led us to a hasty conclusion about Bottom. I would argue to the contrary that there is no literal metamorphosis into an ass in *A Midsummer Night's Dream*. Puck apparently has magical powers at his disposal, at least those granted to him by Oberon; and Puck's description of what happens is perfectly straightforward: "When I did him at this advantage take, / An ass's nole I fixèd on his head" (III.ii.16–17). He does indeed conclude by saying "Titania waked, and straightway loved an ass" (l. 34); but since Bottom is an ass to begin with, this would be true metaphorically even if Puck had not put the ass's nole on Bottom's head. If Shakespeare had intended that Bottom should be literally metamorphosed into an ass, he surely could have managed it better than this—Lyly seems to have had no trouble at all with such onstage metamorphoses.[13] Only Bottom's colleagues, at least one of whom admits to being "slow of study," assert that he has been "translated"; and Titania's response to Bottom is governed by love at first sight, demonstrating once more that "Things base and vile, holding no quantity, / Love can transpose to form and dignity" (I.i.232–33).

But if Bottom is not literally metamorphosed into an ass, he is indeed, as Quince rightly says, "translated"—into something "strange and admirable." The most appropriate model for what Bottom becomes is neither the Ovidian nor the Apuleian metamorph, but the mythological griffon to which Helena refers—half one animal (bird) and half another (lion). Compare "Here come two noble beasts in, a man and a lion" (V.i.214–15).[14] Under this unnatural guise Bottom becomes the comic equivalent of the artificial bird in the last stanza of Yeats's "Sailing to Byzantium":

> Once out of nature I shall never take
> My bodily form from any natural thing,
> But such a form as Grecian goldsmiths make
> Of hammered gold and gold enamelling
> To keep a drowsy Emperor awake;
> Or set upon a golden bough to sing
> To lords and ladies of Byzantium
> Of what is past, or passing, or to come.

Though the man-ass Bottom never rises to the heights of Yeats's final stanza, he speaks some of the most wonderful lines in the play. When Titania declares her love for him, he responds, "Methinks, mistress, you should have little reason for that. And yet, to say the truth, reason and love keep little company together nowadays. The more the pity that some honest neighbors will not make them friends. Nay, I can gleek, upon occasion" (III.i.129–33).

In this speech and others, Bottom seems to speak for his creator in a special way. The hybrid creature cannot pass up the opportunity to equivocate: within a dozen words the meaning of *reason* shifts from "cause" to "rational faculty." He also seems concerned to "make the facts fit the dream," to reconcile reason and law, which dominate the court of Theseus, with love and imagination, which have free rein in the forest outside of Athens. And of course he "can gleek, upon occasion." In earlier speeches he had shown an irrepressible desire to "run the whole show"; he would, if he could, play every actor's part. And when he finally returns to his natural and normal condition, he finds himself utterly unable to communicate the substance of his "most rare vision." But for a time his voice had been prophetic; without the least impediment he had sung, or at least spoken, "of what is past, or passing, or to come."

Bottom is probably Shakespeare's greatest purely metaphoric characterization. The man Bottom is an ass. His humanity is everywhere apparent: "For Bottom and his fellow artisans Shakespeare needed no literary source since he doubtless found them in the villages of his native shire."[15] And his asininity is likewise unmistakable; because we can see that Bottom is an ass, "this metaphor is latent in his characterization from the start."[16] Shakespeare raises this metaphor from the hackneyed to the genuinely poetic by recasting it as a time-lapse metaphor: Bottom the man becomes Bottom the man-ass, and by making use of the "ass's nole," the poet maintains the double nature of his creation. The whole point is not that Bottom is literally metamorphosed into an ass but that he is represented throughout, first inchoatively and then visibly, as this marvelous hybrid creature, the man-ass. And at his best, he is simply oracular. One might say that Shakespeare's man-ass is parallel to Wittgenstein's word-picture: "A sentence is a picture of reality." But just as that statement would be of no help to someone who did not know the difference between an independent clause and a photographic image, so the statement "Bottom the man becomes Bottom the man-ass" is not very helpful to someone who does not know, or who prefers to ignore, the difference between a man with an ass's nole on his head and a four-footed braying beast. The literal and the metaphoric are beautifully intermingled in the characterization of Bottom, but they can be sorted out. Within the context of *A Midsummer Night's Dream*, the sentence "Bottom is an ass" is a twice-true statement of a very interesting kind. It is true metaphorically—(at least one characteristic of) Bottom is (the same as at least one characteristic of) an ass; and it is true visually—he wears an ass's nole. But it is *not* true literally—there is no four-footed braying beast in the play. (Moonshine's dog is the only literal animal that appears on the stage.) And Bottom's unconsciousness that he is wearing an ass's nole blurs the distinction between the literal and the metaphoric even further. One may say that he is "literally translated," but he never becomes a four-footed beast.

Compared to his spectacular success as a metaphoric characterization, Bottom's function in relation to the structure of the play is modest, but still very important. Like Proteus in *The Two Gentlemen of Verona*, he plays a prominent role in both stories that go into the making of the play (in this case, plot and subplot, rather than two stories that are combined to make a single main plot). But unlike Proteus, his transition to a second role becomes a source of delight, rather than a source of uneasiness, to the audience. The incongruity of Bottom as lover of Titania is so gross and palpable that we accept it without batting an eye, as it were. There are no twinges of conscience on Bottom's part as there were on Proteus's (why should there be?); and he plays this new role of Titania's lover with greater self-assurance than he plays that of Thisbe's lover in the play within the play. He is always delightful as the self-intoxicated actor, and his resourcefulness is nearly inexhaustible. In the process, we may not even notice that he welds plot and subplot so closely together that, as with the stories of Echo and Narcissus, we can hardly imagine the two stories existing separately.

The plot structure of *A Midsummer Night's Dream* is perhaps the neatest that Shakespeare ever constructed. The purely mechanical elements—doubling, mistakes, reversals, and hybridization—are not difficult to analyze; but the play's texture and quality depend upon other things as well. The double setting provides, for the first time in the Shakespeare comedies, a meaningful contrast between mundane court and enchanted forest; and the presence of fairies in the second setting gives a certain credibility to the magic associated with the metamorphosed plant. The dreamlike quality of the entire proceedings, generated almost entirely by the poetry of the play, effectively removes whatever lingering objections the audience may have to the play's lack of realism; and the net result is a "most rare vision." Remarkably, the entire structure appears to have been built upon nothing more substantial than 140 lines of Arthur Golding's rather pedestrian verse. It is surely a masterpiece of understatement when Helena declares that "the story shall be changed." The story is of course not only changed, but amended; and consequently, the lovers' elopement, "bootless" in Ovid, shall "speed" in Shakespeare. In short, the main plot of *A Midsummer Night's Dream* is a kind of "antiparody," whose function is the opposite of Ben Jonson's antimasque. As a result, *A Midsummer Night's Dream* is as far above Golding's version of Ovid's story as Quince's "Pyramus" is beneath it.

SHYLOCK stands out as conspicuously in *The Merchant of Venice* as Bottom does in *A Midsummer Night's Dream*. But unlike Bottom, he is excluded from the play's second world. As a Jew and a usurer he has no access to Belmont or to the society it represents, and he quite naturally harbors resentment against the Gentiles with whom he has business dealings. Through much of the play Shylock says in effect, as Malvolio finally does in fact, "I'll be revenged on the whole pack of you!"; but since *The Merchant of Venice,* unlike *Twelfth Night,* has a transformation plot, he no longer says so at the end. And because he has no contact with the play's second world, Shylock's change comes about in the manner of the first two transformation comedies—like Kate he must be chastened by experience, and like Proteus he must be caught in the act. This time, however, the transformation is more complex. We see more deeply into the workings of his mind and heart than we do with Kate, and his defeat at the hands of those who "catch him in the act" is more complete than is the case with Proteus.

Although most of the critical discussion of Shylock's change has focused upon the externally imposed transformation (his enforced conversion to Christianity), Shylock's change is internal as well as external. His reluctant acquiescence in the court's decision ("I am content") is best understood in the light of this internal change. The supposedly magical transformation that is embedded in this play comes neither from folklore nor from Ovid, but from Scripture. The passage, usually taken as a justification for the charging of interest or else as evidence of Shylock's earthiness,[17] summarizes briefly some of Jacob's sharp dealings with his uncle (and father-in-law) Laban:

> Mark what Jacob did:
> When Laban and himself were compromised
> That all the eanlings which were streaked and pied
> Should fall as Jacob's hire, the ewes being rank
> In end of autumn turnèd to the rams;
> And when the work of generation was
> Between these woolly breeders in the act,
> The skillful shepherd peeled me certain wands,
> And in the doing of the deed of kind
> He stuck them up before the fulsome ewes,
> Who then conceiving, did in eanling time
> Fall parti-colored lambs, and those were Jacob's.
> This was a way to thrive, and he was blest;
> And thrift is blessing if men steal it not.
>   (MV I.iii.73–86)

Jacob was a pioneering selective breeder, doing this only with the stronger animals—"but for the feebler of the flock he did not lay them there; so the feebler were Laban's, and the stronger Jacob's" (Gen. 30.42, RSV). But Antonio, obviously impervious to Jewish humor, fails to see the relevance of what he regards as a miracle story:

> This was a venture, sir, that Jacob served for,
> A thing not in his power to bring to pass,

> But swayed and fashioned by the hand of heaven.
> Was this inserted to make interest good?
> Or is your gold and silver ewes and rams?
>   (MV I.iii.87–91)

Shylock simply passes off these questions with the reply "I cannot tell; I make it breed as fast"—but the passage is rich in meaning.

The chapters in Genesis that provide Shylock's tale of Jacob and Laban also contain the story of Jacob's deceiving his blind old father Isaac in order to gain his blessing (Gen. 27), which furnishes a subplot of sorts in *The Merchant of Venice*: the farcical encounter between Launcelot and old Gobbo (II.ii), in which the latter, who is not only "sand-blind" but also "high-gravel-blind," likewise recognizes his son by means of the son's hairiness, and the son twice asks his father's blessing (ll. 72, 78). Between these two episodes in Genesis is sandwiched what may well be the oldest example of the bed trick in Western literature. After Jacob had labored for seven years in order to win Laban's daughter Rachel in marriage, the wedding finally takes place: Laban "took his daughter Leah and brought her to Jacob; and he went in to her. . . . And in the morning, behold, it was Leah; and Jacob said to Laban, 'What is this you have done to me?'" Laban innocently answers, "It is not so done in our country, to give the younger before the first-born" (Gen. 29.23–26).

It seems clear that in telling the story of Jacob and Laban, Shylock identifies strongly with Jacob, the breeder-transformer, who later outwits the oppressive Laban and absconds with his daughters and household gods. On at least one occasion, Shylock swears "by Jacob's staff" (*MV* II.v.35); and he tells Tubal that the turquoise ring Jessica took from him was one that he had long cherished—"I had it of Leah when I was a bachelor" (III.i.107–8), indicating that his deceased wife, Jessica's mother, had gone by the name of Leah. The irony of Shakespeare's treatment of the story is that this man who so obviously thinks of himself as Jacob (the "supplanter") learns to his sorrow as the play progresses that he is the counterpart, not of Jacob, but of Laban. It is *his* daughter and *his* ducats that Lorenzo takes from him, as Jacob had taken Laban's daughters (Rachel and Leah) and his "gods" from Laban, who then tries frantically to recover them. Biblical Jacob prospers; and Laban is left to lament the loss of his daughters and his household gods. Shylock, pitifully lacking in self-knowledge, is not the transformer he fancies himself when he says that he makes his gold and silver "breed as fast" as Jacob's ewes and rams; he is instead the one who gets transformed. When Shylock learns to his dismay that he is not Jacob, but Laban, the effect—whether we consider it as the movement of the plot (Shylock's painful learning process) or as the denouement (his unwilling "conversion" at the end)—is for him to be changed.

Shylock's bond, requiring that Antonio give up a pound of his "fair flesh" if he defaults on the payment of the loan, comes of course from Fiorentino's story in *Il Pecorone* and is usually regarded as gratuitous cruelty on the usurer's part. As Alexander Leggatt suggests, "Great stress is laid *within the play itself* on the fact that Shylock is insisting on a bizarre, unnatural penalty."[18] But Shakespeare makes the pound of flesh a complex symbol, reflecting and combining subtleties of motivation and action. The reference and allusions associated with the pound of flesh are never explicit and obvious; but they are there, I think, and they contribute importantly to the meaning of the play. Shakespeare, after all, is not bound to follow his sources in every respect if it would suit his purposes in any way to change them; but Shylock does not insist upon an eye or a tooth, which would be consistent with the idea of retaliation, nor upon something else that might guarantee the death of Antonio. He wants, purely and simply, a pound of Antonio's fair flesh, "to be cut off and taken / In what part of your body pleaseth me" (*MV* I.iii.146–47).

Shakespeare's other intruder into Venetian society, the Moor Othello, has an encounter with the "infidel"—not a Jew, but a "malignant and a turbaned Turk"—which he recalls in his most passionate moment: "I took by th' throat the circumcisèd dog / And smote him—thus" (*Oth.* V.ii.353–56). Traditionally, circumcision sets the Jew apart and marks him as a partner in the covenant with God. In *The Merchant of Venice,* when Gratiano (who is the most rabidly anti-Semitic of the supposed Christians in the play) sees Jessica "transformèd to a boy," he exclaims: "Now by my hood, a gentle and no Jew!" (II.vi.51). According to C. T. Onions, the phrase "by my hood" is "an asseveration as old as Chaucer, but of uncertain reference."[19] Here, within the Gentile-Jew context, it would seem, however, that Gratiano asseverates among other things his own "gentility," or uncircumcision. The passage in which the phrase occurs is heavily laden with double meanings, at least some of which are sexual. Jessica, as torchbearer, says "Why, 'tis an office of discovery, love— / And I should be obscured" (II.vi.43–44). The word *love* functions both as a word of address (Lorenzo) and as a noun in apposition with *it,* as subject of the verb *'tis.* On the surface level, Jessica's first statement means that "the purpose of torch-bearing is to bring things to light"; and on another level it means that "one of love's purposes is to discover (uncover or undress the loved one)." She then demurely says that she herself should not be "discovered," but "obscured." Within such a context, Gratiano's exclamation seems erotic as well as religious (or "racial"); and it is immediately followed by Lorenzo's protestation of love for Jessica.

If Shylock relishes the story of Jacob and Laban, which includes Jacob's marriage to both Leah and Rachel, then he is probably also familiar with the story of David and Goliath, including David's subsequent betrothal to Michal, King Saul's daughter. When Saul learns of David's desire to marry Michal, he sends his servants to David with his terms for the marriage: "Then Saul said, 'Thus shall you say to David, "The king desires no marriage present except a hundred foreskins of the Philistines, that he may be avenged of the king's enemies."' Now Saul thought to make David fall by the hand of the Philistines" (1 Sam. 18.25). Interestingly, according to biblical narrative, Saul's demand for "a hundred foreskins of the Philistines" has behind it a double motive: the ostensible purpose of revenge upon the Philistines and the covert desire to bring about the death of his personal enemy, David, at the hands of the Philistines themselves, so that the responsibility for that death would be theirs, not his.

Whether by accident or design, Shylock's double motive precisely parallels Saul's; and the terms of his demand are only slightly different from those specified by Saul—"a pound of flesh" from "what part of your body pleaseth me," rather than "a hundred foreskins of the Philistines." In the speech that includes the question "Hath not a Jew eyes?" Shylock declares repeatedly that his purpose is revenge: "If it will feed nothing else, it will feed my revenge" (MV III.i.46–47). It is clear to everyone, including Antonio himself, that what Shylock wants is to bring about Antonio's death—"He seeks my life," says Antonio despairingly to Solanio (III.iii.21). But Shylock fails more completely than Saul had done. David has no difficulty in delivering twice the required number of foreskins (1 Sam. 18.27), and Saul therefore fails in his darker purpose of bringing about David's death at the hands of the Philistines. Shylock, of course, fails in both his purposes, as he must if he fails in either, since the two are tied up together in the bond. Taking the pound of flesh would, he had hoped, secure for Shylock both his revenge upon the Venetians in general and the death of Antonio in particular.

The matter of circumcision and its relation to justification remain important within the history of Christianity. The distinction between justification by faith and justification by works of the law is one of the central differences between Christianity and Judaism. It is to this distinction that Portia refers when she says:

> Therefore, Jew,
> Though justice be thy plea, consider this:
> That in the course of justice none of us
> Should see salvation.
>
> (MV IV.i.195–98)

St. Paul, from whose writings this doctrine derives, regards circumcision as one of "the works of the law"; he asserts categorically that "by works of the law shall no flesh be justified" (Gal. 2.16, KJV). In the dispute with those who insist that a Gentile must first be circumcised in order to become a Christian, he says that they "desire to have you circumcised, that they may glory in your flesh" (Gal. 6.13). He concludes that "neither circumcision availeth any thing, nor uncircumcision, but *a new creature*" (Gal. 6.15, emphasis mine).

What happens to Shylock, both internally and externally, is intelligible within this biblical framework. As it turns out, "no flesh [is] justified" by Venetian law any more than by the Jewish law as described by St. Paul. Shylock's attempt to "glory in [Antonio's] flesh" is therefore thwarted, and Shylock must instead become "a new creature" whether he wants to or not. This externally imposed transformation, which by itself would be dramatically insufficient, is combined with an internal transformation that is rooted in Shylock's lack of self-knowledge—he identifies himself with Jacob, but his role turns out to be analogous to Laban's. Like Laban, he loses his daughter (Jessica) and his "household gods" (ducats) to the bright young man of the piece (Lorenzo). Like Laban he is disturbed by a dream at the time of the abduction (II.v.17–18; cf. Gen. 31.24), and again like Laban he tries unsuccessfully to recover his losses. In terms of New Comedy, Shylock the usurer corresponds to a combination of stock characters, the money-lender and the miser; and Shylock the outwitted and defeated father corresponds to the testy old man who is undone as much by his own self-deception as by the cleverness of his young opponent.

Critics object more strongly to the manner of Shylock's conversion than to anything else in the play. Those who found Kate's transformation unconvincing in *The Taming of the Shrew* are understandably even more skeptical about Shylock. Kate delivers a long speech that contains prima facie evidence that she is changed; Shylock says only "I am content" and asks permission to leave the court because he is "unwell." Some commentators simply evade the issue, as Larry Champion does, by saying, "the insistence that Shylock become a Christian need not disturb us, because to most Elizabethans this would be an act of mercy."[20] If we accept the enforced conversion at all, we are apparently to do so for historical reasons, chief among them being the quaint religiosity of our ancestors. Others simply dismiss the matter out of hand, as Granville-Barker does, by asserting that "there is no more reality in Shylock's bond and the Lord of Belmont's will than in Jack and the Beanstock."[21] These suggestions seem inadequate as a commentary upon the play, though each of them is, I think, at least partly correct. Champion is right in suggesting that historical considerations enter into the matter, and Granville-Barker is correct both in connecting "Shylock's bond and the Lord of Belmont's will" and in pointing out the fairy-tale nature of the plot as a whole. (Even the "no reality" assertion is, I think, simply a false inference from the correct observation that the plot is metaphoric, rather than realistic or literal.) It is obvious that the main twist in the play's plot (Shylock's bond) culminates in Shylock's unwilling conversion; and it is for this reason that the other twist (Lord Belmont's will) focuses upon the question of wills, willing, and choosing.

There are of course various ways of analyzing the question of limitations upon human freedom in *The Merchant of Venice*, the most persuasive of which examine that issue by using myth or folklore. In "The Father and the Bride in Shakespeare," Lynda Boose focuses upon Portia and Jessica and examines the relationships between those two characters and their fathers. According to Boose:

> In *The Merchant of Venice*, Shakespeare gives us two versions of the daughter's solution to the repressive demands of the father. In each, the father follows the folktale motif of trying to lock up his daughter and retain her for himself. Portia's physical self has been symbolically locked up inside a lead casket by her dead father's "will," a term that suggests the father's desire to maintain both legal and physical possession of her. Jessica, meanwhile, is literally locked up inside her father's house—a house that becomes, through Shylock's calling it "my sober house" and its casements "my house's ears" (2.5.36, 34), an anthropomorphic refiguration of the father himself.[22]

It is true that Jessica serves as a foil to Portia and that both of them are represented as constrained in their actions by domineering fathers. But the question of freedom in this play is larger than any analysis limited to this particular aspect of human relationships would suggest. Certainly that relationship, parallel to the one between mother and son, is crucial; but both relationships are part of the more inclusive relationship between parent and child, between those who wield power and those who are subject to the control of others, regardless of age or family relationship. In short, the play addresses the question of freedom of the will, of human freedom (or the lack of it), always within a complex pattern of relationships but not exclusively defined by one or more of those relationships. The play, that is, examines not only the constraint placed upon daughter by father (Portia and the Lord of Belmont, Jessica and Shylock), the constraint placed upon Jew by Gentiles (Shylock and Antonio, Gratiano, Portia, etc.), or that upon penniless young man by those who have money (Bassanio and Shylock,

Antonio, etc.)—notice how the various relationships interlock—but also the constraints upon all human beings in all of their relationships, not only to each other but to existence itself.

Pre-Shakespearean literature frequently touches upon the relationship between "free will" and "necessity," as Chaucer does in "The Nun's Priest's Tale." It remains of course a live issue for John Milton, and even in the twentieth century the dispute continues unabated if we may judge by the works of Jean-Paul Sartre, B. F. Skinner, and others. But in the sixteenth century the most important theological debate leading up to the Reformation came to focus on the question of free will, and Henry VIII played a leading role in that debate. In 1521 Henry wrote his *Assertio septem sacramentorum adversus Martinum Lutherum* (which Geoffrey R. Elton describes as "certainly Henry's own work") in response to Luther's *De captivitate Babylonica ecclesiae praeludium* and his *Assertio omnium articulorum,* both of which had appeared in the previous year. When Luther replied to Henry's *Assertio,* Sir Thomas More, at Henry's request, wrote his *Responsio ad Lutherum* (1523). A year later, focusing upon Article 36 of Luther's *Assertio,* which declared that "the free will is really a fiction and a label without reality," Erasmus entered the fray with his *Freedom of the Will* (*De libero arbitrio,* 1524), for which he received Henry's congratulations. To this, Luther responded with *The Bondage of the Will* (*De servo arbitrio,* 1525). Within the context of these latter works Erasmus offers the following definition: "By freedom of the will we understand in this connection the power of the human will whereby man can apply to or turn away from that which leads unto eternal salvation." Erasmus maintained that human beings did in fact have at least some degree of freedom in this crucial matter; Luther, of course, that they had none at all, that the will was enslaved and utterly powerless, reaffirming his earlier claim (in Article 36) that in these matters "everything takes place by absolute necessity." Just as the Christian Church at its inception was divided on the question of circumcision, so it was also divided, at the time of the Reformation, on the question of whether people had free will in the matter of their own conversion and salvation.[23]

If we may judge by his representation of Hamlet's dilemma, by 1600 or 1601 Shakespeare seems to have become seriously preoccupied with the bondage of the will; and Portia reflects an early version of that concern in her conversation with Nerissa at her first appearance in *The Merchant of Venice.*

> **Portia** If to do were as easy as to know what were good to do, chapels had been churches, and poor men's cottages princes' palaces. It is

a good divine that follows his own instructions; I can easier teach twenty what were good to be done than to be one of the twenty to follow mine own teaching. The brain may devise laws for the blood, but a hot temper leaps o'er a cold decree; such a hare is madness the youth to skip o'er the meshes of good counsel the cripple. But this reasoning is not in the fashion to choose me a husband. O me, the word 'choose'! I may neither choose who I would nor refuse who I dislike, so is the will of a living daughter curbed by the will of a dead father. Is it not hard, Nerissa, that I cannot choose one, nor refuse none?

Nerissa Your father was ever virtuous, and holy men at their death have good inspirations. Therefore the lott'ry that he hath devised in these three chests of gold, silver, and lead—whereof who chooses his meaning chooses you—will no doubt never be chosen by any rightly but one who you shall rightly love. (I.ii.12–31)

In this passage the word *will* appears three times and has a different meaning each time—twice as a noun, once meaning "choice" ("the will of a living daughter") and once meaning "testament" ("the will of a dead father"), and once as a verb, the sign of the simple future ("will . . . be chosen"). It is quickly replaced by "the word 'choose,'" and the whole question of "choosing" is represented in the plot by the "lottery" of the three caskets. A suitor can succeed in his quest for Portia's hand only by "choosing" (i.e., "deciphering") her father's meaning as expressed in the mottoes displayed upon the caskets according to the father's "will" (testament).

Any "choice" among the three caskets is obviously not a choice in the ordinary sense, though Nerissa's word *lottery* is not quite appropriate either. The three mottoes provide a clue, of course, but because the mottoes involve irony, one cannot be sure how to interpret them. The one who "chooses" can depend neither upon what he desires nor upon what he deserves; he can only "give and hazard all he hath" and hope for the best. This Bassanio does, and quite predictably within the confines of Shakespearean comedy, he gets both more than he expects and more than he deserves. In *The Merchant of Venice*, the "will" of individual characters—including that of the manipulator Portia—can hardly be described as "free." The crucial difference, which is most clearly displayed in the contrast between Portia and Shylock, is between "willing submission" to the terms of one's own existence on the one hand and proud defiance on the other. Portia, finding her own will "curbed by the will of a dead father," reluctantly but gracefully accepts the conditions and limitations imposed upon her. When her own happiness is most at risk, she says "I stand for sacrifice" (III.ii.57). And again at the trial when Bassanio proposes, in keeping with the unpalatable doctrine of equivocation, that the Venetian law be bent—"To do a great right, do a little wrong, / And curb this cruel devil of his will"—Portia insists, "It must not be. There is no power in Venice / Can alter a decree establishèd" (IV.i.214–17).

Conversely, when Shylock's "happiness" is most at stake, he proudly and confidently declares, "I stand for judgment" (IV.i.103) and "I stand here for law" (IV.i.142). As a corollary of this defiant attitude, he asserts that

> by my soul I swear
> There is no power in the tongue of man
> To alter me. I stay here on my bond.
> (IV.i.238–40)

Ironically, Shylock, more than any other character in the play, finds that when all is said and done, he is "altered" and "changed" almost beyond recognition. He has gone forth to do battle with the Philistines on their own ground and is dismayed to discover that not only is he unsuccessful, but these same Philistines have captured him and converted him into one of themselves. Like the other characters, Shylock gets more of what he calls for in his relationship with others than he has any right to expect. He gives and hazards nothing that really matters to him; and consequently, he loses all. Portia puts the matter succinctly when she says to him, "For, as thou urgest justice, be assured / Thou shalt have justice more than thou desir'st" (IV.i.314–15).

The third twist in the main plot of *The Merchant of Venice,* and the only one that carries over into the fifth act, involves the rings that Portia and Nerissa first give to Bassanio and Gratiano, and that they in turn surrender to the "lawyer" and "his clerk." The rings are not nearly so significant as Shylock's bond and Belmont's will, but they resonate to some extent with Bassanio's earlier "choice" among the three caskets. Bassanio does indeed make a solemn pledge not to part with the ring except at the cost of his life:

> But when this ring
> Parts from this finger, then parts life from hence;
> O then be bold to say Bassanio's dead!
> (III.ii.183–85)

And according to Nerissa, Gratiano makes a similar promise to her (IV.ii.13–14, V.i.151–56). Thus, in giving away their rings, Bassanio and Gratiano "give and hazard all." By comparison, when Shylock hears that Jessica had parted with his precious turquoise ring in exchange "for a monkey," he tells

Tubal, "I would not have given it for a wilderness of monkeys" (III.i.108–9); and there is no reason to think that he is either exaggerating or lying. At the risk of moralizing, one cannot help noting that Shylock's ring is of course lost to him forever, whereas Bassanio's and Gratiano's are returned to them with interest, as it were.

The rings are charged with sexual meaning, as is appropriate in the fifth act of a romantic comedy. When Portia produces the ring to the astonishment of Bassanio, she teasingly asks his forgiveness:

> Pardon me, Bassanio,
> For by this ring the doctor lay with me.
> (V.i.258–59)

Nerissa teases Gratiano in parallel fashion:

> And pardon me, my gentle Gratiano,
> For that same scrubbèd boy, the doctor's clerk,
> In lieu of this last night did lie with me.
> (V.i.260–62)

Gratiano ends the play with the asseveration that "while I live I'll fear no other thing / So sore as keeping safe Nerissa's ring" (V.i.306–7). But coming from Gratiano, this promise sounds more like an expression of proprietary interest than like a pledge of loving fidelity. Earlier, of course, Gratiano had exclaimed that "Would he were gelt that had it" when Nerissa chides him about having given away the ring; and when she taunts him with the possibility of her sleeping with the fictitious clerk, he cries, "Let not me take him then! / For if I do, I'll mar the young clerk's pen" (V.i.236–37). Such banter no doubt disgusted Leo Tolstoy, but within the comic framework of the play, Gratiano's idle threat serves as a reductio ad absurdum of Shylock's much more serious attempt to "mar Antonio's pen," motivated not by sexual jealousy but by the desire for revenge.

Even though Shylock threatens to steal the show, there is a good deal more to *The Merchant of Venice* than the story of Shylock. At least three other characters change significantly in the course of the play. Bassanio, who at his first appearance is simply a man who has squandered his own resources and who appeals to his friend for enough money to court an heiress in hopes of restoring his fortunes, becomes one who is willing to sacrifice everything in order to deliver that friend from the threat of death: "The Jew," he says, "shall have my flesh, blood, bones, and all, / Ere thou shalt lose for me one drop of blood" (IV.i.112–13). He changes, that is, from parasite or "sponge" to self-sacrificing friend. Antonio, though he seems to his friends a splendid fellow at the beginning of the play, is perfectly willing to admit the truth of Shylock's claim that he had called Shylock "misbeliever, cutthroat dog," had "spit upon [his] Jewish gaberdine," and had voided his "rheum upon [Shylock's] beard." He goes even further and says, "I am as like to call thee so again, / To spit on thee again, to spurn thee too" (I.iii.126–27). By the end of the play, however, his disdain is considerably lessened; he allows Shylock to keep at least part of his possessions when he might deprive him of everything. According to Larry Champion, "in Antonio one perceives in a small way the kind of moral rehabilitation which Shakespeare will later emphasize in his comedies of transformation."[24] In Portia, too, Champion sees considerable change—from snobbish heiress who mocks her suitors and dotes upon their absence to loving wife who exerts all her powers in the effort to save her husband's friend.

The play alerts us to these changes almost from the beginning. Besides Antonio's prediction that Shylock will change radically ("The Hebrew will turn Christian; he grows kind," I.iii.174), we are led to believe that other important changes have already taken place, or at least are under way, when the play begins. Gratiano tells Antonio, "Believe me, you are marvellously changed" (I.i.76), and old Gobbo exclaims to his son, "Lord, how thou art changed!" (II.ii.92). *The Merchant of Venice* goes further than any of the earlier comedies in combining and contrasting these changes, sometimes even within a single role. As I have already suggested, Shylock's transformation is no less externally imposed than Kate's in *The Taming of the Shrew*; but with Shylock we see much more deeply into the corresponding inward change that accompanies the outward one. Likewise Portia deliberately masquerades as a professional person (lawyer) in the manner of Lucentio (teacher) in order to gain certain ends; but unlike Lucentio, she herself undergoes a considerable change in the process. And Jessica's willing conversion to Christianity contrasts, of course, with Shylock's unwilling conversion. Because Shylock has no contact with Belmont, his change is brought about by plot alone as in the earlier comedies; the other character-changes are wrought as much by the romantic atmosphere of Belmont as by the plot itself. The bond and the will are peculiar to the plot of *The Merchant of Venice*, but the ring motif will figure importantly again in *All's Well That Ends Well*.

THE plot of *As You Like It* is perhaps the slightest of Shakespeare's comic plots, but what there is of it is transformational. Once we are introduced to the forest of Arden at the beginning of Act II, there are no serious plot complications resembling those in *A Midsummer Night's Dream* or *The Mer-*

chant of Venice. As Alexander Leggatt suggests, "the only movement [in the forest scenes] is a back-and-forth shuttling as the various characters wander in, confront each other and wander out again."[25] Two of the most memorable characters, Jaques and Touchstone, are superimposed upon the plot borrowed from Lodge's *Rosalynde*; and except for the fact that Touchstone becomes one of the marriage partners at play's end—a rather cynical one, to be sure—their impact upon the plot is minimal. They serve as commentators upon persons and events in Arden rather than as catalysts for what little action there is in the play.

The one plot device that operates throughout the forest scenes is of course Rosalind's male disguise, which she originally assumes in the interest of safety (*AYL* I.iii.104–6) as Julia had done in *The Two Gentlemen of Verona* (II.vii.39–43). Rosalind's disguise is more purposeful, however, than the same device in any of the earlier comedies. In *The Taming of the Shrew*, none of the disguises involve cross-dressing except for the Page, who poses briefly as Sly's wife, and that of course remains on the purely farcical level. There is no cross-dressing in *A Midsummer Night's Dream* unless we regard Flute's impersonation of Thisbe in that light. Portia in *The Merchant of Venice* tends strictly to lawyer's business while disguised as a male, except for the matter of the ring. Nerissa's disguise as the lawyer's clerk has no more sexual significance than Portia's as the lawyer, and Jessica is temporarily "transformèd to a boy" (II.vi.39) only in order to escape from her father's house. Rosalind's disguise and cross-dressing are therefore more significant than the same device in any of the comedies before *Twelfth Night*; and, except for the element of simultaneity, it corresponds roughly to Tiresias's double transformation, first into a female and then, seven years later, back into a male (*Metamorphoses* 3). Because Tiresias is able to speak from the vantage point of both sexes, he is acceptable to both Juno and Jove as an authority on the subject of love and sex.

Likewise, Ganymede speaks for both sexes in *As You Like It*. Her advice to Silvius and Phebe is unbiased: she tells the "foolish shepherd" that " 'tis such fools as you / That makes the world full of ill-favored children"; and with equal frankness, she exhorts Phebe, "Know yourself. Down on your knees, / And thank heaven, fasting, for a good man's love" (III.v.49–58). She has no difficulty in persuading Orlando, who is head over heels in love with "Rosalind," to "imagine me his love" (III.ii.382–408). And Phebe, after hearing Ganymede's chiding, declares, "I had rather hear you chide than this man [Silvius] woo" (III.v.65)—a clear indication that Phebe is falling in love with the supposed Ganymede. The mythological Ganymede is of course androgynous (*Iliad* 20.230–35; *Metamorphoses* 10.161–67); and Rosalind, in disguise, exploits both sides of the characterization. Just as Bottom becomes a man-ass in *A Midsummer Night's Dream,* Rosalind becomes a man-woman in *As You Like It.* The convention of the impenetrable disguise is of course preposterous from the literal or realistic point of view, but as metaphor it presents no particular difficulty. The device requires only that we accept the idea that different people, having different perspectives and expectations, may regard the same person in entirely different ways. Making use of Wittgenstein's phrase "seeing as," we may say that Celia sees "Ganymede" as her old friend Rosalind; Phebe sees the same character as an ideal male lover; and Orlando sees her-him as experienced mentor. The audience sees Rosalind-Ganymede throughout the forest scenes as a skillful actor playing a double role.

Even the most realistic theatrical representation rests upon the willingness of the audience to make the assumption that actors "are" the characters that they represent. The double convention of disguise and cross-dressing makes a much greater demand upon such willingness; it requires that we make the assumption conscious and extend it to include various perspectives other than our own. If we are willing to grant (as Shakespeare's original audience surely did) that a male actor "is" Rosalind, then we should also be willing to grant that from another perspective (Phebe's) this same actor is a possible male lover, and that from still another (Orlando's) he is an experienced mentor possessing characteristics of both sexes. And the device itself is consistent with the content of the speeches delivered by the character in question. Ganymede's advice to Phebe, "Know yourself," is implicitly directed to the audience, since in order to understand what the characters are saying we must raise to the level of consciousness the assumption that the actors "are" the characters that they impersonate and that these characters are one person or another, depending upon the perspective from which they are seen and heard. We may of course reject the play's invitation to expand our self-knowledge, regard the whole representation as patently unrealistic, and congratulate ourselves on our own clear-sighted vision of "reality." But if we do so, we miss the whole point and unconsciously reinforce our lack of self-knowledge.

As I indicated earlier, the actual plot of *As You Like It* is comparatively slight; but if one defines plot rather loosely as what happens in the play, measured by the difference between situations at the beginning and at the end, then the plot of *As You Like It* is by no means insignificant. That difference is best illustrated by the transformations that take place in three of the characters—Duke Frederick, Oliver, and Orlando—all of whom change radically in the course of the play. These three transformations are interdependent, and each of them derives at least part of its meaning from one or both of the others. Duke Frederick's transformation, like that of the hag in "The Wife of Bath's Tale," is represented as mysterious and astonishing; and Orlando's, like that of Chaucer's knight in the same story, is gradual and realistic, at least by comparison with Duke Frederick's. Oliver's, midway between the other two, is sudden as compared with Orlando's and believable as compared with Duke Frederick's.

Duke Frederick's conversion, and perhaps Oliver's as well, do indeed place something of a strain upon audience credibility. According to William Carroll, "the miraculous conversions of Duke Frederick and Oliver at the end of the play seem deliberately contrived and unconvincing; other transformations, through the power of love for example, are enacted quite seriously."[26] Such a comparison suggests that these "miraculous" conversions are hardly serious; and indeed, when we juxtapose them with those of Kate, Shylock, or even Proteus, it would appear that Shakespeare is consciously moving further and further away from realistic representation in this matter. The earlier transformations are represented, at least to some extent, as the result of a cause-and-effect pattern; and all of them take place onstage—they are not simply reported by a messenger who has no other function in the play. Here, on the contrary, the audience is presented with an apparently gratuitous fait accompli:

> Duke Frederick, hearing how that every day
> Men of great worth resorted to this forest,
> Addressed a mighty power, which were on foot
> In his own conduct, purposely to take
> His brother here and put him to the sword;
> And to the skirts of this wild wood he came,
> Where, meeting with an old religious man,
> After some question with him, was converted
> Both from his enterprise and from the world,
> His crown bequeathing to his banished brother,
> And all their lands restored to them again
> That were with him exiled. This to be true
> I do engage my life.
>
> (AYL V.iv.148–60)

The speaker's last sentence reveals his awareness that the news he brings would be hard to believe even on the testimony of an eyewitness; and he himself does not actually claim to be such a witness. In short, how he got the information is just as mysterious as the information itself.

As in "The Wife of Bath's Tale" and New Testament conversion stories, a more or less realistic transformation (corresponding to Orlando's in *As You Like It*) is sometimes juxtaposed with miraculous ones in a way that makes all such transformations intelligible, as they might not be if considered separately. In the Wife's tale, for instance, Chaucer takes pains to make the hag's transformation into a beautiful bride depend upon the young knight's response to the choice offered him between having his wife be ugly and faithful or beautiful and quite possibly unfaithful. As Robert Meyer points out, "in the analogues the bewitched hags display their magical power to transform themselves *before* the knight is confronted with the dilemma. Chaucer, though, does not have the hag change until *after* the bachelor has made his decision. Thus Chaucer emphasizes the depth of the bachelor's humility, enhances the significance of the leap of faith, and suggests a closer, cause-and-effect-like relationship between the two transformations."[27] In the New Testament accounts of St. Paul's conversion (Acts 9) and St. Matthew's ordination (Matt. 9), both transformations are juxtaposed with miracle stories, which are remarkably similar in the two accounts. And in both cases the juxtaposition produces a curious double effect: on the one hand the religious conversion seems quite ordinary by contrast with the healing of cripples or the raising of dead persons; and on the other, such conversions are just as astonishing in their own way as the more spectacular changes against which they are displayed. Within the biblical context, any such transformation results in "a new creature," whether the person is called to faith, cured of paralysis, or raised from the dead.

Orlando's transformation is, by comparison with Duke Frederick's, carefully documented and gradual. In the play's first speech, Orlando complains bitterly that he is kept "rustically at home" and that the treatment he receives at his brother's hands is no different from "the stalling of an ox." He protests to Adam, "I will no longer endure it, though yet I know no wise remedy how to avoid it" (*AYL* I.i.1–23). By play's end, thanks both to the atmosphere of Arden and the tutelage of Ganymede, he has become an acceptable romantic hero and a suitable marriage partner for Rosalind. His progress is reflected in his increasing capacity to express his love for her. When he falls in love at first sight, he is distressed to find himself almost incapable of speaking to her: "What passion hangs these weights upon my tongue? / I cannot speak to her, yet she urged conference" (I.ii.238–39). Later he manages both to write hackneyed love poetry, which Touchstone parodies for the amusement of the audience (III.ii.95–109), and to speak of his love to Rosalind in disguise as Ganymede. The last line he speaks is the one in which he recognizes her through her disguise: "If there be truth in sight, you are my Rosalind" (V.iv.113); but there is some hope, on the basis of his eloquence on other subjects, that he will now be able to articulate his love more adequately. The manner in which, according to Oliver's own testimony, Orlando rescues his detested older brother from the threat of death (IV.iii) also indicates how much Sir Rowland's youngest son has changed since the beginning of the play.

Orlando and Duke Frederick thus stand at opposite ends of a transformational continuum—Duke Frederick's change is sudden and mysterious, Orlando's gradual and carefully traced. Oliver's transformation stands midway between these two, less gradual than Orlando's and less spectacular than Duke Frederick's. In response to the questions of Rosalind and Celia, Oliver describes the action that brought about his own change of heart when Orlando delivers the "wretched ragged man, o'ergrown with hair" (IV.iii.107) from the threat of serpent and lioness. Impelled at first to save the man, Orlando then recognizes him as his hateful older brother and twice turns away:

> But kindness, nobler ever than revenge,
> And nature, stronger than his just occasion,
> Made him give battle to the lioness,
> Who quickly fell before him; in which hurtling
> From miserable slumber I awaked.
> (IV.iii.129–33)

In short, it is what Portia, in *The Merchant of Venice,* had called "deeds of mercy" (or "gentil dedes," to use Chaucer's term) that transform individual human lives—lives ordinarily governed by the simple desire for revenge or, in comic terms, by the delight we take in seeing "poetic justice" done to the "bad personages" of the play.

When Oliver shifts in his narration of these events from third person ("a wretched ragged man") to first person ("I awaked"), Rosalind and Celia suddenly realize that Oliver is telling his own story as well as Orlando's. The women then ask him if he is indeed the brother "that did so oft contrive to kill" Orlando, and his response is succinct and self-conscious:

> 'Twas I. But 'tis not I. I do not shame
> To tell you what I was, since my conversion
> So sweetly tastes, being the thing I am.
> (IV.iii.136–38)

The word *it* (contracted to *'twas* and *'tis*) refers to both the "wretched ragged man" threatened by serpent and lioness and to the brother that "did so oft contrive to kill" Orlando. Oliver's first statement (" 'Twas I") identifies the speaker with that person; his second one (" 'tis not I") denies the identification not only by negating it but also by shifting the verb tense from past to present. The "I," that is, has undergone a transformation, a "conversion" which the speaker finds enormously gratifying, "being the thing I am." Without the shift in verb tense, the two statements would simply contradict each other. But with that shift, they condense an important element of the play's meaning into half a dozen words, two main clauses standing in stark contrast with each other.

Character-changes in *As You Like It* are wrought either by Rosalind-Ganymede, by Arden itself, or by a combination of the two influences. At their first appearance, Silvius and Phebe are simply stock characters out of pastoral romance—he nearly sick with love for the adorable shepherdess, and she disdaining him as an unworthy suitor. Because Arden is presumably their native habitat, their transformation, which qualifies them to be one of the wedding couples at play's end, is due more to the influence of Ganymede than to the pastoral environment. As the play's manipulator figure, Rosalind speaks more directly and more bluntly to them than to anyone else. She does not mince words when she asks Silvius, "You foolish shepherd, wherefore do you follow her, / Like foggy south, puffing with wind and rain?" (III.v.49–50). And Phebe sorely needs the advice that Rosalind gives her in the same speech. Duke Frederick's conversion, on the other hand, is represented as the result of contact with Arden itself, since he never sees Rosalind after her departure from the court. Orlando's subtler change from country bumpkin to "gentil man" (who delivers Oliver from the threat of death) and suitable husband for Rosalind arises from both influences. Ganymede teaches him that "men have died from time to time, and worms have eaten them, but not for love" (IV.i.96–98); and in Arden he learns that kindness is "nobler ever than revenge."

IN all three of the plays we are considering, transformation is central to the plot. The happy ending of *A Midsummer Night's Dream* comes about from transformed relationships that result in turn from the effect of a metamorphosed flower; and the main plot is itself a transformed and amended version of the Pyramus and Thisbe story. The transformation, both internal and external, of the comic villain is indispensable to the happy ending of *The Merchant of Venice*; and if it were not for the multiple transformations in *As You Like It*, the play would have very little plot of any sort after the events of the first act. Because playgoers are most comfortable with characters whose "labels" stay in place once they are attached, these plays make a considerable demand upon the audience; and the time-lapse metaphor, which is the principal vehicle for representing character-change, requires that we apprehend such changes with the imagination, rather than translate them into something literal in order to make them comprehensible to "cool reason." Character-change and cool reason keep little company together nowadays, but fortunately in each case the play functions as an "honest neighbor" in making them better friends.

During this same period (1595–99), Shakespeare begins to experiment even more boldly with the transformation plot than he does in these three comedies and to make correspondingly greater demands upon the imagination of the audience. The time-lapse metaphor works well enough, in the comedies, as the basis for a purely fictional plot. When we have the impression that "there is no more reality" in the comic plot "than in Jack and the Beanstalk," we can respond, though perhaps with some reservation, to the playwright's suggestion, "Imagine this changed like this, and you have this other thing." But when he has the audacity to propose that we take much the same view of an actual English king who is represented as achieving remarkable victories at Shrewsbury and Agincourt, we balk—if not at the sixteen-year-old victor at Shrewsbury, then certainly at the twenty-eight-year-old conqueror of the French at Agincourt. Nineteenth- and twentieth-century criticism contains a whole litany of objections to *Henry V.* We take the youthful Prince of Wales to our hearts, but we recoil from seeing him changed into "this other thing." Like Hippolyta as she watches Peter Quince's production of "Pyramus and Thisbe," we enumerate the faults so glaringly displayed in this final play of the *Henriad,* seldom if ever doubting that it is indeed the author's imagination, and not ours, that fails to make the leap required by superimposing the transformation comic plot upon the events of English history.

SIX

History as Personal Reformation
Prince Hal, Harry Monmouth, and King Henry V

◆

> Presume not that I am the thing I was,
> For God doth know, so shall the world perceive,
> That I have turned away my former self.

SUPERIMPOSING the transformation comic plot upon historical events and persons creates certain dilemmas and involves special risks for the playwright. The two patterns, of course, do not always coincide; and when they do not, one of them must yield to the other. Moreover, a personal transformation that is not historically well documented—as it is, for instance, in the case of St. Francis of Assisi—will seem to the audience even more improbable, more difficult to accept, than the transformation of a purely fictional character. And most important of all, when the historical person in question is an English king, the roles of hero and manipulator must be combined—otherwise the hero would be no king at all in Renaissance terms—and consequently all of the objections that readers and viewers make to the manipulator figure in Shakespearean comedy will come to focus on the protagonist himself. Unfortunately, such objections will also be magnified in the process, because what may pass for benevolent concern and aggressive good will on the part of a peripheral manipulator will seem smug self-interest and calculating self-aggrandizement when the roles of hero and manipulator are combined.

Critical disagreement about the *Henriad* as a whole is most clearly seen in the division of opinion about *Henry V*, the "capstone" of the whole tetralogy. Over the past two and a half centuries critics who view the play positively have tended to fall into two groups—those who regard Shakespeare's

Henry V as authentically heroic and those who see the characterization as a deeply ironic portrayal. A third group, most ably represented half a century ago by Mark Van Doren, contends that the play is simply a potboiler, a failure not only of dramaturgy but of taste and imagination as well. Those who take into account the play's comic element usually locate that emphasis in particular characters rather than in the structure of the play, and tend therefore to regret the loss of Falstaff. Others who scrutinize the protagonist's moral character detect certain faults that would disqualify such a person from leadership in a modern democratic society. Some, however—and this view probably finds its most eloquent expression in the Olivier film version of the play—are quite willing to overlook these faults and to see the protagonist as a splendid and cheerful example of the kind of hero-king that an English-speaking nation would surely need if threatened by aggressive foreign powers.

Norman Rabkin analyzes the critical situation clearly. According to him, the critics of *Henry V* "have gathered into rival camps which could hardly disagree more radically."[1] He quotes Karl P. Wentersdorf's description of the rival camps, one of which claims that the play "presents the story of an ideal monarch and glorifies his achievements" (the "epic" view), and the other of which asserts no less emphatically that "the protagonist is a Machiavellian militarist who professes Christianity but whose deeds reveal both hypocrisy and ruthlessness" (the "mordant satire" view).[2] Rabkin regards the two views as equally valid in their reductive ways and accounts for the split by arguing that *Henry V* is "a work whose ultimate power is precisely the fact that it points in two opposite directions, virtually daring us to choose one of the two opposed interpretations it requires of us." He likens the play—not just the protagonist, but the whole play—to the ambiguous duck-rabbit figure, which comes to him, not from Wittgenstein, but from E. H. Gombrich's *Art and Illusion*.[3] He then argues that in this particular case,

> We are made to see a rabbit or a duck. In fact, if we do not try obsessively to cling to memories of past encounters with the play, we may find that each time we read it it turns from one shape to the other, just as it so regularly does in production. I want to show that *Henry V* is brilliantly capable of being read, fully and subtly, as each of the plays the two parts of *Henry IV* had respectively anticipated. Leaving the theater at the end of the first performance, some members of the audience knew that they had seen a rabbit, others a duck. Still others, and I would suggest that they were Shakespeare's best audience, knew uneasily that they did not know what to think.[4]

This hypothesis seems to me to be highly ingenious; but in the long run it is, alas, no more successful than the other three attempts to reconcile those opposite interpretations that Rabkin outlines briefly and then dismisses by saying, "All of them are wrong."[5]

First of all, Rabkin's use of the duck-rabbit analogy is, I think, inappropriate. Those who hold the "epic" view and those who hold the "mordant satire" view do not vacillate in their interpretation: one claims that the play is a duck and *only* a duck; the other claims that it is a rabbit and *only* a rabbit. Each camp regards the other as mistaken, and each focuses upon somewhat different elements in the play. That is, one camp does not read a particular line or speech as the duck's bill, and the other camp read that same line or speech as the rabbit's ears. They concentrate upon at least slightly different sets of data within the play as a whole. And perhaps most important, despite the use of the word "ideal" in connection with the "epic" view of Henry, both views are (at least unconsciously) realistic interpretations of the play—that is, they see the play as a representation of life (or history), rather than as an artistic composite, which may indeed have only a limited correspondence to the world of politics and human strife.

Moreover, the observer's response to the duck-rabbit figure can hardly be said to involve a "choice." We see it as one thing or the other at any given moment, but it seems odd to suggest, in the analogy with *Henry V*, that the figure "points in two opposite directions, virtually daring us to choose one of the two opposed interpretations it requires of us." This is like suggesting that a pun virtually dares us to choose one of the two opposed meanings implicit in the word being played upon. But if we make such a "choice," then we are simply getting rid of the pun and missing the whole (combined) point. The most salient characteristic of Shakespearean writing is indeed its reflection of the author's tendency to see everything "with parted eye, / When everything seems double" (*MND* IV.i.188–89)—hence the abundance of puns, which exploit the multiple meanings of individual words; the emphasis upon metaphor, which juxtaposes dissimilar things; and (within the comedies) double-faceted characters, that appear first in one guise and then later in a very different, even opposite guise. The value of such doubleness is of course the tension that is generated between the two opposites, corresponding to the difference in potential between the positive and the negative poles in a storage battery. If we "choose" one of the poles and eliminate the other, then we are left with simply a dead battery.

What then is the source of the "two opposed interpretations" that *Henry V* seems to elicit from readers and audiences? It is another manifestation of the "parted vision"—a double attitude, reflected in the text itself, toward the heroic tradition in literature.⁶ The text both pays homage to and parodies the conception of the royal–military–religious–wise–efficient king–commander in chief–high priest–philosopher–conqueror–chief executive we see in such historical figures as King David and King Solomon of Israel and "Alexander the Pig" of Macedonia. In this respect, the historical comedy *Henry V* resembles the fictional comedy *As You Like It,* which both honors and spoofs the pastoral tradition in literature. But to claim that such parody involves "mordant satire" is to suggest that Shakespeare, at least in this play, is more closely akin to Juvenal and Swift than to Horace and Chaucer—a dubious claim at best.

A more appropriate visual emblem for Rabkin's hypothesis would be, I think, the griffon (*1H4* III.i.150), the centaur (*MND* V.i.44), or perhaps "two-headed Janus" (*MV* I.i.50), the Roman god of gates and doorways, whose two faces look in "two opposite directions," as do the two interpretations of *Henry V* as described by Rabkin. Each interpreter inspects part of the data, and (to use the pictorial analogy of the griffon) sees only a lion's body (epic view) or a bird's head (mordant-satire view); and each conveniently ignores the data insisted upon by the other camp. Each camp assumes that what it sees is a "real" bird or a "real" lion; and the obvious fact that what both are looking at is an artistic composite, rather than an accurate representation of any "real creature," escapes not only both camps as described by Rabkin but what he calls "Shakespeare's best audience" as well, who leave the theater knowing "uneasily that they did not know what to think." They would not know what to think only if they supposed that the function of art was to represent reality photographically, rather than to combine images taken from nature in a fashion that culminates sometimes in a hybrid, or a juxtaposition of images, which can exist only within the work of art.

I have said that both views are at least unconsciously realistic; that is, they regard the portrait of Henry V in Shakespeare's play as an attempt to represent a particular historical person, rather than an imagined composite with certain points of correspondence to the fifteenth-century monarch. It is probably not necessary to document the assertion that those who hold the mordant-satire view regard the play as an attempt to portray what Henry V was "really" like; but the word *ideal* used in connection with the epic view calls for some explanation. Rabkin repeatedly refers to Olivier's film version of the play as a prime example of the heroic view, involving a "prettied up" atmosphere and a "fairy-tale world of the Duc de Berry."⁷ But at least one change that Olivier introduces into the text will show that he was concerned to make the film historically accurate and genuinely credible. In the last scene of Act IV, Henry announces the casualties on both sides: "This note doth tell me of ten thousand French / That in the field lie slain," the king says solemnly. He then names four Englishmen who have been killed and goes on to say, "None else of name; and of all other men / But five-and-twenty. O God, thy arm was here!" (IV.viii.100–101). Olivier dutifully corrects this exaggeration by adding the word "score" after "five-and-twenty." That is, he puts the number of English dead not at twenty-nine, as Shakespeare would have it (in both the quarto of 1600 and the First Folio of 1623, and in most modern editions), but at 504. This emendation "sets the record straight" by the most liberal of modern estimates. According to Christopher Hibbert, "the most recent English historian" has put the number of French dead at "10,000. . . . In contrast the English casualties were negligible. The highest estimates put them at no more than 500 in all, and more reliable ones at 100; and most of these were wounded."[8] Say what you will about Olivier's "prettified" version of *Henry V*, he apparently tried, at least in this instance, to improve the "historical accuracy" of Shakespeare's text by multiplying the poet's estimate of English dead by twenty.

The opposite view asserts that "the protagonist is a Machiavellian militarist who professes Christianity but whose deeds reveal both hypocrisy and ruthlessness," and those who hold such a view regard the characterization as an example of mordant satire. This description of the heroic Henry V might be more damaging to the characterization than it is if it did not apply even more accurately (except for the word *Christianity*) to another hero, who perhaps served as one of Shakespeare's models for Henry—King David of Israel. David is a hero of the Judeo-Christian tradition if there ever was one: "Saul has slain his thousands, And David his ten thousands" (1 Sam. 18.7, RSV). His refusal to wear heavy armor and his trick of dispatching Goliath with a stone from his slingshot, rather than taking him on face to face and toe to toe, "like a man," was certainly Machiavellian (1 Sam. 17.38–50). He professed Judaism and claimed to be a servant of the Lord. He was of course a good king, but he stole away another man's wife—though he already had plenty of wives of his own—and sent the woman's husband to the war front to be killed (2 Sam. 11). "The thing that David had done displeased the LORD," of course, but it did not make him any less of a hero to his people. Surely, David's behavior with Bathsheba and Uriah demonstrates enough "hypocrisy and ruthlessness" to ruin the career of any modern politician, but it seems to have done David's popularity no damage whatever. Even the Prophet Nathan's rebuke seems not to have caused him any serious political problems.

The reader of Samuel and Kings could no doubt articulate either or both of the "two opposed interpretations [the story] requires of us"—one of David as the splendid young shepherd boy who rose to be king by virtue of his heroic exploits and then served his nation faithfully for many years (Sunday-school version) or, quite differently, as the despicable rapist and cold-blooded murderer who rode roughshod over his subjects while chanting Davidic psalms to the greater glory of God (soap-opera version). But it would be inappropriate, I think, to suppose that the biblical narrator was "virtually daring us to choose one of the two opposed interpretations." Any conception of that narrator as either uncritical hero-worshiper or mordant satirist is out of the question: he was apparently a chronicler of ancient Israel who was concerned to represent this particular character, warts and all, as they say; but there can be no doubt that he regarded King David as an authentic national hero.

Our judgment of the *Henriad* should depend not on how well we like (or how much we dislike) the protagonist as an actual person, but on our estimate of the poet's success in synthesizing the disparate elements that go into the plays—historical events and literary patterns, shrewd politician and comic manipulator, English king and comic hero. In general, the poet's attempt at synthesis will seem bold in proportion to the dissimilarity and inflexibility of the elements to be synthesized, just as the strength of a metaphor depends upon the oppositeness of its subject and predicate terms and upon the logical structure of the metaphoric statement. Because there is less similarity between historical record and literary form than between the forms of two invented stories and because historical fact is less flexible than fictional story, what Shakespeare undertakes to do in the Henry plays is bolder than anything he had attempted in earlier comedies. And I would argue that if we grant the playwright's premises, we will have to concede that he is successful in all three attempts—to combine historical events with transformation comic plot, to represent a historical figure as comic hero, and to fuse the roles of manipulator and protagonist in one boldly autocratic popular hero who manages to combine self-interest and national interest in triumphant fashion.

A more serious problem for any interpreter of the *Henriad* as a whole than the split between critics who embrace either the epic view or the mordant-satire view of *Henry V* is the attack upon that play—which serves, after all, as the capstone of the whole tetralogy—as a potboiler and a shabby piece of work. Though he wrote half a century ago, Mark Van Doren is perhaps still the most articulate spokesman for this view of the play. He suggests among other things that "Henry is Shakespeare's last attempt at the great man who is also simple. Henceforth he will show greatness as either perplexing or perplexed; and Hamlet will be both."[9] But we cannot have it both ways: Henry succeeds in "redeeming time" by means of heroic action; and if we grant Hamlet's point that "the native hue of resolution / Is sicklied o'er with the pale cast of thought" and that consequently "enterprises of great pitch and moment / . . . lose the name of action" (*Ham.* III.i.84, 88), then we can hardly complain that the Shakespearean protagonist whose chief merit is his capacity for heroic action in the comic manner is not also a profound thinker in the tragic fashion. We will deal much more fully with the negative view of *Henry V* somewhat later. But first we should consider the overall structure of the *Henriad* and the appropriateness of *Henry V* as the conclusion to that large structure.

The important question about any literary work, including the *Henriad*, is whether the author succeeds in giving adequate artistic form to the subject matter chosen—whether, in this case, Shakespeare successfully recasts the events of history in the form of heroic comedy. And all the elements of Shakespearean comedy are here in the Henry plays—a usurper who proves unkind, even (and especially) to those who helped him to power; a second world, where certain characters (including some who are favorites with the audience) find refuge from a troubled and hostile court; disguises that figure importantly in both worlds of the play; a young hero who seems most unpromising at first but who later triumphs over both his enemies and his critics; a manipulator who shrewdly takes into account everything that might prevent a happy ending; and a high degree of self-consciousness on the part of all the main characters. In addition to these, the Henry plays exploit one other element of comic structure to a greater degree than any of the earlier comedies, an element which, according to L. J. Potts, is the fountainhead of all comic form and meaning—"the contrast and balance of characters." Such a "grouping of characters," says Potts, is more important than plot, which is simply an onward "march of events."[10] But in dealing with the Henry plays there is no need to assert the priority of either element; the plays depend for their success equally upon transformation comic plot and upon the balance and contrast of characters.

At the heart of the Henry plays is of course the prince's transformation. Some readers and commentators may discount the significance of Hal's "reformation," but it is insisted upon repeatedly in *Henry IV* and again at the beginning of *Henry V*. And the key to that regeneration is the couplet that concludes the much-discussed soliloquy at the end of the first scene in which Hal appears: "I'll so offend to make offense a skill, / Redeeming time when men think least I will" (*1H4* I.ii.204–5). The crucial phrase *redeeming time* is sometimes glossed as "saving time from being lost"; and although that gloss rests upon the authority of the *Oxford English Dictionary*, it is not very helpful for the simple reason that the gloss itself is ambiguous. One cannot be sure whether it means "preventing time from becoming lost" or "ransoming time already past from its status as lost time." The second meaning sounds distinctly modern and Proustian, rather than Shakespearean—even though Moncrieff's English title for Proust's novel is simply borrowed from Shakespeare. And the first meaning makes very little sense because there is no need to "redeem" something that is not yet lost. (This is like defining "to ransom a captive" as "to prevent someone from being captured.")

In an interesting essay entitled "'Redeeming time' in *Henry IV*," Paul A. Jorgensen summarizes editorial glosses on the phrase and rejects them all, preferring to understand the phrase within the context of earlier religious drama and the Homilies. He rightly associates the phrase with the biblical passage "See then that ye walk circumspectly, not as fools, but as wise, Redeeming the time, because the days are evil" (Eph. 5.15–16, KJV; cf. 2H4 II.ii.131–39) and concludes that "to the Elizabethan audience, to redeem (or 'rescue') time would be clearly understood as meaning to take full advantage of the time that man is given here on earth for salvation." He argues that this is precisely "what Hal actually does in *Henry IV*," that he redeems time not simply by defeating Hotspur or rejecting Falstaff, but rather that "his redeeming of time is going on almost constantly." It may be true that Hal's personal reformation is best understood in religious terms; strangely, however, Jorgensen ends up "agreeing with those critics . . . who argue that Hal undergoes no radical reform."[11] But I for one do not understand how, in Christian terms, one can "take full advantage of the time that man is given here on earth for salvation" and at the same time "undergo no radical reform"—unless what we are actually describing is "a radical reform that is no radical reform." There are, moreover, at least two other objections to Jorgensen's argument: the final clause of Hal's speech, "when men least think I will," apparently refers to one or more particular occasions rather than to a continuous process; and Jorgensen's view suggests that the main significance of Hal's role, and therefore of the play as a whole, is not so much national and historical as it is personal and religious.

More useful than the Homilies as a guide to the meaning of the biblical phrase "redeeming the time" is the marginal comment in the Geneva Bible of 1560, the Bible that Shakespeare apparently used. It reads as follows: "In these perilous dayes & crafte of the aduersaries, take hede how to bye again the occasions of godlines, which the worlde hathe taken from you."[12] We notice first that the conception of time is made specific by reference to present historical time. The biblical words "because the days are evil" are considerably intensified and are brought closer to home by use of the demonstrative adjective: "In *these perilous* dayes." Second, *buy again* is offered as a synonym for the word *redeem;* and this is consistent with the etymology of the word—*re(d)*, meaning "backward, over again" and *em*, meaning "take; later, buy" (as in "caveat *emptor*").[13] Thus, *redeem* is synonymous with "buy again," "buy back," or "ransom" and is also closely akin to "pay back," "pay the debt," "restore," and even "revenge." (The Jerusalem Bible renders the familiar KJV line "I know that my Redeemer liveth" as "This I know: that my Avenger lives," Job 19.25.) Third, the commentary refers not to a process, but to specific "occasions of godliness."

The *Henriad* represents England as having fallen upon evil days as a consequence of the incompetent administration of Richard II and the usurpation of Henry IV. At the beginning of the second play of the tetralogy, Henry IV laments that the "opposèd eyes" of warring factions,

> All of one nature, of one substance bred,
> Did lately meet in the intestine shock
> And furious close of civil butchery.
> (1H4 I.i.9–13)

He of course proposes to change all this and to begin by undertaking a crusade "As far as to the sepulchre of Christ" (l. 19). But even he acknowledges that little will come of his resolve: "And bootless 'tis to tell you we will go" (l. 29). It therefore falls to Prince Hal, who, as he later admits, has "a truant been to chivalry" (1H4 V.i.94), to "redeem the time" by ransoming England from civil chaos. And he proceeds to do so by confronting his adversaries the Percies "in the adventure of *this perilous day*" at Shrewsbury (1H4 V.ii.95), which becomes for him an "occasion of godliness" if we accept Vernon's description of the prince as he prepares for battle:

> I saw young Harry with his beaver on,
> His cushes on his thighs, gallantly armed,
> Rise from the ground like feathered Mercury,
> And vaulted with such ease into his seat
> As if an angel dropped down from the clouds
> To turn and wind a fiery Pegasus
> And witch the world with noble horsemanship.
> (1H4 IV.i.104–10)

The prince's godliness on this occasion is both classical ("like feathered Mercury") and Christian ("As if an angel dropped down from the clouds")—another nice example of Shakespearean synthesis. A suggestion of the occult ("witch the world") is even tossed in for good measure. Moreover, if this "Harry" is the same person as the "Hal" who had formerly been "a truant to chivalry," then I think it is safe to say that he has undergone a radical reform.[14]

In the scene that follows Hal's promise about redeeming time, two of the other principal characters declare their own attitudes toward the possibility of redeeming or ransoming persons or things temporarily lost or held hostage. When Hotspur refuses to surrender his prisoners until the king ransoms his brother-in-law Mortimer, the king swears that he has no intention whatever of doing so:

> Shall our coffers, then,
> Be emptied to *redeem* a traitor home?
> Shall we *buy* treason? and indent with fears
> When they have *lost* and *forfeited* themselves?
> No, on the barren mountains let him starve!
> For I shall never hold that man my friend
> Whose tongue shall ask me for one penny cost
> To *ransom* home revolted Mortimer.
> (1H4 I.iii.85–92, emphasis mine)

And after the king has taken his leave, Hotspur's anger rises—not only at the king but also at his father and uncle for having planted "this thorn, this canker, Bolingbroke" upon the throne:

> And shall it in more shame be further spoken
> That you are fooled, discarded, and shook off
> By him for whom these shames ye underwent?
> No! yet *time serves* wherein you may *redeem*
> Your banished honors and *restore* yourselves
> Into the good thoughts of the world again;
> *Revenge* the jeering and disdained contempt
> Of this proud king, who studies day and night
> To answer all the *debt* he owes to you
> Even with the bloody *payment* of your *deaths*.
> (1H4 I.iii.177–86, emphasis mine)

The parallelism of the two speeches is obvious, and they alert us to the various synonyms for *redeem* that echo through the play. The *debt-death* pun that Hotspur exploits (cf. Hal's "And pay the debt I never promisèd," I.ii.197) becomes a means of relating the subject of mortality to "redeeming time." Falstaff's position on such matters is clearly articulated when Hal tells him that the money stolen at Gadshill has been paid back again. "O, I do not like that paying back! 'Tis a double labor," Falstaff responds (*1H4* III.iii.171–72). And just before the battle of Shrewsbury, Hal's reminder "Why, thou owest God a death" introduces Falstaff's "catechism" on honor, which begins, "'Tis not due yet: I would be loath to pay him before his day. What need I be so forward with him that calls not on me?" (*1H4* V.i.126–29).

Perhaps the most important function of the redeem-ransom-debt-death theme is that it becomes the verbal (rather than the dramatic) means for displaying the balance and contrast of characters that is essential to the structure of *Henry IV*. As a usurper, the king of course does not want to "ransom home revolted Mortimer," whom Richard had named as his successor, because Mortimer's presence would pose a threat to his own power: "No, on the barren mountains let him starve!" Hotspur's position, though on the surface it seems more positive than the king's, is in fact equally negative: "No! yet time serves wherein you may redeem / Your banished honors." He proposes not to redeem time, but to make time a servant in buying back his own personal honor; and, as becomes clear later (III.i), he is perfectly willing to carve up England and divide it among his fellow rebels in payment of the debt he feels is owed to him. Falstaff's manner of settling debts is best described by Mistress Quickly: "You owe me money, Sir John, and now you pick a quarrel to beguile me of it" (*1H4* III.iii.63–64; cf. *2H4* II.i.113–16). Hal alone promises to "redeem time." He does so by buying back England from the evil days upon which it had fallen; and by this means he "pays the debt he never promisèd."

Falstaff himself is of course a special challenge for the interpreter of *Henry IV*. Like Shylock in *The Merchant of Venice,* he seems to stand head and shoulders above the play in which he appears, so completely does he transcend his role in the plot. Again like Shylock, he may be seen as a composite of various New Comedy stock characters (the big-bellied glutton, the drinker, the braggart soldier, the parasite, and the clever servant), and he ultimately serves as a kind of scapegoat. But, unlike Shylock, he does not actually participate in the transformation aspect of the plot even though he himself is a protean character. He represents the kind of characterization that Aristotle refers to specifically when he requires that a character be "consistent and the same throughout"—for he adds that "even if inconsistency be part of the man before one for imitation as presenting that form of character, he should still be consistently inconsistent."[15] C. L. Barber's description of Falstaff seems apt: "It is the essence of his character, and his role, in *Part One,* that he never comes to rest where we can see him for what he 'is.' He is always in motion, always adopting postures, assuming characters."[16]

Falstaff is of course constantly changing, but always the same. Even his capacity to wriggle out of any predicament depends upon his switching from one aspect of his multifaceted personality to another almost at will. When he is questioned about the adventure at Gadshill, Falstaff at first assumes the role of braggart soldier. That he had planned in advance to do so is obvious from Peto's admission that Falstaff had "hacked [his sword] with his dagger, and said . . . he would make you believe it was done in fight, and persuaded us to do the like" (1H4 II.iv.290–93). When this fails completely, he immediately leaps to the role of clever and faithful servant: "Was it for me to kill the heir apparent? . . . I was now a coward on instinct" (II.iv.254–58). Then, because he is not really comfortable as self-confessed coward and underling, he switches again, this time to his favorite role as master of the revels: "What, shall we be merry? Shall we have a play extempore?" (II.iv.264–65). When even that culminates in another humiliation for Falstaff—Hal's assertion that (as king) he will "banish plump Jack"—a knock at the door is all that delivers the fat knight from the necessity of still another switch; and he seeks refuge from the law behind an arras, where he promptly falls asleep.

Falstaff is much written about—testimony, no doubt, to the truth of his own claim that he is not only witty in himself "but the cause that wit is in other men." Our concern with Falstaff, however, has to do with his relation to the plot; and it would be best if we did not, as often happens, let his personal charm overwhelm our view of his function in the play. Reading some of the older critics, one gets the impression that Falstaff is the chief character and center of interest in *Henry IV*; and more recent critics seem at times to lean in that direction. M. A. Shaaber, for instance, concludes his introduction to the Pelican edition of the play by saying that Falstaff "comes within an ace of turning Shakespeare's history of Henry IV into the comedy of Falstaff." Such a view of the play suggests that comedy ought certainly to be subordinated to history in any dramatic representation of Henry IV's reign and that Shakespeare, by making Falstaff so amusing, seems to have gotten his priorities and perhaps even his genres mixed.

But history, in and of itself, has no literary quality. Dividing the Shakespeare plays into comedies, histories, and tragedies, in the manner of the First Folio, obviously involves what is called "cross-ranking"—two entirely different principles of division are used. The distinction between comedy and tragedy is on the basis of plot; the distinction between history and the other two types, however, is on the basis of subject matter—all ten of the histories have as their subject matter the "modern" history of England. (Thus, legendary history—*King Lear, Cymbeline*—and non-

English settings—*Julius Caesar, Macbeth*—fall outside the scope of the "history play.") The historiographer presents history *as history;* the dramatist presents it as comedy or as tragedy (e.g., *The Tragedy of King Richard the Second*), and the historical subject matter comes in as an "added attraction." What this all means is that *Henry IV* is not a comedy because Falstaff is in it; rather, Falstaff is in the play because it is a comedy.[17]

The plot which extends over all three of the Henry plays we may capsulize, as we did those of earlier comedies, in a series of time-lapse metaphors. In *Henry IV, Part 1,* the Prince of Wales, long a truant to chivalry, becomes Harry of Monmouth, victor over the Percies at Shrewsbury. In *Henry IV, Part 2,* Harry Monmouth, the victor at Shrewsbury, becomes Henry V, the mirror of all Christian kings. And in *Henry V,* this mirror of all Christian kings becomes the victor over the French at Agincourt, and in a remarkable dramatic coup involving politically expedient love at first sight, he becomes the suitor to Princess Katherine of France. This last manifestation of Henry's transformational prowess has been an embarrassment to many, including Dr. Johnson, who observed, "The truth is, that the poet's matter failed him in the fifth act, and he was glad to fill it up with whatever he could get; and not even *Shakespeare* can write well without a proper subject."[18] Dover Wilson and others have sought to defend this last act, among them J. H. Walter, who argues that "the Christian prince to complete his virtues must be married."[19] But such interpretation makes the form of the play depend entirely upon its content, which in this view is didactic; the marriage proposed at the end of the play rounds out this portrait of the heroic medieval king.

There is, however, a simpler explanation, which arises out of the play's form rather than its content. Shakespeare's comedies characteristically end with the celebration of at least one wedding and sometimes with as many as four of them. Two exceptions come to mind: *The Comedy of Errors,* which has few if any romantic overtones, and *Love's Labor's Lost,* in which any possible weddings are postponed for a year. As I indicated earlier, these plays are two of the three Shakespeare comedies that make no use of the transformation plot. All of the other comedies, including *Twelfth Night,* end with such a union or at least the promise of one. In *Henry V,* because the protagonist is an English king, the marriage at the end of the play is of national and dynastic importance. If Dr. Johnson was correct in his judgment of the last act, then he was incorrect in his explanation: "the poet's matter" did not fail him; *that* came to him directly from English history. What failed him (if the last act is indeed a flop) was his conception of form—his belief that he could adequately represent the career of Henry V by means of a transformation comic plot with the requisite festive wedding at the end.

But Henry's courtship of Katherine at the end of the play—which is also the end of the whole *Henriad*—serves other literary purposes besides providing a happy ending for the comic plot. Sexual potency was an indispensable qualification for the hero-king of literary tradition. We are told that Solomon "loved many foreign women.... He had seven hundred wives, princesses, and three hundred concubines" (1 Kings 11.1–3). Such "heroic potency" was no doubt one of the reasons why Solomon's father, David, escaped popular condemnation when he abducted Bathsheba and arranged for the death of her husband. That such potency was indispensable to the monarch and not merely a desirable attribute is confirmed in the story of King David's forced abdication. When the people saw that he was becoming old and perhaps impotent, "they sought for a beautiful maiden throughout all the territory of Israel." Finding that he was unable to perform adequately with this "very beautiful maiden," they realized that the time had come for him to abdicate; and Adonijah "exalted himself, saying, 'I will be king'" (1 Kings 1.1–5). Thus did political power change hands in ancient Israel.

Henry's "ursine wooing" of the French princess both establishes the king's heroic potency and preserves his reputation as a moral man, happy within the confines of a Christian marriage. Just as he combines his own self-interest ("commodity") with the national and imperial interest, he manages to publicize his potency and confirm his reputation as a "Christian king" at the same time. Shakespeare handles the same problem no less adroitly (but of course without the comic overtones) half a dozen years later when dealing with the question of succession in *Macbeth*. On the one hand, we hear repeated references to the tyrannical Macbeth's "infirmity," his having "no spur / To prick the sides of [his] intent," his wife's chiding him for his failure to be the same in his own "act and valor" as in "desire," and her urging him to "screw [his] courage to the sticking place." And on the other hand, we hear Malcolm (who is to be Macbeth's successor as king) confess that

> Your wives, your daughters,
> Your matrons, and your maids could not fill up
> The cistern of my lust.
>
> (IV.iii.61–63)

Macduff's response to Malcolm's question about whether such a one would be "fit to govern" is unequivocal: "Fit to govern? / No, not to live!" (IV.iii.102–3).

Malcolm's later disavowal of that confession (IV.iii.120–26) satisfies what I have called the moral-man requirement for an Elizabethan-Jacobean (or modern) hero-politician; but for an audience familiar with the heroic tradition both in the Bible and in literature generally, it is as if the judge at a trial should instruct the jury to "disregard" a crucial piece of evidence that has just been forcefully presented. The distinct implication, when all is said and done, is that Malcolm shows promise of becoming a much more adequate king than Macbeth, precisely because of his discreetly disavowed potency. Otherwise it would simply not be true, as Macduff claims at the end of the play, that "the time is free." It would instead just be a matter of exchanging a blood-thirsty tyrant for an unknown quantity.

Thus, the final scene of *Henry V*, so much maligned for its supposed irrelevance and vacuity, serves a multiple literary purpose—and it does so very neatly. Other crucial moments in the transformation plot likewise furnish the beginnings and endings of the three plays. Perhaps the most remarkable of these (other than Hal's prediction of his own "reformation" near the beginning of *Henry IV, Part 1*) is the newly crowned Henry V's rejection of Falstaff at the end of *Henry IV, Part 2*. If there is any one deed by means of which Henry secures the enmity of critics and audiences alike, it is surely this rejection speech, in which the new king "casts off the old man" and banishes him forever:

> I know thee not, old man. Fall to thy prayers.
> How ill white hairs become a fool and jester!
> I have long dreamed of such a kind of man,
> So surfeit-swelled, so old, and so profane,
> But, being awaked, I do despise my dream.
> Make less thy body hence, and more thy grace.
> Leave gormandizing. Know the grave doth gape
> For thee thrice wider than for other men.
> Reply not to me with a fool-born jest.
> Presume not that I am the thing I was,
> For God doth know, so shall the world perceive,
> That I have turned away my former self.
> So will I those that kept me company.
> When thou dost hear I am as I have been,
> Approach me, and thou shalt be as thou wast,
> The tutor and the feeder of my riots.
> Till then, I banish thee, on pain of death,
> As I have done the rest of my misleaders,
> Not to come near our person by ten mile.
> For competence of life I will allow you,
> That lack of means enforce you not to evils.

> And, as we hear you do reform yourselves,
> We will, according to your strengths and qualities,
> Give you advancement. Be it your charge, my lord,
> To see performed the tenor of our word.
>
> (2H4 V.v.48–72)

The speech itself is extremely interesting from a technical point of view; its structure resembles that of Oliver's speech in *As You Like It* (" 'Twas I. But 'tis not I.") in that it makes use of shifting verb tenses to distinguish between the various "selves." But it is more complex than Oliver's speech because it involves three stages of development rather than two, and it reflects both the private and the public sides of Henry's personality by means of the personal "I" and the royal "we." In general, the past tense corresponds to Prince Hal, the present to Harry Monmouth ("Presume *not* that *I am* the thing *I was*"), and the future to Henry V ("For competence of life *I will allow* you"), while the present perfect tense represents the transition between the first two selves ("That I *have turned away* my former self"). The transition between the private "I" and the royal "we" is facilitated by associating a verb that suggests the exercise of royal power ("banish") with the singular pronoun and then going on in the same clause to the royal plural: "Till then, *I banish* thee, on pain of death, / . . . / Not to come near *our* person by ten mile."

This speech, like Prince Hal's earlier prediction of his own reformation, has indeed been characterized as "priggish"; but that seems rather like describing Falstaff as "obese." Autocrats seldom make pleasant and easy-going companions—especially those who have remolded their characters in order to become great rulers. Shakespeare apparently recognized, as Confucius had done two thousand years earlier, that "if a man can reform his own heart, what should hinder him from taking part in government? But if he cannot reform his own heart, what has he to do with reforming others?"[20] Whatever our response to the fictitious personality that utters this rejection speech, the speech itself is a masterpiece of the synthesizing imagination— it brings together five different character elements within twenty-five lines, and it does so without the least confusion or ostentation on the author's part. The diction is extremely simple—only a few words (such as "gormandizing" and "tenor") are even slightly unusual. There is very little figurative language ("I have long dreamed . . . / But being awaked.") and very little subtlety of rhythm; nearly every line ends with a punctuation mark of some sort, and more than half the lines contain no internal punctuation.[21]

Whether or not the new king sounds priggish when he publicly casts off the old man, C. L. Barber makes a much more serious charge—that the rejection of Falstaff the man does not justify "the rejection of Falstaff as a mode of awareness." According to Barber, "In *Part One*, Falstaff reigns, within his sphere, as Carnival; *Part Two* is very largely taken up with his trial." And later he says,

> The result of the trial is to make us see perfectly the necessity for the rejection of Falstaff as a man, as a favorite for a king, as the leader of an interest at court.
> But I do not think the dramatist is equally successful in justifying the rejection of Falstaff as a mode of awareness.

Barber's explanation for the "drastic restriction of awareness" which supposedly characterizes the end of *Part 2* is that it "goes with the embracing of magical modes of thought, not humorously but sentimentally." He comments upon particular lines of the rejection speech and says: "If ironies about Hal were expressed by the context, we could take the scene as the representation of his becoming a prig. But there is simply a blur in the tone, a blur which results, I think, from a retreat into magic by the *dramatist*, as distinct from his characters."[22] If I understand Barber's point correctly, he is saying that the difficulty with the ending of *Henry IV, Part 2* is not simply a matter of a dramatic character's becoming a prig at the time of his coronation. Rather it would seem that by sentimentally embracing magical modes of thought the dramatist himself enthusiastically turns prig at the same time.

But Shakespeare does not "reject Falstaff as a mode of awareness" at the end of *Part 2* any more than he rejects chivalry and honor when Hotspur is killed at the end of *Part 1*. Indeed, the two events—Hal's victory over Hotspur and his rejection of Falstaff—are precisely parallel in the structure of the *Henriad*. As Hugh Dickinson suggests, the prince learns from both of his "foils" and develops "as if taking from Falstaff the cunning a king must have, and from Hotspur the courage."[23] The evidence for asserting that the young king has incorporated elements of Hotspur's attitude and character into himself is contained principally in *Henry V*. Before the battle of Shrewsbury, Hotspur, like Henry before the battle of Agincourt, finds himself and his army badly outnumbered, and he overhears his followers wishing for more men to fight in their cause. Hotspur, as one would expect, makes the best of a bad situation (*1H4* IV.i.75–83); but the young Henry V makes a rousing speech that echoes both the long-dead Hotspur and the young prince's own promise to reform: "But if it be a sin to covet honor, / I am the most offending soul alive." And he outdoes his old rival by offering money and safe passage to anyone who has no stomach for the uneven fight (*H5* IV.iii.18–67). The speech has of course a superpatriotic ring to it; but it helps us greatly in any attempt to understand the now nearly defunct conception of the "hero."

Likewise, the evidence for Falstaff's lasting influence upon his protégé is contained in the last play of the *Henriad*. Barber represents Falstaff's "mode of awareness" primarily as an "attitude" when he asserts that "the trouble with trying to get rid of this attitude merely by getting rid of Falstaff is that the attitude is too pervasive in the whole society of the play, whether public or private."[24] The attitude itself is of course fairly complex, but chief among the elements that go into its making are an enormous capacity for rationalization and self-justification (Purse-taking? "Why, Hal, 'tis my vocation, Hal. 'Tis no sin for a man to labor in his vocation," *1H4* I.ii.98–99; cf. Eph. 4.1) and a no-nonsense view of such abstractions as "honor" ("Can honor set a leg? No. Or an arm? No. . . . What is honor? A word. What is that word honor? Air!" *1H4* V.i.131–34). Such Falstaffian philosophy seems harmless enough, and amusing too, largely because it is expressed in a vacuum—nothing is at stake for the simple reason that Falstaff wields no power.[25]

The young King Henry V repeatedly demonstrates how well he has learned from the master of rationalization and self-justification, when for instance he attaches so much significance to the advice of the bishops—as if it would never have occurred to him to invade France but for their assurance that his cause was perfectly righteous (*H5* I.ii). Or, when he expresses his innocent concern to the citizens of Harfleur as he stands before the gates of that embattled town:

> What is't to me, when you yourselves are cause,
> If your pure maidens fall into the hand
> Of hot and forcing violation?
>
> (*H5* III.iii.19–21)

Or again—most interesting of all—when Henry, in disguise, explains to Bates, Court, and Williams that if they should die in battle, it is certainly not the fault of the king who brought them there (*H5* IV.i.82–215). A king, after all, must sometimes sacrifice the lives of his subjects; Henry is, by vocation, a king, and " 'Tis no sin for a man to labor in his vocation." The syllogism is worthy of Falstaff, and there is no reason at all to think that the master logician would "deny his pupil's major" in this case (cf. *1H4* II.iv.471). Falstaff, we remember, regarded conscripts he himself had gathered as "food for powder, food for powder," saying, "They'll fill a pit as well as better" (*1H4* IV.ii.58–64).

The most interesting verbal echo of Falstaff's teaching comes in Henry's discourse, or soliloquy if you will, on the eve of the battle of Agincourt. In a self-pitying mood more characteristic of the master than of the pupil, Henry debunks the whole conception of "ceremony," the honor paid to a king by deferential subjects, who in all other respects (according to the king) are better off than he is. Henry displays the same contempt for ceremony that Falstaff had shown earlier for honor in general; and he even uses some of the same imagery and catechistic form. Henry's attitude is apparent almost from the beginning by such devices as the *idol-idle* pun: "And what art thou, thou idol Ceremony?" (*H5* IV.i.226). Like Falstaff, Henry raises questions about ceremony's "skill in surgery": "O, be sick, great greatness, / And bid thy ceremony give thee cure!" (*H5* IV.i.237–38). And a few lines later, he asks, "Canst thou, when thou command'st the beggar's knee, / Command the health of it? No" (*H5* IV.i.242–43). In *Henry IV, Part 1*, Prince Hal exits moments before Falstaff's catechism on honor, and he is certainly not present when Hotspur delivers his brief pep talk before the battle of Shrewsbury; but the parallelism between their speeches and Henry's is unmistakable. Henry V, as popular hero, manages to incorporate all of the best characteristics of his models into himself and at the same time to avoid their chief faults. He has all of his father's political shrewdness, but none of his guilt "in compassing the crown." He has all of Hotspur's capacity for courage and self-sacrifice, but none of his blindness to the nation's interest while pursuing his own. And he possesses in abundance Falstaff's capacity for self-justification as well as his no-nonsense attitude toward pomp and ceremony, but none of his indifference to "time" and to how the world may fare outside the tavern walls.

The Henry plays are certainly Shakespeare's most ambitious undertaking in the comic mode, because in them a single transformation plot, extended over three entire five-act plays, becomes the vehicle for representing the career of an authentic national hero. It is no exaggeration to say that in these plays one transformation comic plot is expanded to epic proportions; historical figure and comic hero are united in one of the most remarkable syntheses of fact and fiction that world literature has to offer. The facts, of course, are subject to some exaggeration and distortion. Even if Shakespeare's account of the casualties at Agincourt is reasonably accurate, it is difficult to suppose that the sixteen-year-old Prince Hal's role at the battle of Shrewsbury was quite so brilliant as Shakespeare represents it as having been. But to quibble with the accuracy of Shakespeare's facts and numbers is to miss the point. To represent the facts simply and accurately is the business of chroniclers; to represent those facts as the consequence of certain social, political, and economic forces is the function of historians; to show forth historical figures as triumphant national heroes is the purpose of comic dramatists who choose events and persons out of a national past as the subject matter for their plays.

Indeed, no matter how magnificent the actual English victory at Agincourt, it would still have been necessary to maximize the French losses and to minimize the English casualties in order for the writer to achieve his comic and heroic purpose. (It is for this reason that Olivier's emendation—"five-and-twenty score"—is misguided.) Henry's triumph at Agincourt, against enormous odds, and his marriage to Katherine of France again suggest a parallel with King David's early career—his astonishing victory over Goliath and his subsequent betrothal to King Saul's daughter Michal. Simple doubling, as we saw in *The Comedy of Errors* and *A Midsummer Night's Dream,* is common enough in the elaboration of comic plot. It is likewise standard practice in heroic tale. As we observed earlier in connection with Shylock, when the young David is required to bring in "a hundred foreskins of the Philistines" so that he might become the king's son-in-law, he goes out and slays *two hundred* Philistines and delivers their foreskins to the king's servants (1 Sam. 18.25–27). From any conservative and realistic point of view, this is of course ridiculous; and *The Interpreter's Bible* hastens to tell us that "the killing of two hundred Philistines is an unnecessary and unoriginal exaggeration."[26] The prose part of the story is, nonetheless, fairly conservative—it simply doubles the number of slain enemies as an indication of the youthful hero's strength and courage.

When poetry and song enter in, however, the numbers are not doubled but multiplied by ten in an effort to show forth the young hero's prowess and popularity:

> When David returned from slaying the Philistine, the women came out of all the cities of Israel, singing and dancing, to meet King Saul, with timbrels, with songs of joy, and with instruments of music. And the women sang to one another as they made merry,
>
> "Saul has slain his thousands,
> And David his ten thousands."
> (1 Sam. 18.6–7, RSV)

Again the commentary explains, "The song here is an example of Oriental exaggeration, not to be taken literally, so that no difficulty need be felt about its use at this early stage in David's military career."[27] What the biblical narrator says of young David in an effort to make him seem heroic may indeed be "an example of Oriental exaggeration"; but the same statement is literally true of the twenty-eight-year-old King Henry V—at Agincourt he actually did slay his "ten thousand." The poetic device, then, is not to double the number but simply to add on a zero and thereby to multiply by ten—the process to which the Prologue refers, in *Henry V,* when he calls the theater "this wooden O" and goes on to point out that "a crooked figure may / Attest in little place a million," calling himself and his audience "ciphers to this great accompt" (Prol. i.13–17).

Such comic doubling and heroic multiplying by ten goes some distance toward explaining what Mark Van Doren objected to as "a radical and indeed an astounding inflation in the style."[28] As we have seen, the rhetoric of *Henry V* is in some ways akin to what we find in the story of David and Goliath, which is full of "Oriental exaggeration" or, less charitably, "unnecessary and unoriginal exaggeration." Even if (as is highly doubtful) the stripling David had indeed slain his "ten thousands," it seems most unlikely that "the women came out of *all* the cities of Israel," singing to one another and making merry, especially at a time when long-distance communications were almost nonexistent. I suppose such claims, as Van Doren says of the boasting and exhortation in *Henry V,* "have a forced, shrill, windy sound, as if their author were pumping his muse for dear life."[29] As I have already suggested, *Henry V* both honors and mocks the heroic tradition in literature—hence the "rival camps" among the play's single-minded critics. Fluellen's attempt to honor his king by comparing him with "Alexander the Pig" (*H5* IV.vii) is clearly ridiculous; and the longer he pursues it, the more ridiculous it becomes. But that parodic interlude comes right in the midst of the battle of Agincourt, an episode that is sufficient, by itself, to establish Henry's credentials as an authentic hero.

Van Doren's other main objections to *Henry V,* in an essay that may be regarded as the culmination of two centuries of negative reaction to the play, rest upon his refusal to accept the comic mode as being appropriate for representing the career of this triumphant medieval monarch. He says first that "the prologues are everywhere apologetic" and that they insist, in tiresome fashion, that what cannot be realistically represented on the stage "will simply have to be imagined." He then says that "the author of 'Romeo and Juliet' had not been sorry because his stage was a piece of London rather than the whole of Verona, and the storm in 'King Lear' will begin without benefit of description."[30] But those plays are tragedies, not comedies, and Van Doren seems to forget that Puck, speaking as epilogue, apologizes profusely for the "weak and idle theme" of *A Midsummer Night's Dream,* which he begs us not to "reprehend," or that Theseus reminds us that "the best in this kind [plays] are but shadows, and the worst are no worse if imagination amend them" (*MND* V.i.209–10). If this sort of description and exhortation (which certainly cannot, as Van Doren rightly observes, "turn tableau into tragedy") is inappropriate in Shakespearean drama, then surely Prospero's epilogue to *The Tempest* is a most regrettable lapse in taste on the dramatist's part.

Another complaint registered by Van Doren has to do with "the note of gaiety that takes the place here of high passion." Again, I suppose one might cite *Romeo and Juliet* and *King Lear* as evidence that the playwright in his more inspired moments did not allow the note of gaiety that is appropriate to comedy to displace the high passion that one looks for in tragedy. But it seems almost perverse to keep insisting that a play that is so clearly constructed on the comic pattern should evoke the feelings we associate with tragedy. Van Doren's irritation is obvious when he describes Henry's speech "about matching rackets and playing sets—his idiom for bloody war," or characterizes the French camp as "a locker room, littered with attitudes no less than uniforms," or refers to "the scenes where Katherine makes fritters of English."[31] One would almost think, from reading the play itself, that the dramatist was trying to suggest in comic fashion that the French leaders were foolish and misguided and that the French princess was a delicious prize for a conquering hero, a "morsel for a monarch," as it were.

Van Doren's last objection, to a "direct and puerile appeal to the patriotism of the audience," is closely akin to E. K. Chambers's suggestion that in Henry one sees "the prototype of the blatant modern imperialist."[32] But the particulars of Van Doren's objection are not impressive. According to him, the play lacks unity, and therefore "Shakespeare must grow lyrical about the unity of England; politics must substitute for poetry." But like most of the Shakespeare comedies, this play depends for its unity upon its own version of the transformation comic plot; and that unity becomes difficult to see if we insist upon regarding the play, not as transformational heroic comedy, but as some sort of tragedy manqué. "The traitors Scroop, Cambridge, and Grey are happy to lose their heads for England," says Van Doren. But part of the point of this episode is surely to show how much more effectively the comic hero–king Henry V deals with traitors and conspirators than either of his predecessors, Richard II and Henry IV, had done. And of this difference, all the comic hero–king's subjects (even the bad ones) must surely be glad. Also, says Van Doren, "the battles in France, even though the enemy's host is huge and starvation takes its toll, are bound to be won by such fine English fellows as we have here."[33] But this suggestion conveniently ignores the fact that the English, in 1415, did indeed win the battle of Agincourt against a vastly more numerous French army; and we can only ask the critic if he would prefer, since we cannot change the outcome of such a celebrated battle, that it had been won by cads and bounders rather than by "such fine English fellows as we have here" in Shakespeare's *Henry V*.

Seen in perspective, these four main objections to *Henry V* come across as reasons why the critic dislikes the play rather than as literary faults in either the play itself or the author's method. They point to the play not as an example of bad dramaturgy, but as an example of bad taste. *Henry V* has of course had its defenders and apologists; but the negative view, which goes back at least to Dr. Johnson, reappears with considerable regularity. My own response to those criticisms is that they single out characteristics of the play that are corollaries of the author's decision to superimpose the transformation comic plot upon events and persons from English history and to represent the most important of those persons as an effective champion of national interest—a real-life comic hero. That superimposition becomes one of the premises upon which the play is based, and the critic's refusal to accept such a premise is an objection not to the playwright's artistry, but to his outmoded or inappropriate view of historical events.

The transformation comic plot appears to work best in connection with purely fictional characters that tend to be simple and amusing, such as Kate in *The Taming of the Shrew* or Bottom in *A Midsummer Night's Dream*. It begins to create problems for the critic as the characters become more realistic, either because they are complex, in the manner of Shylock, or because they are historical, in the manner of Henry V. Shakespeare apparently attempted to compensate for this difficulty by "distancing" the realistic characters—by making the complex character a social outcast and by choosing a historical figure that was removed from his audience by nearly two hundred years of tumultuous history. Nevertheless, some influential critics have responded to the plays either by denying that the plot involves any significant transformation or else by ignoring the transformation itself, as if it were not really central to the play's meaning and form.

But the transformation plot is less foreign to historical material than one might at first suppose, and Shakespeare apparently foresaw the possibility of synthesizing the two before he ever embarked upon the *Henriad*. When time-lapse metaphor becomes the basis for plot, as it does in all but three of the Shakespeare comedies, it accomplishes the greatest of all syntheses—it actually fuses time and eternity. The truly successful work of art, which in the case of poetry is based upon metaphor, finally (as Hippolyta tells Theseus) "grows to something of great constancy." It breaks free of time and becomes eternal. But comedy itself (as the Page tells Christopher

Sly) is indeed "a kind of history." And history is inconceivable apart from time. The Page's word *history* means of course "story," but in most European languages one word conveys both meanings. The important distinction between the two words in English is that *history* usually implies factuality whereas *story* often suggests imaginative composition; but both words refer to "a sequence of events." At its best, simple metaphor raises statement to the level of art, which transcends time. Likewise, the time-lapse metaphor at its best incorporates time into art. The *Henriad* differs from the other Shakespeare comedies primarily in this respect: the "history" it represents is presumably factual, whereas the other comedies do not pretend to any basis in fact; they have "no more reality," as Granville-Barker suggests, "than Jack and the Beanstalk." In the *Henriad* Shakespeare gives us some "reality" by making his comic "history" more or less factual, though some are inclined to think that he was guilty of lapses in taste largely because his imperialism in *Henry V*, like his conception of the ideal wife in *The Taming of the Shrew*, is now sadly out of date. But the disappointment of those who read poetry for its political and sociological content should not be surprising, especially when the poetry they read is nearly four hundred years old.

The *Henriad* was not, of course, Shakespeare's first attempt to superimpose the transformation comic plot upon historical events. In some ways, *King John* prefigures within a single play the structure of the entire *Henriad*. The career of John as set forth in Shakespeare's play recounts "the fall and wretched death of an eminent person" in a way that roughly parallels *The Tragedy of King Richard the Second*, which was written only a year or so later. And Philip the Bastard, though he is illegitimate, consciously chooses his own identity and, after a period of cynicism, emerges as a heroic figure who almost single-handedly delivers England from lying "at the proud foot of a conqueror." Salisbury can quite truthfully say of the "reformed" Philip, "That misbegotten devil, Faulconbridge, / In spite of spite, alone upholds the day" (*Jn.* V.iv.4–5). Like Prince Hal, Philip learns somehow to combine his own self-interest with the national interest; and like Henry V, he becomes in his own way the savior of his country, or at least its deliverer from the evil days upon which it had fallen.

The *Henriad* does, however, take the transformation comic plot as far as it can possibly go in representing historical events—not in "turning tableau into tragedy," as Mark Van Doren would prefer, but in expanding comic drama to epic proportions. Clearly, if Shakespeare is to make further use of the transformation plot, he must strike out in a different direction. He can—as he does in *The Merry Wives of Windsor*—return to farce; but even then, if we may judge by the more or less contemporary setting of the play, he remains committed to a more realistic representation than he had been when he wrote *The Comedy of Errors* and *The Taming of the Shrew*. More important, though, he will experiment with the transformation plot as a vehicle for portraying the aberrant behavior of otherwise normal people—the charming young nobleman who is suddenly revealed as an insufferable snob, the morally upright governor who uses his position to harass a beautiful and pure young woman, the loving husband who inexplicably falls into a jealous fury, and the honorable prince who willingly takes part in a conspiracy to usurp another ruler's power. Having nearly exhausted the possibilities of the transformation plot as a structure for farce, romantic comedy, and heroic comedy, he next adapts it to problem comedy and romance.

❧ SEVEN ❧

Transformation in Problem Comedy and Romance

Bertram, Angelo, and Leontes

◆

>'Tis time; descend; be stone no more; approach;
>Strike all that look upon with marvel. Come,
>I'll fill your grave up. Stir, nay, come away;
>Bequeath to death your numbness, for from him
>Dear life redeems you. You perceive she stirs.

The *Merry Wives of Windsor* and *Twelfth Night,* both of which may be dated about 1600, recall the earliest Shakespeare comedies in that one of them is purely farcical and the other nontransformational. The comedies written after these two tend to be more "serious" than the earlier farces, romantic comedies, and heroic comedies, which are by definition frolicsome, amorous, and overblown. There is of course continuity within the comedies as a group, and the later ones are sometimes likewise playful, erotic, and exaggerated. But they are in general more deeply concerned with the problems of ordinary living and with the representation of values such as one person's devotion to another and that person's willingness to forgive even the most dire offenses. A play's seriousness depends upon neither how realistic the plot nor how disastrous the conclusion, but upon whether the issues dealt with in the play are ones that really matter and whether they get serious attention within the framework of the play. Paradoxically, the play's lack of realism and its happy conclusion may actually augment the seriousness of its overall effect.

Of the comedies written about 1600, *Much Ado About Nothing* may be regarded as transitional. The tone of the play, created in part by the bantering dialogue of Beatrice and Benedick, is akin to that of the high romantic comedies, but its structure, which involves a serious situation arising from the young protagonist's "misprision" and which culminates in repentance and forgiveness, looks forward to the problem comedies and romances. Claudio does indeed acknowledge his responsibility for the turmoil that leads to Hero's supposed death, but at the same time he suggests that almost anyone else would have made the same mistake in such circumstances. He throws himself upon Leonato's mercy while intimating that Leonato would be unjust to withhold that mercy:

> Choose your revenge yourself;
> Impose me to what penance your invention
> Can lay upon my sin. Yet sinned I not
> But in mistaking.
> (*Ado* V.i.259–62)

To be sure, Claudio undergoes a change of heart; he begins by smugly proclaiming Hero's supposed guilt and ends by acknowledging, however reluctantly, his own undeniable offense. For reasons such as these Robert Hunter regards *Much Ado* as the first of the comedies of forgiveness, different in structure from the comedies that come before, but less serious in its implications than the ones that follow.[1]

Several of the late comedies do in fact share thematic material with the great tragedies that were written at about the same time. *Troilus and Cressida*, a play of this period and of doubtful classification, articulates one such theme very clearly. When Hector says of the beautiful Helen, "Brother, she is not worth what she doth cost / The keeping," Troilus inquires cynically, "What's aught but as 'tis valued?" And Hector replies:

> But value dwells not in particular will;
> It holds his estimate and dignity
> As well wherein 'tis precious of itself
> As in the prizer.
> (*Tro.* II.ii.51–56)

This distinction between intrinsic worth and estimated value is central to the meaning of *Othello* and *King Lear*. In both plays the enormous intrinsic worth of one character (Desdemona, Cordelia) stands as a given, and in both plays the protagonist radically misprizes that character. Lear's "devaluation" of Cordelia (this "unprized precious maid") is sudden and angry, and Othello's "estimate" of Desdemona is gradually and completely eroded. Similarly, in *Much Ado* Claudio misprizes Hero, whose innocence the audience never has reason to doubt, as a result of Don John's malicious deception. Likewise in *All's Well That Ends Well* the king and countess, who serve as guardians of the play's traditional values, repeatedly assert Helena's intrinsic worth, although Bertram through sheer snobbery stubbornly refuses to recognize her value. And in *The Winter's Tale* Leontes devalues Hermione in corresponding fashion, acting as suddenly as King Lear and as irrationally as Othello.

Moreover, the late Shakespeare comedies—*All's Well, Measure for Measure, The Winter's Tale,* and *The Tempest*—place considerable emphasis upon story elements and plot devices that are patently unrealistic. The two so-called problem comedies are the only ones in the Shakespeare canon that make use of the bed trick, the coarsest and most improbable device in the farcical repertory.[2] The two romances also depend heavily upon what might be called authentic miracle, as opposed to fairy magic or Old Testament tall tale. When we compare the bed trick with other comic conventions, we realize that love at first sight, for instance, requires only that we regard the normal process of falling in love as taking place within a much-reduced time frame. The bed trick, on the other hand, requires that we suppose the person upon whom the trick is played (and it is the male protagonist in both plays) to be deaf, dumb, and blind, at least during the rendezvous itself; and one would ordinarily think that his senses would be especially keen just then, even if the light was a little dim. As for the authentic miracles in the romances, we need only compare the effect of Sebastian's line "A most high miracle!" in the last act of *The Tempest* with Lucentio's laughter-producing claim "Love wrought these miracles" near the end of *The Taming of the Shrew* to see that the "comic distortion" we noted earlier in the meaning of the word *miracle* has somehow evaporated in the intervening seventeen years.

These two things—important subject matter and unrealistic story elements or plot devices—combine to produce the seriocomic effect characteristic of the late plays which the First Folio classifies as comedies.[3] Subject matter of the type referred to earlier (intrinsic worth versus estimated value) lends itself to either tragedy or comedy, the crucial difference being whether or not the characters suffer irreparable loss in the course of the play; because Helena and Hermione are alive and well at the end, the final effect is "comic," however "serious" the proceedings up to that point. And the use of miracle, not to mention utterly incredible plot twists, makes it clear to reader and viewer well before the end of the play that the manipulator is in firm control and that all will end well. In short, the subject matter is serious enough to be genuinely interesting for its own sake, and the plot is clearly metaphoric rather than straightforwardly realistic.

The other elements of Shakespearean comedy—reflexive structure, strongly contrasted settings, and self-consciousness on the part of characters that change—are not so consistently prominent in the late comedies as in the middle plays. Only one of the four late comedies has a recognizable play within the play (*The Tempest*). Only one emphasizes the contrast between two settings (*The Winter's Tale*), while another is set entirely in the existential world (*Measure for Measure*) and still another entirely in the pastoral world (*The Tempest*). The characters in all four plays vary from the foppishly self-important to the harshly self-critical, and in all four plays (which in this respect are fundamentally different from the earlier comedies) a character who is thought to be dead is, if not resurrected, at least recalled to life in a meaningful way.

The first of the four comedies, *All's Well That Ends Well*, treats us to a triple portion of the unbelievable. First we have a miracle in Helena's curing the king. When the miracle worker says, "Heaven hath through me restored the king to health," all respond, "We understand it, and thank heaven for you" (II.iii.63–64). Such king-curing smacks of medieval romance. Next, Bertram requires that Helena get the ring from his finger and a child from her body that he is father to—only then, he says, will he be her husband. He does not believe that she will ever succeed in these "impossible" tasks: "In such a 'then' I write a 'never,'" he tells her (III.ii.55–59). Carefully worded requirements of this sort resonate with the riddling prophecies in other Shakespeare plays, including the prediction that Henry IV will "not die but in Jerusalem" (*2H4* IV.v.237) and the witches' assertion that "none of woman born / Shall harm Macbeth" (*Mac.* IV.i.80–81). Finally, there is the bed trick, in which the sportive young Bertram never suspects that his partner for the occasion is his childhood acquaintance turned unwanted bride. Such obtuseness on the part of a young man who is presumably in full possession of his faculties would seem to cry out for metaphoric, rather than literal, interpretation.

According to Northrop Frye, we should regard the plot of *All's Well* as a reversal of the usual New Comedy pattern. He offers a brief Freudian analysis of New Comedy in general and then concludes with a specific reference to *All's Well*:

> New Comedy unfolds from what may be described as a comic Oedipus situation. Its main theme is the successful effort of a young man to outwit an opponent and possess the girl of his choice. The opponent is usually the father (*senex*), and the psychological descent of the heroine from the mother is also sometimes hinted at. The father frequently wants the same girl, and is cheated out of her by the son, the mother thus becoming the son's ally. The girl is usually a slave or courtesan, and the plot turns on a *cognitio* or discovery of birth which makes her

marriageable. Thus it turns out that she is not under an insuperable taboo after all but is an accessible object of desire, so that the plot follows the regular wish-fulfillment pattern. . . . Whether this analysis is sound or not, New Comedy is certainly concerned with the maneuvering of a young man toward a young woman, and marriage is the tonic chord on which it ends. The normal comic resolution is the surrender of the *senex* to the hero, never the reverse. Shakespeare tried to reverse the pattern in *All's Well That Ends Well*, where the king of France forces Bertram to marry Helena, and the critics have not yet stopped making faces over it.[4]

But perhaps the critics are still "making faces over it" for the same reason that the inheritors of Mark Van Doren's point of view are still making faces over *Henry V*—they want the play to be something it is not.

Anne Barton, like Frye, regards the play as an inversion of the regular New Comedy pattern. According to her, "It is virtually axiomatic in comedy since the time of Menander that when a young man or woman wishes to marry purely for love, overleaping disparities of birth, wealth, and position, the older generation represented by fathers, mothers, uncles, and guardians will strenuously oppose such an attempted infringement of the laws of established society. *All's Well That Ends Well*, with no help whatever from its source, insists upon inverting this pattern."[5] And Robert Hunter, who sees later Shakespearean comedy as being rooted in medieval drama rather than in New Comedy, considers that Shakespeare radically changed the emphasis of Boccaccio's novella, though he apparently thinks of that story as being well within the tradition of romantic comedy: "Like the anonymous author of *Calisto and Melebea*, Shakespeare has changed his narrative source into a play of forgiveness, and it is as a comedy of forgiveness rather than as a purely romantic comedy that *All's Well* should be examined and judged. . . . As a purely romantic comedy, *All's Well* is unquestionably a failure; as a comedy of forgiveness it may be only partially successful, but the successes it does achieve are frequently of a high order."[6] In my view, *All's Well* represents neither an inversion of the New Comedy pattern nor a romantic comedy converted into a comedy of forgiveness. It is instead a transformation comedy involving a synthesis of three separate but closely related elements: the Boccaccio novella "Giletta di Nerbona," probably by way of Painter's *Palace of Pleasure*, the generic plot of the Loathly Lady story, probably by way of Chaucer's "Wife of Bath's Tale," and the intrinsic worth—estimated value theme, most clearly articulated in *Troilus and Cressida* (II.ii.53–60). These three elements, I suggest, provide story, plot, and theme for one of Shakespeare's most difficult comedies.

There is of course a sense in which the Loathly Lady story is a reversal of the normal New Comedy pattern, but the king in *All's Well* is no more a New Comedy *senex* than is Arthur's queen in "The Wife of Bath's Tale," who also forces a young man to marry a woman he most emphatically does not want. Borrowing Frye's terminology, we may say that in New Comedy the girl is an object of desire, and at first she is inaccessible to the bright young man. Later when the obstacles are removed and she becomes marriageable, the young man gains access to her and the plot follows the regular wish-fulfillment pattern. In the Loathly Lady story the girl is an object of aversion, and at first the young man finds that she is inescapable. Later, when her ugliness is transformed into beauty and the young man realizes what is available to him, he no longer desires to escape, and this plot similarly follows the wish-fulfillment pattern. In both cases, marriage is the tonic chord on which the story ends; and in both cases there are two variables in the preliminary part of the story: desire-aversion and access-escape. In New Comedy the girl is desirable throughout, and the plot consists in removing the obstacles that block the young man's access to her. In the Loathly Lady story the girl is accessible throughout, and the plot consists in getting the young man to regard her as an object of desire. Such a plot presupposes of course that the young man is either incredibly stupid or else terribly antisocial—in Chaucer's story he is a rapist and a "cherl" ("For vileyns synful dedes make a cherl"); and in Shakespeare's play he is an insufferable snob and a boor.

What Shakespeare does—and in this he makes a significant departure from the generic plot, but not from Boccaccio's story—is to make the lady's loathsomeness the result of a purely subjective response to her, rather than an objective characteristic that produces disgust or aversion in anyone who sees her. In "The Wife of Bath's Tale" and all the medieval analogues, it is perfectly obvious that the lady's loathsomeness strikes consternation into the hearts of all who look upon her. Likewise in the feminized version of the same plot, the eighteenth-century French tale "Beauty and the Beast," Beauty's father finds Beast every bit as repulsive as Beauty herself does. In both the masculine and the feminine versions of the plot, the "miracle" comes at the *end* of the story: when Chaucer's knight gives the lady "sovereignty," he discovers that she becomes beautiful and desirable; when Beauty learns "not to be deceived by appearances" and consents to marry Beast, she discovers that he is in fact the handsome and charming prince of her dreams, who has had the misfortune to be under an enchanter's spell for a very long time.

Thus, Shakespeare follows Boccaccio in limiting the young man's objection (and the basis for his aversion) to the girl's being lowborn: Giletta is both "giovane" and "bella," as opposed to Chaucer's hag, who besides being lowborn ("of so lough a kynde") is both "oold" and "loothly." But he follows Chaucer in having the young man lectured sternly on the true meaning of "gentillesse" (AWW II.iii.116–43), and he follows the generic plot (as does Chaucer) in making use of "miracle." In Boccaccio, Giletta's curing the king is nothing very spectacular. She is glad to learn that others have abandoned the attempt to cure him, because she expects by this means "not only to have a legitimate reason for going to Paris, but, if that illness was what she believed it to be, easily [*leggiermente*] to be able to bring it about to have Bertram for her husband."[7] (Her use of the phrase *collo aiuto d'Iddio*, when she speaks to the king, seems merely formulaic, equivalent to "with God's help" or *Deo volente*.) Interestingly, however, Shakespeare uses the generic plot's miracle in this play exactly as he had used Ovid's metamorphosed plant in *A Midsummer Night's Dream*—he transposes it to the early part of the story and changes its function. Bertram's transformation at the end of the story is hardly miraculous; indeed, some critics claim that it is non-existent. But Helena's cure is clearly represented as a miracle (II.iii). This miracle serves to establish, beyond the shadow of a doubt, Helena's intrinsic worth shortly before Bertram makes it perfectly clear to the king that he estimates her value to be little more than zero.[8]

Within this framework the rest of Shakespeare's plot unfolds. The principal event is of course the transformation of the male protagonist, which marks this comic plot as typically Shakespearean. The Bertram who says, "I cannot love her, nor will strive to do't" (AWW II.iii.144) becomes the Bertram who says "If she, my liege, can make me know this clearly, / I'll love her dearly—ever, ever dearly" (V.iii.312–13). Those who claim that Shylock remains unchanged or that the Duke Frederick's conversion seems "deliberately contrived and unconvincing" will of course find this transformation extremely disappointing. According to Jonas Barish, "What may chill us is that the Bertram who perpetrates this new offense [in the final scene] remains the same Bertram as before—not one capable of feeling a deeper shame when his evasions are exposed, but the same self-willed, self-satisfied adolescent of the earlier scenes, ready to trivialize all of his experience. . . . Shakespeare seems to go out of his way to insist that the conversion we thought we were witnessing was no conversion at all."[9] Apparently for Barish, as for Dr. Johnson, Bertram is "dismissed to happiness," and Shakespeare's refusal either to show us another miracle or to edify us with a display of poetic justice in this final scene is cause for regret. My own view is that any person (or character) who moves from saying "I cannot love her, and I will not even try" to saying later, with reference to the same person, "If this is true (and it is), I'll love her dearly from this time forward" has undergone one of the most profound changes in human experience, from being totally alienated to being at least partly socialized. It is of course true that Bertram has to be "nailed to the wall" before he begins to "suffer the change" we see in him, but then so do Angelo, and Leontes, and Alonso. So does the knight in "The Wife of Bath's Tale." And so do we all.

The remaining details of Shakespeare's synthesized plot fall into place quite naturally. Verbal equivocation and the bed trick solve any remaining difficulties. Even if we are unfamiliar with the riddling prophecies of other Shakespeare plays, Helena demonstrates that the supposedly impossible tasks that Bertram sets for her may postpone, but certainly will not destroy, the young couple's happiness. The letter that spells out the requirements about ring and child concludes mournfully, "Till I have no wife, I have nothing in France" (*AWW* III.ii.73). The countess provides the first clue when she transposes the sentence elements and shifts the verb in the dependent clause to a subjunctive: "Nothing in France until he have no wife!" (III.ii.77). Shortly thereafter, Helena again quotes the line as it appears in the letter, then immediately transposes its order as the countess had done, but makes the second verb indicative rather than subjunctive. She then transposes the phrase *in France* so that it modifies *wife* rather than *nothing* and thus solves the problem—at least verbally, in a fashion that reminds us of Falstaff's way with words:

> 'Till I have no wife I have nothing in France.'
> Nothing in France until he has no wife!
> Thou shalt have none, Rossillion, none in France;
> Then hast thou all again.
> (III.ii.97–100)

She then proceeds to give the words substance by removing herself from France, and the audience is left with the distinct impression that Bertram will soon "have all again."

Much has been written, some of it quite recently, about the endings of the problem comedies, especially *All's Well That Ends Well*.[10] David Scott Kastan says for instance that "in spite of its title, [*All's Well*] refuses to end well, indeed virtually refuses to end at all; but, pointedly, it is the desire for comic endings that has informed—and deformed—the action throughout."[11] In short, we are told that *All's Well That Ends Well* doesn't "really" end well, and that some misguided desire to shape the play's content to an inappropriate pattern or some darker purpose on the author's part has resulted in a pseudoresolution of the problems presented in the play. At the very least, these uneasy endings have given rise to all sorts of conjectures as to the significance not only of the endings but also of the characters, and the plays as a whole. But anyone who appreciates puns knows that a "perfect" pun (involving exact homophones) is hardly ever a "good" pun. If two word-sounds coincide exactly so that no wrenching or deformation is involved, the pun not only loses much of its force, but it is also likely to go unnoticed or to be regarded as a simple case of unintentional ambiguity. Likewise, if the rough edges of human experience are filed away in order to make that experience seem to coincide with the smooth outlines of comic form, then the audience is led, consciously or unconsciously, into thinking that life itself is comic, that moral appropriateness and wish fulfillment actually do go hand in hand (or to think that the author believes that this is the case), when all writers worth their salt know that such a representation is utterly false to human experience—that it is only within the limits of pure farce or of out-and-out fantasy that they can even pretend that adult human experience and undistorted comic form ever coincide exactly. Although of course not all incongruities are laughter-producing, Schopenhauer's observations about the relationship between laughter and incongruity should provide some help in coming to terms with Shakespeare's incongruous, and therefore disturbing, comic endings.[12]

In a recent article entitled "*All's Well That Ends Well* and the Triumph of the Word," Maurice Hunt argues that this particular comic ending (among other things in the play) is brought about by the power of language, rightly used, to transform persons and events. "The prosperous ending," says Hunt, "occurs mainly through several transformational virtues inherent in language."[13] He refers, not to metaphor, but to religious values associated with the creative power of the Word (John 1.1–4) and to analysis of these values by means of speech act theory. This argument is certainly a welcome antidote to the kind of interpretation that asserts, for instance, that "the holier Helena's language becomes, the less we should believe her," but it is less helpful than it might be in convincing those who are fundamentally skeptical about the connection between religious values and Shakespearean language.[14]

At least two other matters require some comment—the part played by Parolles, because he seems distinctly foreign to the transformation plot, and the "quickening" of Helena, because the emphasis upon being recalled to life runs through these four late comedies. Anne Barton quite rightly says that Parolles is ultimately "subjected to a public exposure and humiliation that is crushing in a manner more usually associated with the 'comical satires' of Ben Jonson than with Shakespeare."[15] Parolles (whose name means "words," especially as in "word of honor") seems in fact, both by name and by temperament, to be a fugitive from one of the nontransformational Shakespeare comedies, such as *Love's Labor's Lost* or, more probably, from the phantom play *Love's Labor's Won*. He is a verbal show-off: the phrase "Bajazet's mule" (*AWW* IV.i.41), for instance, has always seemed to me to be a blundering reference to Balaam's ass, whose mouth "the Lord opened" when Balaam smote the poor creature (Numbers 22.22–35); and he is certainly a vindictive coward.[16] The chances of his ever being anything else seem small indeed. His role is, I think, the best evidence that *All's Well* is a hybrid play, the main part of which is rather ineptly transformational and the other part of which is more closely akin to *The Comedy of Errors, Love's Labor's Lost,* and even to *Twelfth Night,* in which Malvolio likewise suffers public exposure and humiliation.

As for Helena's "quickening," it looks forward to the last of the comedies as Parolles' part looks back to the first of them. To a certain extent, it looks both forward and backward, since it depends as much upon wordplay as it does upon authentic miracle. Helena's "revival" is part of a riddle that involves a pun:

> So there's my riddle: one that's dead is quick—
> And now behold the meaning.
> *Enter Helena and Widow.*
> (*AWW* V.iii.300–301)

The word *quick* means of course both "alive" and "pregnant" because the sentence Marriage brings life is a twice-true statement—it "revives" those who marry, and it "begets" new lives. Helena's response to Bertram's declaration that he will "love her dearly" has a similar double meaning: "If it appear not plain, and prove untrue, / Deadly divorce step between me and you" (V.iii.314–15). According to the Riverside editor, "deadly divorce" means "divorcing death," and this of course is true, since the 1559 *Book of Common Prayer* includes the clause "so long as you both shall live" in the wedding vows.[17] But when Helena says, "Deadly divorce step between me and you," she is not promising to drop dead; she is pledging rather to accept "deadly divorce" if what she says "proves untrue," and she is acknowledging that for her, divorce brings "death" in its wake, just as marriage brings "life."

IN *Measure for Measure* we have a different alternative to the basic New Comedy pattern. The lady (Isabella) is certainly not loathly; she is, to be sure, the object of (Angelo's) desire. But marriage is not a real possibility: the young man, like Ovid's gods in their affairs with mortal women, has no interest in marriage; and the young woman wishes to enter a convent as soon as possible. At the opposite pole from the Wife of Bath, Isabella is hardly one of those women who desire to be "at oure large"; on the contrary, she finds herself "wishing a more strict restraint / Upon the sisterhood, the votarists of Saint Clare" (I.iv.4–5). And Angelo has already broken off his engagement to one woman (Mariana), using the loss of her dowry and reputation as excuses (III.i.205–25). Here, as in *All's Well*, the desire is felt by only one person, and the main obstacle to wish fulfillment is internal and subjective on the other person's part. But in *Measure for Measure*, the odds against a happy ending seem staggering, since the aversion to marriage is mutual and the society represented in the play officially regards sexual activity outside of marriage as whoredom and lechery, punishable by death. Unlike Bertram, who feels an aversion to one particular person, Isabella avoids all members of the opposite sex; and unlike Helena, whose resources are limited, Angelo wields enormous power.

On the surface, parts of the two plots seem remarkably similar: in both plays a young man (Bertram, Angelo) makes sexual advances to a young woman (Diana, Isabella) outside the marriage relationship, and both times the young man is hoodwinked by means of a bed trick. And in both cases two young men (Bertram, Parolles; Angelo, Lucio) are publicly exposed and humiliated in a way that seems not to be typical of Shakespearean comedy. But more important, the plot of *Measure for Measure* reverses an element in the plot of *All's Well*: whereas only Bertram feels an aversion to Helena, and he does so purely because she is lowborn, only Angelo desires Isabella, and he wants her merely as bed partner, not as wife. Just as Helena differs from the Loathly Lady of romance by being objectionable only to the hero, while everyone else seems to regard her as eminently suited to be the young count's wife, so Isabella differs from the heroine of New Comedy by being (until the end) the "object of desire" only to the young deputy, while everyone else, including even the lecherous Lucio, regards her as

> a thing enskied and sainted,
> By [her] renouncement an immortal spirit,
> And to be talked with in sincerity,
> As with a saint.
> (MM I.iv.34–37)

The plot of *Measure for Measure*, like the plots of earlier transformation comedies, may be set forth most simply in a series of time-lapse metaphors: Angelo the self-righteous Puritan becomes Angelo the lecher; and Angelo the lecher becomes Angelo the repentant sinner, who says,

> But let my trial be mine own confession.
> Immediate sentence, then, and sequent death
> Is all the grace I beg.
>
> (V.i.368–70)

The skeptic may of course say in this case, as in others, that Angelo has not changed "one whit" or that there is no real reformation in Angelo. In other words, the Angelo who pronounces sentence upon himself at the end of the play is the same rigid Puritan who condemns Claudio at the beginning; he has merely found another person to condemn, and that person is himself. But surely Mariana comes closer to the truth and to the point of the play when she says,

> They say best men are moulded out of faults,
> And, for the most, become much more the better
> For being a little bad; so may my husband.
>
> (V.i.435–37)

Self-knowledge is the fundamental subject matter of comedy, and if we implicitly deny, or seriously underestimate, the value and significance of self-knowledge, then we will certainly assign no great importance to the difference between Angelo the self-righteous Puritan and Angelo the repentant sinner, in which case we will probably find a "confusion of values" in the play and a good many "unresolved conflicts" as well.

But to find fault with *Measure for Measure* because it contains unresolved conflicts and reflects a confusion of values is like objecting to Shakespeare's puns because they depend upon equivocation and ambiguity, or to his metaphors because they involve incongruity and self-contradiction. And to regard the Duke as "a kind of comic dramatist" is merely to substitute one allegorical interpretation for another. According to Anne Barton, "Almost all of Shakespeare's comedies before *Measure for Measure* end with the formation of what Northrop Frye has called a 'new society.' . . . *Measure for Measure*, by contrast, does not really create anything that can be understood as a new society. Of the three marriages set up in its final moments, only the previous bond between Claudio and Juliet has any reality for us. The other two are ciphers. Most important of all, the play has admitted in its fifth act that it is only a play, a false geometry."[18] First, there is a total of *four* marriages implied at the end of *Measure for Measure*: Claudio-Juliet, Angelo-Mariana, Lucio-Kate, and the Duke–Isabella. In relation to the plot of the play, Claudio and Juliet are of course New Comedy lovers: their attraction is mutual, and the obstacle to their union is external and objective. To say that "only the previous bond between Claudio and Juliet has any reality for us" is merely to specify New Comedy plot as the standard of reality in the play and to argue that consequently "there is no more reality" in the other marriages "than in Jack and the Beanstock." And second, Shakespeare has an irritating penchant for admitting, at the end of the play or in the epilogue, that "this is only a play." He has done so before *Measure for Measure,* and he will do so again. I would regard this tendency, however, not as a fault, but as evidence of honesty and straightforwardness (not to mention self-knowledge) on the part of the playwright. After all, authors of plays are artificers, "playwrights," and they should have no illusions about the illusions they create.

Like *All's Well That Ends Well, Measure for Measure* may be described as a synthesis of three different elements: the Cinthio novella of Juriste, Epitia, and Vico, probably by way of Whetstone's *Promos and Cassandra;* a special version of New Comedy plot, perhaps by way of Plautus and Terence; and the biblical theme, "Judge not that ye be not judged" (Matt. 9.1–2, Luke 6.37–38), probably by way of St. Paul, who specifically associates the idea of judgment (Rom. 2.1) with both the matter of self-knowledge and the question of adultery (Rom. 2.19–22). The biblical theme "Judge not" is perhaps best understood as a historical example of the intrinsic worth–estimated value theme, since *judging* is simply a synonym for "appraising a person's value"; within a Christian context no one can do that but God himself. It is to this fact that Isabella refers in her first interview with Angelo when she says:

> Why, all the souls that were were forfeit once,
> And He that might the vantage best have took,
> Found out the remedy. How would you be,
> If He, which is the top of judgment, should
> But judge you as you are? O think on that,
> And mercy then will breathe within your lips,
> Like man new made.
>
> (*MM* II.ii.73–79)

This last phrase seems also to refer to St. Paul's assertion that "neither circumcision availeth any thing, nor uncircumcision, but a new creature" (Gal. 6.15, KJV); and the Geneva Bible's marginal comment indicates that here the word *new* means "which is regenerate by faith."

The marriages at the end of *Measure for Measure* do indeed have a close relationship to plot and theme. The one between Claudio and Juliet, as I suggested before, is the appropriate conclusion to a New Comedy plot: because the obstacles to their marriage have been removed in the course of the play, they are now free to marry and live "happily ever after," as one would expect in New Comedy. The marriage between Lucio and Kate Keepdown is rooted in another aspect of New Comedy—that of moral appropriateness or "poetic justice." When Lucio objects, "Marrying a punk, my lord, is pressing to death, whipping, and hanging," the Duke replies, "Slandering a prince deserves it" (V.i.517–19). Poetic justice is the New Comedy equivalent of the Old Law, which the play "fulfills" rather than "destroys" (cf. Matt. 5.17). Third, the marriage between Angelo and Mariana has elements of poetic justice, since Angelo had earlier abandoned Mariana, partly because her dowry fell short,

> but in chief
> For that her reputation was disvalued
> In levity.
> (V.i.218–20)

(Here as elsewhere in the Shakespeare plays, "disvaluing" leads to rejection and betrayal.) But more important, this marriage also involves forgiveness, since the wedding could not take place at all if Angelo were not forgiven for his gross offenses against Isabella, Mariana, the Duke, and the people of Vienna. And fourth, the implied marriage of the Duke and Isabella adds a nice touch—marriage, not repression, is the answer to the problem posed by the play. Neither Jewish rabbi (Old Law) nor Christian prince (New Law) is a complete person until he is married.[19] From the standpoint of the play, the home is more appropriate than the convent as a sphere of activity for the woman who would live and love most fully. Marriage is the beginning of socialization, and comedy is the most social of literary genres.

Both *All's Well That Ends Well* and *Measure for Measure* involve a bed trick, and both of them represent a character as being recalled to life (Helena, Claudio), though there is nothing miraculous about the recall in either case. Instead, it is simply a matter of deliberate concealment—as in *Much Ado About Nothing*, in which the manipulator (Friar Francis) allows the other characters to think that the young woman (Hero) is dead, in order to bring the young man (Claudio) to repentance. Like the earlier transformation comedies, these two contain explicit references to significant change on the part of the protagonists. In *All's Well*, an anonymous lord asserts that upon reading his mother's letter Bertram "changed almost into another man" (IV.iii.4), and later Bertram refers to his own "high-repented blames" (V.iii.36). Moreover, when Bertram responds to Diana's statement of her "opinion" and says, "Change it, change it" (IV.ii.31), he sounds rather like Oberon and Theseus in *A Midsummer Night's Dream* on the subject of "amending" whatever is offensive or inappropriate (*MND* II.i.118, V.i.208–14). Likewise in *Measure for Measure*, Isabella is simply predicting in Act II what will happen to Angelo in Act V when she says to him,

> How would you be,
> If He, which is the top of judgment, should
> But judge you as you are?
> (II.ii.75–77)

In her prediction, Isabella is of course referring to God and Christ, and the "judge" in Act V turns out to be the Duke; but this is a bit of typically Shakespearean substitution.[20] And clearly, we are to understand that Angelo is a "man new made" at story's end, whether we think of him as a comic figure who is no longer "ridiculous" because he has gained self-knowledge or because, in biblical terms, he is "regenerate by faith" when he perceives that the Duke, "like power divine, / Hath looked upon [his] passes" (V.i.365–66).

THE last two plays which the First Folio lists as comedies are of course *The Winter's Tale* and *The Tempest*, though modern editors and critics prefer to lift them out and place them in a fourth category (with *Pericles*, *Cymbeline*, and even *The Two Noble Kinsmen*). If my analysis is correct, it is not these two plays that are fundamentally different from the other Shakespeare comedies, but the three that have nontransformational comic plots: *The Comedy of Errors*, *Love's Labor's Lost*, and *Twelfth Night*. As I indicated earlier, the Folio classification already involves cross-ranking, since the comedies and tragedies differ from each other in terms of plot whereas the histories differ from both of those in terms of subject matter. To create a fourth category on the basis of philosophical content, fantastic plot elements, or some other such distinction seems to me to muddy the waters even further. It is better, I think, to do in such cases as the editors of the Pelican and Riverside editions have done with *Troilus and Cressida*—one group of editors places it among the tragedies, and the other, among the comedies. They disagree with each other as to what kind of play it is, but they do not emulate Polonious in creating still another category to accommodate differences of emphasis within particular plays. In my view, one might (as Robert Hunter does) move *Cymbeline*, which is listed among the tragedies in the First Folio, to a revised comedy category; but we should not resort to a fourth classification by introducing still another basis of division.

The type of personal transformation we first saw in *The Taming of the Shrew* reaches the final stages of its development in *The Winter's Tale*. In the first of the transformational comedies, attention is focused almost entirely upon the outward appearance of the main character—Kate the shrew becomes Kate the ideal wife, and we get very little insight into Kate's own thought processes. Here, the dramatist concentrates instead upon the protagonist's changing consciousness. The time-lapse metaphor which *The Winter's Tale* dramatizes may be stated as follows: the Leontes who jealously exclaims "Too hot, too hot!" (I.ii.108) when he sees his wife holding hands with his childhood friend becomes the Leontes who happily murmurs "O, she's warm!" (V.iii.109) when the "statue" of his long-lost wife moves to embrace him. As if to remind us of the first exclamation and prepare us for the second one, Leontes muses, when the "statue" is first revealed to him:

> O, thus she stood,
> Even with such life of majesty—warm life,
> As now it coldly stands—when first I wooed her!
> I am ashamed. Does not the stone rebuke me
> For being more stone than it?
>
> (V.iii.34–38)

When we hear him confess that he perceives his own hardness of heart in the "statue" that stands before him, we know that the happy ending that grace brings in its wake cannot be far behind. Only when he has made this confession can the "statue" be "stone no more," recalling Leontes himself to life and love.

Two recent studies of *The Winter's Tale* deal separately with poetry and time as central concerns of the play. In "Poetry and Plot in *The Winter's Tale*," Russ McDonald argues persuasively that there is an important connection between the structure of the blank verse in the late plays and the nature of the plots. He uses the word *periodic* to characterize both poetry and plot, observing that, in both, meaning is withheld until the end—"convoluted sentences or difficult speeches become coherent and meaningful only in their final clauses or movements." Likewise, this same (or a kindred) principle "governs the arrangement of dramatic action: the shape and meaning of events become apparent only in the final moments of the tragicomedy."[21] Stated more compactly, "the shape of the verse reflects the shape of the plot." In another essay, entitled "Time and Presence in *The Winter's Tale*," Stanton B. Garner, Jr., emphasizes the double nature of human experience of time as represented in the play—the relationship between (what I would call) "now" and "then." According to Garner, "On the one hand, man lives in the present, a moment so complete in its immediacy that it seems to escape time entirely." And on the other hand, this immediate and virtually timeless experience stands in contrast to a "then," which involves both "memory and anticipation, nostalgia and eagerness, regret and foreboding." Moreover, says Garner, this "temporal double vision" is "strangely reminiscent of the opening lines of a fourth-century Chinese poem: 'Swiftly the years, beyond recall. / Solemn the stillness of this fair morning.'"[22]

Both of these interpretations seem to me to be exactly right though incomplete. It is by means of the poetry—and especially the time-lapse metaphor—that Shakespeare constructs the plot not only of the late comedies but of the early ones too, and that poetic device is also the means for expressing the "temporal double vision" that emerges most clearly in these late plays but characterizes the early ones as well. We might say that the "then" in *The Winter's Tale* is prospective, whereas in *The Tempest* it is retrospective. When the earlier play opens, Leontes has not yet committed the act that yields such dreadful consequences; the play dramatizes the manner in which his heart, hardened virtually to stone by jealousy, becomes living flesh again. What is stone "now" becomes, once more, the seat of affection "then." Conversely, Alonso's gross offense against Prospero "then" (in the years almost beyond recall) is redeemed "now" (in the solemn afternoon of this fair island). In both cases, the audience is invited to "imagine this changed like this, and you have this other thing." And all by means of the poetry, which in its most compact form shows us the transformation from "this" to "this other thing" through the medium of time, holding the best for last, whether we are considering the structure of the time-lapse metaphor (eyes, pearls) or the play as a whole, with its comic (i.e., "best for last") denouement.

Shakespeare's principal source for *The Winter's Tale* is Greene's *Pandosto: The Triumph of Time* (1588). But *The Winter's Tale*, like *All's Well*, may be regarded as a version of the Loathly Lady story; and after the third act, the plot owes very little to Greene. Like Bertram, Leontes rejects and despises his wife, not because she is lowborn but because he imagines that she is guilty of adultery with Polixines. Again, it is only the lady's husband who regards her as loathly; everyone else in the play—including this time even the oracle of Apollo—comes to her defense and asserts her intrinsic worth and purity. Ultimately of course the aberrant husband recovers his senses, and after many years of penitence is restored to happiness in a scene that comes closer than anything else in the Shakespeare comedies to an authentic miracle. The "stone" Hermione comes to life, and though she and Leontes suffer the loss of one child, another that had been lost is found; and the couple is reunited in happiness that is even greater than that of the New Comedy lovers Perdita and Florizel, who are youngsters and innocents by comparison. In other ways, the plot resembles that of *The Tempest*. More than a dozen years elapse during the course of each plot; but *The Winter's Tale* is presented in linear fashion, with a sixteen-year gap between Acts III and IV, whereas *The Tempest*, which makes use of a narrative flashback technique, directly represents only the final hours of the twelve-year period covered by the play.

The oracle's pronouncement in *The Winter's Tale* is less mysterious than the one in *Cymbeline* and less cryptic even than Bertram's enigmatic letter to his mother in *All's Well That Ends Well*. All but the final sentence of it is as plain and clear as can be: "Hermione is chaste, Polixines blameless, Camillo a true subject, Leontes a jealous tyrant, his innocent babe truly begotten; and the king shall live without an heir if that which is lost be not found" (WT III.ii.131–34). As one would expect, the "jealous tyrant" immediately declares that "there is no truth at all i' th' oracle"; but the news, a few lines later, that his son is dead causes Leontes to relent, saying "Apollo's angry, and the heavens themselves / Do strike at my injustice" (III.ii.146–47). This of course marks the turning point of the action and the beginning of Leontes' long period of repentance, which culminates finally in the "revivification" of Hermione and the reunion of the aging spouses. Perhaps the most remarkable thing about the play, other than the statue scene, is the long pastoral episode (IV.iv), which is much admired but which does not advance the plot in a way that is proportional to the episode's length.

The supposed improbabilities and inaccuracies of these final plays are sometimes defended as being "not, as often assumed, the defects of carelessness, but charming if not essential characteristics of an old folk-tale."[23] The main "improbabilities" in *The Winter's Tale* include a complete lack of motivation for Leontes' jealousy, the message from the oracle of Apollo, and the revivification of Hermione. But under close examination these seem less improbable than the ghost in *Hamlet* or the witches in *Macbeth*. First of all, we are told that "by presenting only the last day of Polixines' visit and by freeing Hermione of the imprudent behavior of her prototype [Shakespeare] discards the obvious motivation of Leontes' jealousy."[24] But the whole point of the early scenes is precisely that there is no basis outside Leontes' own psyche for his rejection of Hermione. If his suspicions of his wife were actually justified to any extent at all, then his behavior might be correctly understood as righteous indignation. But because his suspicions are unjustified and unmotivated, we can only attribute them to sexual jealousy—a devaluation of the person in question, which has nothing whatever to do with justifiable cause or with the spouse's intrinsic value.

As for the other "improbabilities," the oracle's message contains nothing but facts that are plain as day to all the characters except Leontes himself, and his irrationality is the point of departure for the whole play. Finally, the statue scene may of course be understood as the culmination of the discussion in act IV, scene iv, of the relationship between nature and art. The statue is a work of art; Hermione herself is the work of nature. Polixines states:

> This is an art
> Which does mend nature—change it rather—but
> The art itself is nature.
>
> (WT IV.iv.95–97)

This prepares us for "art becoming nature," which is what happens in the statue scene. Or, if one prefers a biblical interpretation, Leontes is clearly represented in the final scene as a "new" man; and when Paulina tells him, just before the supposed statue begins to move, that "it is required / You do awake your faith," she is apparently drawing upon the biblical idea that the "new creature" is one "which is regenerate by faith."

My own view, simpler than either of those just mentioned, is that the statue scene represents the dramatization of a time-lapse metaphor parallel to, but different from, the "translation" of Bottom in *A Midsummer Night's Dream*. Just as it is inaccurate to say that Bottom is metamorphosed into an ass, so it is inappropriate to say that Hermione's statue comes to life. The figure in question is a woman-statue, just as the creature in *A Midsummer Night's Dream* is a man-ass. It exists only within the confines of a work of art, and its precise meaning cannot "be translated into a literal paraphrase without any loss of cognitive content." Just as the loathly lady becomes a beautiful bride at the end of "The Wife of Bath's Tale," so the woman-statue becomes a miraculously recovered wife at the end of *The Winter's Tale*. The plot of this play, like others of Shakespeare's last period, is an ingenious synthesis of several sources, including at least these three—*Pandosto*, the Loathly Lady story, and Pygmalion. The Loathly Lady story provides the basic framework for the entire play; *Pandosto* furnishes the events of the first three acts, and Ovid's Pygmalion supplies the spectacular ending.[25] These three, and perhaps others, are combined by means of "an art / Which does mend nature—change it rather."

WE have already analyzed, in earlier chapters, the plot structure of *The Tempest*; but we should consider an aspect of these late plays that comes to a clear focus in *The Tempest*—namely, some loose ends in connection with the forgiveness of the principal character and their relation both to traditional comedy and to the kind of transformation comic plot that Shakespeare makes use of in most of his comedies. Traditional comedy shows of course a marked preference for "poetic justice" as reflected in the Aristotelian double plot, which has an opposite issue for the good and the bad characters. In the later Shakespeare comedies, such justice comes to be viewed as analogous to the Old Law; and it gives way to the New Law, "Judge not that ye be not judged," as finally expressed in Prospero's parting words, "As you from crimes would pardoned be, / Let your indulgence set me free." The transformation of the offending character and his humility in asking for either justice (Angelo) or forgiveness (Alonso) enable the manipulator figure to suspend what would otherwise be an appropriate sentence and to bring the play to a happy conclusion. Obviously, however, there are some loose ends, some incomplete transformations (Bertram) and some characters who show almost no sign of remorse (Lucio; Antonio, Sebastian) but who nevertheless benefit from the general amnesty at the end of the play. How do these loose ends fit into the pattern of Shakespearean comedy? Does forgiving these untransformed characters constitute a blemish upon the structure of the transformation comedy?

The simple way of dealing with such characters as Lucio, in *Measure for Measure,* and Antonio, in *The Tempest,* would be either to expel them from the new society (in the manner of traditional comedy) or else to transform them, repentant or not, into suitable members of that society (in the manner of completely unrestrained transformational comedy). But Shakespeare does neither, and for some readers the grudging forgiveness these characters receive is not a satisfactory resolution. Prospero's words to Antonio illustrate the problem clearly:

> For you, most wicked sir, whom to call brother
> Would even infect my mouth, I do forgive
> Thy rankest fault—all of them; and require
> My dukedom of thee, which perforce I know
> Thou must restore.
> (*Tmp.* V.i.130-34)

In this speech, Prospero apparently both pardons and does not pardon his brother; and we are somewhat puzzled by the position he takes. If he actually forgives him, why does he not do so more graciously? And if he does not forgive him, why does he make the pretense of doing so?

Though it is certainly not funny, Prospero's speech to Antonio involves an incongruity that is similar in structure, but not in content, to the incongruity described by Schopenhauer as being the cause of laughter. According to the German philosopher, we laugh when we suddenly perceive "the incongruity of sensuous and abstract knowledge," as when we see Don Quixote respond to the prompting of his mind rather than that of his senses by attacking windmills as if they were giants. But literary comedy includes imagination and the moral sense as well as the physical senses and the mind, with the result that Schopenhauer's framework is incomplete. In *Analytical Psychology: Its Theory and Practice*, C. G. Jung offers an analysis of the ectopsychic functions of consciousness that is more helpful for our purposes. He lists and defines four such functions. The first of these, sensation, "tells us that a thing *is*"; the second, thinking, "tells us *what* that thing is"; the third, feeling, "tells us what it is *worth* to us"; and the fourth, intuition, is "a sort of divination, a sort of miraculous faculty." Jung represents these functions schematically by means of two intersecting lines. The vertical line, which connects the rational functions, has thinking at the top and feeling at the bottom; the horizontal line, which connects the nonrational functions, has sensation at the left and intuition at the right. At the point of intersection is the ego, "which has a certain amount of energy at its disposal, and that energy is the will-power."[26]

If we superimpose Schopenhauer's laughter theory upon this framework, we see that the incongruity of which he speaks is represented by the quadrant at the upper left, which is bounded by sensation ("sensuous knowledge") on the left and by thinking ("abstract knowledge") at the top. We also see that there is an exactly corresponding incongruity represented by the quadrant at the lower right side of the figure, bounded by intuition on the right and by feeling at the bottom. If we regard Jung's *intuition* as being equivalent to Shakespeare's term *imagination*, which the dramatist associates, in *A Midsummer Night's Dream*, with madness, love, and poetry, and if we regard Jung's *feeling*, which tells us what something "is *worth* to us," as being equivalent to the human inclination to judge and condemn, then we discover that this unfamiliar incongruity between the dictates of "intuition" (forgiveness) and "feeling" (judgment) is every bit as native to comedy as the more familiar incongruity between sensuous and abstract knowledge, which according to Schopenhauer is the principal cause of human laughter. The one is, in fact, a mirror image of the other in terms of the human psyche as described by Jung.

It is primarily in this respect that the last four Shakespeare comedies differ from the earlier ones: *All's Well, Measure for Measure, The Winter's Tale*, and *The Tempest* probe the human psyche much more deeply than do *The Taming of the Shrew, The Two Gentlemen of Verona*, and *A Midsummer Night's Dream*. The crucial matter in a Shakespearean comedy is not how much older the protagonist may be at the end of the play than at the beginning, but how much and in what ways that character is *changed* from what he or she had been when the play began. In short, the main significance of a Shakespeare comedy resides not in what transpires between "now" and "fifteen years later" but in the difference between "before" and "after." Alonso's transformation takes place in three hours at most; Leontes, who, like Snug, is somewhat "slow of study," requires some sixteen or seventeen years to achieve similar results. The "stories," the characterization, and the poetry of the later plays are much changed and much improved, but the plots remain closely akin to those of the earlier comedies for the simple reason that nearly all of the plots are dramatizations of time-lapse metaphors—tentative and experimental at first, "And ever best found in the close."

EIGHT

Conclusion

◆

> Therefore the poet
> Did feign that Orpheus drew trees, stones, and floods;
> Since naught so stockish, hard, and full of rage
> But music for the time doth change his nature.
> The man that hath no music in himself,
> Nor is not moved with concord of sweet sounds,
> Is fit for treasons, stratagems, and spoils;
> The motions of his spirit are dull as night,
> And his affections dark as Erebus.
> Let no such man be trusted. Mark the music.

IF it were true, as Kenneth Muir insists, that "there is no such thing as Shakespearian Comedy; there are only Shakespearian comedies," then either it makes no sense for C. L. Barber to analyze *Henry IV* as one of "Shakespeare's festive comedies" and for Robert Hunter to regard *Cymbeline* as one of the "comedies of forgiveness," or else the compilers of the First Folio were hopelessly inept in listing one of those plays as a history and the other as a tragedy, not both of them as comedies.[1] If we accept Muir's statement as true, then we should probably either toss out two of the most important books on the Shakespeare comedies, or else we should discard the Folio classification and find some other way to identify the "Shakespearian comedies" that Muir is referring to. But if the Folio classification is untrustworthy and if "there is no such thing as Shakespearian comedy," then how do we determine which of the plays are in fact "Shakespearian comedies"? Muir's critical position is thus less helpful than either Barber's or Hunter's, whatever the limitations or shortcomings of *Shakespeare's Festive Comedy* and *Shakespeare and the Comedy of Forgiveness*.

Part of the difficulty is that Muir takes an all-or-nothing approach and emphatically rejects the notion that three-fourths of a loaf is better than none. In enumerating the obstacles to articulating an adequate theory of Shakespearean comedy, he announces the impossibility of devising what he calls "a magic formula—except one so broad as to lack particularity—which can be applied with equal suitability to *The Comedy of Errors* and

The Two Gentlemen of Verona, Twelfth Night and *Troilus and Cressida, The Taming of the Shrew* and *The Tempest*."[2] This may be true, of course, but it hardly serves as significant evidence for the assertion that "there is no such thing as Shakespearian Comedy." The most obvious red herring in this list of "Shakespearian comedies" is *Troilus and Cressida,* which has the word "history" in the full title and which was originally intended by the First Folio editors to be printed after *Romeo and Juliet* but was withdrawn for reasons that are not entirely clear and later placed between the histories and the tragedies. Surely no theory of Shakespearean comedy should be judged upon its ability to account for *Troilus and Cressida*. Second, as I have shown at some length, *The Comedy of Errors* and *Twelfth Night* are fundamentally different from the other Shakespeare comedies in that they both have twin-plots and they make no use of the transformation plot that is common to sixteen of the Shakespeare plays (eleven of the comedies, four of the histories, and one of the tragedies—according to the First Folio classification). Those two plots are based upon simile rather than metaphor; and though Aristotle minimized the difference between the two in Greek, the consequences of that difference for dramatic plot in English are highly significant. Of Muir's six recalcitrant examples, this leaves only *The Taming of the Shrew, The Two Gentlemen of Verona,* and *The Tempest,* all three of which are interesting examples of the transformation plot, even though one is a farce, the second a romantic comedy (albeit a rudimentary one), and the third a romance.

Moreover, if we combine the two types of comic plot based upon the two rhetorical figures—sixteen based upon the time-lapse metaphor and two more based upon simile—we can account for the plots of fully half the thirty-six plays in the First Folio. I have argued that the type based upon metaphor was far richer than that based upon simile, that it provided many more opportunities for related and supporting subplots and for parodic representations. And if we may assume that the number of plays of each type accurately reflects that relative richness, then we cannot help observing that there are eight times as many plots based upon metaphor as upon simile. The two based upon simile—*The Comedy of Errors* and *Twelfth Night*—are of course very good plays, the one an extremely successful farce and the other as splendid a festive comedy as Shakespeare ever wrote. But apparently he much preferred the transformation plot, not only because of the more numerous possibilities it provided but also because by its very nature it produced a mellower and more humane effect, less harsh and satiric than the kind of comedy associated with the morally appropriate endings characteristic of nontransformational comedy.

Thus, the terms *Shakespearean comedy* and *Shakespeare's comedies* (which

I prefer to "Shakespearian comedies") are both perfectly legitimate though they differ from each other in both signification and comprehension. *Shakespeare's comedies* are those plays written by Shakespeare that are, for the most part, of a light and amusing character and that have a happy conclusion to their plots. They include the fourteen plays listed as comedies in the First Folio. *Shakespearean comedy,* on the other hand, means the particular kind of comedy that Shakespeare most often wrote, which typically, but not invariably, involves punning dialogue, a transformation plot, and a wish-fulfilling denouement. On all three counts, Shakespearean comedy differs from traditional, neoclassical comedy, which shows a marked preference for unambiguous language, straightforward (nontransformational) plots, and morally appropriate endings. The term *Shakespearean comedy* comprehends not only the fourteen plays listed as comedies in the First Folio but *King John, Henry IV (Parts 1* and *2), Henry V,* and *Cymbeline* as well.

These three main characteristics of Shakespearean comedy are by no means arbitrarily combined—the second arises naturally from the first, and the third follows necessarily from the second. As I have said before, character transformation is to human personality as the pun is to word meaning. Shakespearean wordplay emerges from the exploitation of multiple word meanings, and the representation of comic character derives from the observation of multifaceted human personality. Just as the pun is generated within the context of a sentence (a sequence of words), so character transformation takes place within the context of a plot (a sequence of events); and the play itself becomes a vehicle for the display of multifaceted words and multifaceted personalities. Because character-change in Shakespearean comedy is typically a change for the better, the requisite "happy ending" comes about not as the culmination of the traditional double plot, which has, according to Aristotle, "an opposite issue for the good and the bad personages," but rather as the result of the main character's change from a "bad" character into a "good" one.

In a recent book entitled *Comic Persuasion: Moral Structure in British Comedy from Shakespeare to Stoppard,* Alice Rayner characterizes wish-fulfilling comedy in connection with cathartic laughter. In her view,

> theories of humor often focus on the cathartic function of laughter, suggesting that laughter integrates the human community and that laughter itself has a unifying or healing capacity. The cathartic effectiveness of laughter need not be the explosive release of excess emotions alone but might be, metaphorically, the creative explosion that unifies contradictory elements and embraces meaning and emotion as well. If we imagine such "present laughter" turning into a structure of comedy,

we would find those plays that take "men as they are" through fictional situations and turn them into "men as they ought to be." This is the comic form in which desire is fulfilled.[3]

She mentions no specific examples of such comic structure, however; and since she undertakes to include Shakespearean comedy within a more or less historical framework that emphasizes a particular moral structure, she bases her observations of "Shakespeare's *poesis*" primarily upon *Twelfth Night*—the only mature Shakespeare comedy that has a nontransformational plot and that thus enables the critic to relate (this *one* example of) Shakespeare's comedies to traditional neoclassical comedy more closely than would otherwise be possible. That analysis is based on the unarticulated assumption that *Twelfth Night* has a typically Shakespearean comic structure; and such an assumption, as I have argued, is both mistaken and misleading.

Nevertheless, Rayner's theoretical description of wish-fulfilling comedy is accurate, and it illuminates the structure of nearly all the Shakespeare comedies. Typical Shakespearean comedies do indeed "take 'men as they are' through fictional situations and turn them into 'men as they ought to be.'" That is to say, each of the transformational comedies presents, in time order, two widely contrasting views of a particular character—first, a more or less realistic view of the character as lacking or flawed in a way that interferes with his or her relation to the rest of society, and then later, an idealized view of the same character with that impediment to socialization removed or corrected. Such a double view is, as Rayner suggests, metaphoric, juxtaposing radically different, rather than realistic or literal, images of the same object, representing some "actual" progression from one thing to another; and the appropriate response to such metaphoric juxtaposition is one that responds to the plot in accordance with Wittgenstein's suggestion, "Imagine this changed like this, and you have this other thing." Any other response leads inevitably to a quarrel with the text, an objection to the plot on realistic grounds. Like the precocious child who is proud of knowing that of course frogs cannot be changed by the love of a good woman (as represented by a single kiss) into princely human beings, realistic critics of Shakespeare's metaphoric plots simply reject one of the playwright's premises and then blame their own failure of imagination upon the poet who constructed the plot.[4]

The description of transformational comic structure as one that takes "'men as they are' through fictional situations and turns them into 'men as they ought to be'" thus illuminates, in social and moral terms, the plots of the early transformational comedies such as *The Taming of the Shrew* and *The Two Gentlemen of Verona*. But it also enables us to see how such a structure can serve equally well—as it does in the later comedies, such as *Measure for Measure* and *The Tempest*—as a vehicle for representing human experience in religious terms. If we simply reverse the order of images of human character as presented in wish-fulfilling comic structure, then we have a more or less accurate description of the story of the Fall, as detailed in Genesis 2 and 3. That story purports to account for the present, fallen condition of humanity by taking "man as he ought to be"—Adam before the Fall—through fictional situations and turning him into "man as he is now"—at odds with both God and other people. Within the framework of such a story, a person's moral and social problems (being at odds with others) are a direct result of religious alienation (being at odds with God). The inversion of that pattern, as reflected in the structure of wish-fulfilling comedy, enables the playwright to depict the rise, or regeneration, of human beings from the consequences of the Fall by representing them as learning—most often against their will—how to love.[5]

The technical means for developing a metaphoric plot of the sort we are describing is a type of metaphor that Shakespeare adopted from his predecessors, brought to perfection, and applied to comic drama. As I have already indicated, biblical writers (particularly St. John) made frequent use of such metaphors; they are in fact at the heart of Christian doctrine and belief. Among classical poets, Ovid—who qualifies perhaps better than anyone else for the title of "everyone's favorite narrative poet"—exploited them to the fullest in the plots of his *Metamorphoses*. Likewise, medieval writers, particularly Chaucer, made use of them in narrative plots, the most familiar of which is the Loathly Lady story, which became the basis for "The Wife of Bath's Tale." Earlier writers actually developed the time-lapse metaphor itself further than Shakespeare ever took it, as in the biblical statement "For the Lamb in the midst of the throne will be their shepherd." There, the device is carried as far as possible, since both elements that go into the compound metaphor are themselves metaphoric. Consequently, the statement becomes almost cryptic, and this may have been an important part of the author's intention in an age when Christians routinely faced persecution and even martyrdom. But the historical result has been that overzealous readers who are unable to cope with metaphor have not only taken the book of Revelation literally but have allegorized it unmercifully. By making his compound metaphors singly, rather than doubly, metaphoric, Shakespeare has escaped the clutches of all but the most inveterate allegorizers of nonallegorical writing.

Of the three influences upon Shakespeare's conception of the time-lapse metaphor just mentioned, the least recognized but by no means the least important is Geoffrey Chaucer, who, as Nevill Coghill suggests, provides much of the basis for Shakespearean comedy. In a neatly balanced pair of metaphors Coghill summarizes the difference between Jonsonian and Shakespearean comedy: "Ben Jonson knotted his cat-o'-nine-tails. Shakespeare reached for his Chaucer."[6] And in my view, he reached for "The Wife of Bath's Tale" more frequently and to better advantage than for any other Chaucerian work. Nearly all the main features of Shakespearean comedy are prefigured in this one story: two settings, one of which is existential (here and now) and the other of which is idyllic (Arthur's realm); stories within stories, the most important being from Ovid (Midas's ears); the importance of self-knowledge ("Poverte . . . / Maketh his God and eek hymself to knowe"); the "emergence of an ideal attitude" ("gentillesse");[7] a Christian context for the comic experience ("Crist wole we clayme of hym oure gentillesse"); and, perhaps most important of all, neatly juxtaposed transformations (hag and knight), for which the Ovidian interpolated story prepares us but which is astonishing and gratifying nonetheless. Even the word *amend,* which undergoes a dazzling semantic metamorphosis just before the hag's "pillow lecture," seems to have captured Shakespeare's imagination: Puck uses various forms of the word four times (all but one of those times in a rhyme position) in the brief epilogue to *A Midsummer Night's Dream,* echoing Theseus's advice to Hippolyta (and, by implication, to the audience) during the play within the play (V.i.209–10) and Oberon's to Titania even earlier (II.i.118).

Having explored to some extent both the structure and the history of the time-lapse metaphor, we can generalize more adequately about its function in the Shakespeare comedies. The metaphor itself is of course simply a technical device, devoid of any significance until it is invested with meaning and purpose by the writer who uses it. The function of such metaphors in Shakespearean comedy is twofold: to reveal the nature of both the transformed self and its relationship to other persons, and to explore the meaning of time in human experience. This double function provides the basis for distinguishing most Shakespearean comedy from nearly all traditional comedy, which is designed, according to Northrop Frye, "to ridicule a lack of self-knowledge"—to hold the untransformed person, utterly lacking in self-knowledge, up to ridicule. And the consequence of such ridicule (as with Malvolio, in the nontransformational *Twelfth Night*) is almost always to expel the person against whom the ridicule is directed from the society represented by the play. The main emphasis in Shakespearean comedy, on the other hand, is on acceptance and reconciliation. As for the significance of time, in traditional comedy time is for the most part linear and Newtonian; that is, it "flows equably without relation to anything external."[8] In Shakespearean comedy, however, time (except occasionally, as in the nontransformational *Comedy of Errors*) is cyclical and relativistic; and the time-lapse metaphor is the means by which the poet succeeds in "redeeming time when men think least he will."

First of all, the time-lapse metaphor, whether it is applied to persons or events or objects, suggests a shift from the trivial to the meaningful, from the plain to the beautiful, and from the ephemeral to the eternal. Hippolyta's commentary near the end of *A Midsummer Night's Dream* takes the form of such a metaphor:

> But all the story of the night told over,
> And all their minds transfigured so together,
> More witnesseth than fancy's images
> And grows to something of great constancy;
> But howsoever, strange and admirable.
> (V.i.23–27)

The familiar vocabulary of change is present ("transfigured," "grows"), and the emphasis is on the shift from that which fades ("the night," "fancy's images") to that which endures ("something of great constancy"). As a result, the witness (and, by implication, the audience) finds himself in the presence of something unfamiliar and awe-inspiring ("strange and admirable"). And this poetic summary of the play takes the form of a time-lapse metaphor because the play itself is a dramatization of several such metaphors, the most spectacular of which is Bottom's "translation" into the hybrid figure of the man-ass—something that is also "strange and admirable." Similarly Alonso, some fifteen years later in *The Tempest*, is changed "into something rich and strange."

But comedy is nothing if not social, and the transformation of a relationship is at least as important as the transformation of individuals who participate in it. Dramatic utterances by the characters provide evidence for these changed relationships. Early in *The Taming of the Shrew*, Kate and Petruchio engage in what seems to be lighthearted banter:

> *Petruchio* Myself am moved to woo thee for my wife.
> *Kate* Moved? In good time: let him that moved you hither
>   Remove you hence. I knew you at the first,
>   You were a movable.
> *Petruchio* Why, what's a movable?
> *Kate* A joint-stool.
> *Petruchio* Thou has hit it: come sit on me.
> (II.i.194–200)

And they do so again at the end:

> *Kate* [*advancing*]   Husband, let's follow, to see the end of this ado.
> *Petruchio*   First kiss me, Kate, and we will.
> *Kate*   What, in the midst of the street?
> *Petruchio*   What, art thou ashamed of me?
> *Kate*   No sir, God forbid, but ashamed to kiss.
> *Petruchio*   Why, then let's home again.   [*To Grumio*]   Come, sirrah, let's away.
> *Kate*   Nay, I will give thee a kiss. Now pray thee, love, stay.
>
>   (V.i.129–36)

From Kate's point of view, the relationship has changed from "I–it (joint-stool)" to "I–thou"; and her later reluctance to show affection is rooted not in aversion, but in modesty. Such differences as these give substance to Baptista Minola's observation that "she is changed as she had never been" (V.ii.120) and to the play's title as well.

The second function of the time-lapse metaphor in Shakespearean comedy is, as I suggested earlier, to explore the meaning of time in human experience. The linear time of neoclassic drama, "flowing equably" through the play, is very different from Shakespeare's comic time, which is sometimes described as having "an extremely elastic character."[9] But this elasticity is by no means simply a matter of "artistic economy" or a way of accommodating an inconveniently long or short sequence of events. It is indeed true that "time travels in divers paces with divers persons," as Rosalind says in response to Orlando's assertion that "there's no clock in the forest" (*AYL* III.ii.286–316). In the Shakespeare comedies time both expands and contracts; and it does so both subjectively (within the consciousness of individuals) and objectively (with reference to whole episodes, involving several characters). Time expansion (or dilation, to use the term associated with relativity theory) is associated primarily with the pastoral or green world of the comedies, and also of course with the tavern in *Henry IV*.[10] Conversely, its contraction (or, more properly, acceleration) serves mainly to condense into compact symbolic form the significance of events that take place, in realistic terms, over a much longer period of time. The expansion creates a relaxed and comfortable atmosphere, conducive to the acquisition of self-knowledge; and the contraction makes possible sudden resolutions and condensed images of personal growth, which may be either astonishing or laughable, or both.

The time dilation aspect of the Shakespeare comedies is much written about, and, for the most part, well understood. Critics tend to be more skeptical, however, about time acceleration and its relation to comic drama.

They seem to suspect in these cases that the poet is just not being serious—as for instance in bringing the plot of *The Two Gentlemen of Verona* to such a swift conclusion or in having the second brother bring in an utterly incredible report of Duke Frederick's split-second conversion in *As You Like It*. But two facts about our experience of comedy suggest the appropriateness of these episodes and incidents. One is the emphasis which laughter theorists place upon suddenness in their analysis of what makes people laugh: Thomas Hobbes uses the phrase "sudden glory," and Immanuel Kant attaches great importance to "the sudden transformation of a strained expectation into nothing." For both thinkers, suddenness is an indispensable element in the laughter-producing situation. The other fact comes to us from the technology of comedy in the early twentieth century. Because the verbal resources of early movies were simply nonexistent, comedians and directors had to resort to nonverbal equivalents. One of the happy results was the accelerated chase scene, which became a standard feature of silent-movie comedies. The passages to which we are referring in the Shakespeare comedies, all of which involve time-lapse metaphors, are the verbal counterparts of these mechanically accelerated scenes. Though they may seem undignified to some observers, they add a marvelously comic touch—besides being necessary to the dramatic effect.

What Alexander Leggatt says about time in *As You Like It* is true, I think, of the other comedies as well. According to Leggatt, there are "two main ways of seeing time" in the play, the first "as the medium of decay" and the other "as the medium of fulfilment."[11] The former is the realist-satirist view, associated primarily with Jaques and Touchstone; the latter is "embodied not in any one speech, but in the whole movement of the play," and it "suggests that time's progress may be circular." Critical emphasis upon "seasonal myth" is, at least indirectly, an emphasis upon this circularity of time in the Shakespeare comedies; and although such a view of time is indeed embodied in the whole movement of the play, as Leggatt asserts, it is also sometimes beautifully condensed into one speech or even a single line. The time-lapse metaphor, whether dramatized in the entire plot of the play (as in *The Taming of the Shrew*) or compressed into one line (as in "Those are pearls that were his eyes"), is Shakespeare's principal device for representing time as the medium of fulfillment.

The last two comedies—*The Winter's Tale* and *The Tempest*—represent in various ways the culmination of Shakespeare's preoccupation with time. Like *A Midsummer Night's Dream* and *Twelfth Night* earlier in his career, the titles of both plays refer to time and/or season, though winter and tempest are more ominous and certainly less "festive" than the occasions referred to in the titles of those earlier comedies. These last two also have the longest and the shortest time spans of any of the plays; and what Stanton Garner, Jr., says of one of them is equally true of the other: "Literally as well as figuratively, Time stands at the center of *The Winter's Tale*."[12] A character called Time serves as chorus for one play, and the other's title is simply an anglicized version of the Latin word meaning "time, period, season, storm." Both plays give substance to the Page's suggestion in *The Taming of the Shrew* that Shakespearean comedy is in fact "a kind of history" in that events which took place "in the dark backward and abysm of time" give significance to what happens here and now, or conversely, what happens here and now becomes "prologue" to all that follows. Change is what makes the passage of time significant in human experience—"this is changed into that," and drama makes us spectators to the event. "Imagine this changed like this," the dramatist suggests, "and you have this other thing."

The time-lapse metaphor and the transformational comic plot are Shakespeare's artistic responses to the most important social, moral, political, and religious problem in human history: the relationship between self and other. Just as Albert Einstein put the Lorentz transformations to new and better use in understanding the physical world by means of special relativity, Shakespeare implemented the time-lapse metaphor in comedies that point the way to a better understanding of human relations. The endless strife between self and other—which manifests itself in human history as enmity, hatred, sexism, racism, and world war—is resolved only when *self becomes other (than its former self)*. The "new creature" we see at the end of a Shakespeare comedy is presented to us in many ways. Other characters attest to the reformation: "For she is changed as she had never been." The changed character announces it imperiously, "Presume not that I am the thing I was," or asserts it more modestly, " 'Twas I. But 'tis not I." The news of it may even arrive by an invisible messenger before the actual transformation has taken place:

> Nothing of him that doth fade
> But doth suffer a sea-change
> Into something rich and strange.

But only insofar as such transformation represents a genuine possibility in human experience does it make any sense to say, either to one person or to a whole theaterful of them, "As you from crimes would pardoned be, / Let your indulgence set me free."

APPENDIX 1

Comic Structure

Mistakes, Misfortunes, and Happy Endings

FARCE tends to be regarded as literary comedy's "poor relation." The word *farce* usually brings to mind hopelessly ridiculous situations, wit of the crudest kind, and pure physical buffoonery, such as a custard pie in the face or a slapstick on the backside. We often encounter the suggestion that farce bears the same relation to comedy that melodrama does to tragedy; and we can hardly miss the implication that both are rather primitive as compared with "high comedy" and "high tragedy." L. J. Potts, in his excellent little book on comedy, says quite simply that farce "might be described as comedy with the meaning left out; which is as much as to say, with the comedy left out."[1] The subject matter of farce is almost invariably trivial, hardly worthy of serious attention or critical examination; and the words *exaggerated* and *absurd* are frequently used to characterize this most basic form of comedy. Its purpose, after all, is merely to excite mirth. If it fails in this, it is worthless; and if it succeeds, few are inclined to ask for anything more.

On the other hand, a few critics, who may or may not use the word *farce*, define comedy itself primarily in terms of the trivial and indicate either directly or indirectly that "serious comedy" is not really comedy at all. Elder Olson, for instance, asserts in *The Theory of Comedy* that the comic action is "one which is of no account, which comes to nothing, so that, on hindsight at least, it would seem foolish to be concerned about it."[2] He goes on to say that "you could call all comedy 'Much Ado About Nothing.'" Curiously though, when he gets to Shakespeare, he contends that the greatest of English comic dramatists produced only five comedies "in our sense of the word" (*Love's Labor's Lost, A Midsummer*

Night's Dream, and the three obvious farces) and that *Much Ado About Nothing* is not in fact a comedy, its title being "a misnomer."³ As one would expect, Olson finds that the plays of Molière illustrate his theory better than most of Shakespeare's do ("Molière is pure comedian"); but even they require some minor adjustments, since "it is not Tartuffe who is the comic protagonist and the figure primarily ridiculous; it is his dupe, Orgon."⁴ And Olson does not even mention *The Misanthrope*, which many consider to be Molière's greatest play.

On the question of how important farce really is, comic theorists seem to offer us only two basic alternatives. Either farce is a vestige of comedy's ancient and primitive origins, and it makes its appearance in serious comedy only as a decorative element or an added attraction; or else works of literature which transcend the purely farcical to deal with matters of genuine importance do so only by abandoning the realm of comedy and taking on a different, though usually unspecified, form. The main difference between the two views resides in what each considers essential to comedy—Potts regards meaning as central, while Olson insists upon trivial action, temporarily and mistakenly invested with importance, as the heart of the matter. Both views exclude things that most of us suppose would fall within the domain of comedy. Potts would apparently reject the Marx Brothers and Laurel and Hardy, and Olson seems perfectly willing to rule out *As You Like It* and *Much Ado About Nothing*. Each critical view rests on the unexamined assumption that the trivial and the meaningful are mutually exclusive, or that they make what is at best a very awkward pair.

But even a cursory examination of comic masterpieces suggests that comic writers do not hesitate to exploit the trivial for a serious purpose or to use the insignificant as a metaphor for more important things. Shakespeare's Duke Theseus, speaking within the context of *A Midsummer Night's Dream*, which both Potts and Olson regard as a paradigm of comedy, asserts that the poet's pen "gives to airy nothing / A local habitation and a name" (v.i. 16–17). From this point of view, the comic writer's function is precisely to take the trivial and to render it meaningful within the framework of reality. At the risk of oversimplifying, I would suggest that Olson and Potts both ignore or at least minimize the relation between beginnings and endings—Olson insists upon the primary importance of "airy nothing" and Potts demands that we focus our attention upon the "local habitation" and the "name." To emphasize either element at the expense of the other is to distort the nature of comedy in a way that either diminishes its significance or else confuses it with other literary types. Considered separately, the trivial is forever trivial, and meaning is inherent in all of the major literary modes. The special appeal of comedy, however, is that its meaning, which branches out and flourishes no less than its counterpart in tragedy, germinates in the trivial.

Attempts to comment meaningfully on comedy without somehow accounting for the tendency reflected in comic works to have "all things sort so well" at the end not only fail to illuminate this important aspect of form; they also completely ignore the manner in which a departure from that pattern affects the meaning of a particular work. Potts stresses "the contrast and balance of characters" as the source of meaning in comedy; but when he tries to deal with the ending of *Tom Jones,* he encounters a significant interpretive difficulty. According to Potts,

> The way everything is made suddenly to go right for Tom and wrong for Blifil is outrageous; even if we are prepared to grant that in this world dishonesty is usually detected in the end and virtue is upon the whole rewarded in pounds, shillings, and pence, we must boggle at the convenience and neatness with which justice does itself in this story.
>
> Yet once we have grasped the real principle on which the book is constructed these criticisms become irrelevant. . . . The plot of *Tom Jones* is a comic plot, based on the grouping of characters rather than on the sequence of events.[5]

Thus, unfortunately, Potts makes "these criticisms become irrelevant" by the simple expedient of declaring the ending itself irrelevant. But if such an ending is irrelevant, then why should Aristotle have claimed, as he does in his discussion of tragedy, that the pleasure associated with a double plot, which has "an opposite catastrophe for the good and for the bad," is "proper rather to Comedy"?[6] Moreover, why should Coleridge have thought *Tom Jones* one of "the three most perfect plots ever planned"?[7] If such an ending is outrageous and irrelevant, then the endings of plays like Molière's *Misanthrope* and Chekhov's *Cherry Orchard* become simply baffling or perverse, even though one is the masterpiece of a "pure comedian" and the other is specifically labeled a comedy by its author, who was a very careful craftsman.

In dealing with so-called problem plays or tragicomedies it is often more illuminating to analyze their structure in relation to farce than to emphasize their mood or tone in relation to tragedy. To suggest an analogy with games, we might say that comedy corresponds to poker, and tragedy to chess. Pure farce finds its equivalent in penny ante; the game is played almost entirely for the amusement it affords rather than for any money that changes hands. More serious comedy has its counterpart in the five-dollar-limit game and makes a considerably greater demand upon the attention of all concerned. Full-fledged comedy, which exploits the total resources of comic form, corresponds to the no-limit game in which large fortunes pass, or threaten to pass, from one player to another. It would be silly for an observer to claim that a no-limit poker game is "almost chesslike" simply because the players are every bit as serious as those in a major chess tournament. Indeed, it would be nearly as silly for a poker snob to claim that penny ante "might be described as poker with the money interest left out; which is as much as to say, with the poker left out." Poker is one game and chess is another, each with its own particular rules and etiquette.

Comedy originates, both historically and structurally, in farce. Satire usually has a social or political purpose, and parody a literary one; but farce, at least in its purest form, stands completely alone and apparently has no other purpose than to evoke an immediate response from its audience. Its structure is perfectly simple—it consists of a series of mistakes and misfortunes, usually brought to a conclusion either by carrying them to their extreme limit or else by the simple device of correcting them or blotting them out. The basic "mistake" in farce takes the form of mistaken identity or a blundering scheme (or both), and the usual "misfortune" is some sort of minor physical injury or temporary setback. As for the two quite different types of ending, in one type the main character either flees from an aroused opponent (as in many animated cartoons) or collapses under a storm of blows (as in most episodes of *Don Quixote,* Part 1). In the other principal type of ending, any mistaken identities are easily sorted out by a manipulative writer, and the minor injuries or temporary setbacks are quickly forgotten in a joyous revelation of identities (as in *She Stoops to Conquer*). Often the correct identification of all parties to the confusion has the added benefit of removing the obstacles to one or more marriages, and the mood of festivity is thereby heightened. These two types of endings reflect the familiar distinction between comic situations in which we laugh at or laugh with the main character.

The relationship between the three structural elements of farce is not arbitrary, but causal. That is, in comedy the mistakes cause the misfortunes, and the ending must follow from what has preceded it. Moreover, the pattern of causation is not scientific or empirical, but moral. Failure to recognize this distinction often leads critics, as we have already noted, to deplore the endings of comedy as "wildly improbable" or "simply outrageous." Walter Kerr carries this view to its logical conclusion when he asserts in *Tragedy and Comedy* that "the finale of comedy bears no organic relationship to the body of comedy."[8] He (like Potts in commenting on *Tom Jones*) regards the ending of *Tartuffe* as completely arbitrary and decides that "the obvious fact of the matter is that Molière, who possessed as much skill in plotting as any man who ever wrote comedy, is simply being cavalier."[9] Kerr seems not to notice or at least not to care that the ending of *Tartuffe* embodies perhaps the most spectacular example of "poetic justice" ever presented upon the stage, and it does so by a dazzling juxtaposition of two causal patterns, the one empirical and the other moral. Surely it was never more obvious in a comic play that the main characters "get what they deserve"; and at the same time it was never more obvious that this pattern requires a considerable wrenching of any realistic perception of ordinary human experience.

In pure farce the action is not bound by realistic considerations, and the moral pattern—which is basically wish-fulfilling—may operate without any significant inhibition. In serious comedy, however, there is an effort to superimpose the moral pattern on the real world; and this superimposition is effective only when it reflects some other seriously held conviction on the part of the author, such as Molière's apparent faith in the ability of the well-regulated and smoothly running society to protect the well-intentioned but foolish citizen from the machinations of the brilliantly resourceful confidence man. That is to say, the main characters in *Tartuffe* finally get what they deserve as members of a particular society, not as human beings with obvious blemishes upon their characters. Molière, as seems appropriate in a writer who may be described as "pure comedian," regards the significant moral pattern as being rooted in social rather than in what he probably thought of as merely personal values.

Three of the Shakespeare comedies—a pure farce, a romantic comedy, and a problem play—will serve to illustrate the manner in which the farcical pattern is elaborated into serious comedy. *The Comedy of Errors* provides the obvious starting point for any such analysis. Mistakes of identity abound in a play which includes, as this one does, two sets of identical twins in its cast of characters; and the mistakes are compounded by dramatic irony, since neither member of either pair is aware of the other pair's presence in Ephesus. The misfortunes these errors produce are not particularly serious. The two slaves receive various slaps and beatings at the hands of the two masters; Antipholus and Dromio of Ephesus find themselves locked out of their own house; and the same Antipholus is threatened with arrest because he refuses to pay for a gold chain that is mistakenly delivered to his twin. On this level, simple discovery of the errors is sufficient to nullify their effect; but even here one of the characters is under sentence of death through most of the play. Egeon, the father of the two Antipholuses, cannot produce the thousand marks demanded of any Syracusan who sets foot in Ephesus; and it is only when they are on the way to the place of execution that the abbess, Egeon's long-lost wife, identifies him and helps to straighten matters out.

Much Ado About Nothing represents a considerable advance over *The Comedy of Errors*, but the differences between the two plays are those of quality and degree rather than differences of kind. The crucial mistake this time is a mistake of judgment—the important question in *Much Ado* is not who the heroine is but what she is. Further, the answer to this question is made to depend upon a mistake of identity engineered by Don John, who invites Claudio to witness a rendezvous between Margaret and her lover conducted at Hero's window specifically to deceive Claudio. When Claudio confronts Hero at their wedding the following day, he thinks that "her blush is guiltiness, not modesty" (IV.i.40); thus he mistakes a virtuous maid for a "rotten orange" and denounces her publicly. The consequences of his error are obviously more serious than a slap on the backside or the threat of being arrested. At stake in this case are the happiness and reputation of a respectable young woman and her family, not to mention the future of the young man who makes the error. That is to say, the mistake has significant moral implications, as those in *The Comedy of Errors* do not. Moreover, mere discovery is not sufficient to prevent or remove the consequences of the error. The inimitable Dogberry reveals how the error has arisen; but he is hardly competent to bring about a satisfactory resolution.

If the farcical happy ending is to be preserved when the mistakes are more serious than those of identity, the writer must either protect characters from the results (as in *Tartuffe*) or increase their capacity to deal with such consequences (as in *Much Ado*). The first sign of this increased capacity in *Much Ado* is the verbal dexterity manifested in both the bantering dialogue of Beatrice and Benedick and the brilliant malapropisms of Dogberry. In the earlier play the characters labor under the difficulty of having little or nothing to say that matters outside the immediate context of the plot. One would be hard pressed to remember even a few lines from *The Comedy of Errors* that strike the listener as being particularly witty or as reflecting any insight into human experience. In *Much Ado,* however, a good deal is said that persists in the viewer's memory long after the intricacies of plot have become blurred by the passage of time.

A second sign of increased capacity to deal with misfortune—and a more important one as far as structure is concerned—is that the scheming which both creates and resolves the problems of the play is done onstage by the characters themselves, rather than offstage by an omniscient writer. In the main plot, the "plain-dealing villain" Don John concocts the plan that leads to Claudio's mistaken judgment by confusing him about the identity of Margaret and Hero. Working in the opposite direction in the subplot, Don Pedro conceives the stratagem for bringing Beatrice and Benedick together apparently against their will. The third scheme, which makes possible the happy ending, is the work of Friar Francis, who is more expert and certainly more humane than either Don John or Don Pedro. Convinced that Hero lies "guiltless here / Under some biting error" (IV.i.167–68), he lets it be thought that she has died, and by changing "slander to remorse" he begins to correct Claudio's "strange misprision." The mechanics of discovery in the main plot are left on the farcical level with Dogberry's motley crew; and no discovery is necessary in the subplot because the plan itself produces a suitably comic ending, the prospective marriage of the supposedly reluctant lovers.

The third and most important feature of the play that enables the characters to deal effectively with the consequences of errors is their capacity to admit their mistakes and to seek reconciliation and, on the part of those injured by the mistakes, a willingness to be reconciled. The introduction of this conception (which corresponds roughly to Molière's apparent faith in the social order) has profound implications for both the meaning and the form of Shakespearean comedy because it involves substituting the religious idea of repentance and forgiveness for the moral pattern of poetic justice. Even if Dogberry's bungling discovery were communicated more directly and efficiently, it would not be sufficient to remove the guilt Claudio incurs by his error of judgment. Before that can happen, he must accept full responsibility and demonstrate his willingness to make amends. Thinking that Hero has died as a result of his breach of faith, he tells her father,

> I know not how to pray your patience;
> Yet I must speak. Choose your revenge yourself;
> Impose me to what penance your invention
> Can lay upon my sin.
>
> (V.i.258–61)

Such a speech is necessary if the farcical pattern is to accommodate the requirements of real life and if the ending is to be fully satisfactory. Even so, the young offender can conclude his apology to Leonato by claiming with some justification, "Yet sinned I not / But in mistaking"; and his mentor Don Pedro can second him by saying, "By my soul, nor I!"

In *Shakespeare and the Comedy of Forgiveness* Robert G. Hunter has indicated fully the manner in which the repentance-forgiveness pattern affects six of the mature Shakespeare comedies. For our purposes, it is important to see that this pattern modifies farcical form by expanding it to include real human problems as well as the contrived problems of equally contrived characters. As a philosophic doctrine apart from its usefulness in comedy, the conception of poetic justice is obviously untenable. Hamlet is not just being cynical when he asks Polonius, "Use every man after his desert, and who shall scape whipping?" If Hamlet is right, and if the plots of the mature Shakespeare comedies are to be determined by the unmodified requirements of farce, then surely they ought to end with a round-robin of whippings or even a series of executions rather than with the arrangement of various marriages. Indeed, as late as Act IV of *Much Ado* Beatrice pushes matters toward such a conclusion. Asked by Benedick what he can do to prove his love for her, she unhesitatingly responds, "Kill Claudio." But the friar is already at his manipulative work by this time, so that Beatrice's proposed "solution" later becomes not only unnecessary but inappropriate. When Claudio repents and asks forgiveness, Leonato grants it willingly; and Antonio speaks for all of us when he says, "Well, I am glad that all things sort so well." Thus, the way is clear for the marriage of Claudio and Hero as well as that of Beatrice and Benedick.

Despite the religious orthodoxy and the obvious sensibleness of Shakespeare's resolution, it apparently bothers some critics that certain characters benefit as they do from a special dispensation or from a kind of general amnesty at the end of these plays. Moreover, the reasons for their objections are not difficult to specify. Quite simply, the characters do not deserve to be forgiven—they are either too dull or too mean to merit anything but a hard blow of the slapstick. Traditional comedy, as represented by pure farce, justifies these misgivings. In *The Importance of Being Earnest*, Miss Prism obviously has a comic pattern in mind when she describes the novel she has written in her youth, "The good ended happily and the bad unhappily. That is what fiction means." However facetious that comment may be, it would be hard to deny that there has long been a connection between the structure of comedy and what came to be known as the doctrine of poetic justice—hence Aristotle's observation (already noted) that the double ending is particularly appropriate to comedy. Indeed, the objections to forgiveness in the later Shakespeare comedies reflect a genuine uneasiness at seeing this doctrine significantly modified within a comic plot.

The implications of the farcical pattern are even more fully developed in *Measure for Measure* than in *Much Ado*. As one would expect, greater structural complexity requires more elaborate characterization. The functions of governor and friar are compressed into a single role—that of the Duke, who goes about discovering and exploiting the loopholes which make it possible to resolve all the problems. His activity as manipulator begins earlier than that of the friar in *Much Ado*, and his power is greater; indeed, the repentant Angelo characterizes his influence as being "like power divine." Similarly, the roles of Don John, the unscrupulous schemer, and Claudio (in *Much Ado*), the chief though ultimately penitent offender, are combined in the subtler and more realistic personality of Angelo. Moreover, the innocence of Hero and the verbal facility of Beatrice come together in Isabella. As a result, the characters in *Measure for Measure* lose something in charm and sparkle but gain a great deal in credibility and significance.

The mistakes that matter most in this play are not those of identity, as in *The Comedy of Errors*, nor of judgment, as in *Much Ado*, though the play contains several errors of both types. The Duke's identity is concealed under his monk's robe during most of the action; Ragozine's head is substituted for Claudio's when the latter is supposed to be executed; and the "bed trick" involving Isabella and Mariana is among the oldest and most obviously farcical of mistaken identity devices. Angelo discovers in Act II that he has been mistaken in judging his own nature; by the end of Act III the Duke becomes aware that he too has mistakenly judged his deputy; and Lucio misjudges the Duke badly and has the misfortune to communicate that judgment directly to the disguised Duke. These errors would no doubt be sufficient to sustain the action of the play; but in this case they all either spring from, or are necessitated by, mistakes of an even more serious kind—mistakes of attitude toward life.

Wrong-headed attitudes abound in *Measure for Measure*. Angelo is an absolutely rigid Puritan; and Isabella can only be described as a militant virgin. The Duke's deputy is "precise," and he undertakes to enforce the death penalty for any sexual contact outside of marriage; but he does not hesitate for long, when temptation and opportunity present themselves simultaneously, to take sexual advantage of someone who appears to be defenseless against his power and influence. The point is not, of course, that he is a calculating hypocrite, but rather that his lack of self-knowledge, rooted in a serious misjudgment of his own nature, has led him into an utterly mistaken attitude toward life. Until he discovers that he himself is vulnerable to the demands of the flesh, he supposes that his consistency in applying the ban to himself no less than to others justifies his repressive attitude. When Escalus pleads for mercy in Claudio's case, Angelo responds:

> You may not so extenuate his offense
> For I have had such faults; but rather tell me,
> When I that censure him do so offend,
> Let mine own judgment pattern out my death
> And nothing come in partial.
>
> (II.i.27–31)

Far from justifying Angelo's position, this argument merely shows that he has made a sincere though obviously rationalizing effort to be consistent in his wrong-headedness.

Isabella's position is much closer to Angelo's than one might at first suppose—both seem quite willing to sacrifice someone else's life in order to establish and preserve their own conception of proper sexual behavior. Her attitude seems at the outset to be less harsh than his only because she expresses it within a purely personal, rather than social, context. Angelo is a political man and therefore his values must find their justification within the framework of society as a whole. Isabella, who is on the point of entering a convent, need not take anyone but herself into account; and placing her in a social situation reveals the inadequacy of her view, just as placing temptation in Angelo's way reveals the shallowness of his. When Claudio pleads with her to be spared, she lashes out at him:

> O you beast,
> O faithless coward, O dishonest wretch!
> Wilt thou be made a man out of my vice?
> Is't not a kind of incest, to take life
> From thine own sister's shame?
> (III.i.136–40)

Isabella seems not to realize that the question could very well be asked of her: Is it not a kind of fratricide, to take virtue from thine own brother's death? Thus within a social context, Isabella's attitude turns out to be as narrowly self-serving as Angelo's.

Mistaken attitudes in *Measure for Measure* threaten to produce consequences that are plainly disastrous. Claudio is ordered to the chopping block; Isabella must deliver up her virginity to her persecutor; and Angelo ultimately condemns himself to death for his breach of the law which it was his duty and desire to enforce. As we have already seen, within the pattern of pure farce the characters behave in unconscious fashion, and discovery alone is sufficient to rectify matters—once everybody knows who is who, the problems are solved; the insignificant misfortunes simply evaporate; and the play may end happily. On the second level, it becomes necessary to increase the characters' ability to deal with misfortune by making them more articulate, by making them resourceful in scheming, and by allowing them to retrieve themselves through repentance and forgiveness. On the third level, where consequences actually threaten to be fatal, the happy ending is preserved only by making the characters who commit errors fully aware of what they are doing and by allowing forgiveness to come from those who believe themselves to be irreparably injured by the errors in question. In *Much Ado*, Claudio thought that he was behaving honorably when he denounced Hero; but in *Measure for Measure*, Angelo knows full well that he is committing one crime after another. Similarly, Leonato (in *Much Ado*) forgives Claudio, knowing that Hero is alive and well; but Isabella (in *Measure for Measure*) asks that Angelo be forgiven while she still believes that her brother has been executed at the deputy's command. In other words, at this highest level the farcical pattern is kept from bursting apart only by making the characters fully conscious of their behavior and by invoking the deepest meaning of repentance, forgiveness, and reconciliation.

The ending of *Measure for Measure* (like that of *Much Ado*) combines the two basic farcical conclusions—the one in which mistakes are carried to their extreme limit, and the other in which the mistakes are corrected or blotted out. The bed trick enables Isabella to maintain her attitude until the final scene; and since the Duke has managed to conceal both Claudio's escape from the executioner and Isabella's noncompliance with Angelo's demand, the erring deputy thinks that his scheme has been carried through to its end. But fortunately the Duke is no less merciful than powerful, and he is willing both to resolve the sexual problems of the play through marriage and to forgive the earlier errors which had their origin in those problems. Such a combination of endings permits the writer to "have it both ways," as is thoroughly appropriate in comedy. From a realistic viewpoint we see human error moving inexorably forward, and from a comic viewpoint we see a complicated plot brought to a happy ending. It is particularly satisfying that neither pattern is violated in order to meet the requirements of the other. No one could object to the plot on the basis of farcical structure; and the conception of repentance and forgiveness is beautifully illustrated. The offender expresses his willingness to be punished according to the most severe standard, and those who forgive do not merely overlook the offense; they judge it sternly but suspend the sentence. The spirit, rather than the letter, of the law is fulfilled; and the modern audience, which presumably understands that "justice delayed is justice denied," is shown that justice not tempered by mercy is little more than socialized revenge.

For purposes of analysis, we have described the three main kinds of comic mistakes as those of identity, of judgment, and of attitude; and the seriousness of comedy depends upon the type of mistake that it stresses and the validity of the author's method in controlling the consequences of such mistakes. If that method is based upon an attitude or belief which is or can be implemented successfully in human society, then the author is able to expand farcical form to accommodate the demands and problems of human existence. Otherwise, the writer must either be content with the pleasures of farcical form as an end in itself or present human society and its problems by means of some other dramatic pattern. Laughter, by itself, is no reliable indicator of a comic work's seriousness. For this reason, a comic work may be at one and the same time uproariously funny and highly serious; conversely, it is not difficult to imagine a play or a novel that would be utterly frivolous and extremely dull. As an example of the funny-serious work we may take Voltaire's *Candide,* which can be characterized as heavily farcical or genuinely philosophical according to which aspect of the tale one wishes to emphasize. It is overflowing with mistakes of identity and of judgment, but almost all such errors are represented as springing from a fundamentally mistaken attitude toward life—that of rationalistic optimism. Ending as it does with the suggestion that we should work without arguing or "cultivate our gardens," the story implies that the most devastating social problems are in fact created by the conflict of mistaken and belligerent social attitudes rather than by the world itself, however imperfect that world may be.

As a test of the analytical approach to serious comedy that we have been describing, let us look closely at two of Molière's works already mentioned in passing. *Tartuffe* and *The Misanthrope* are both highly structured, and both have generated a body of criticism that leaves one bewildered as he contemplates the plays themselves. In connection with *Tartuffe* we are told on the one hand that Orgon, not Tartuffe, is the comic protagonist, but we are given no explanation as to why the play should be named for a secondary character; and on the other we are asked to believe that Molière was an extremely skillful plotter and that in ending *Tartuffe* as he does, he is "simply being cavalier." Yet his cavalier ending serves no other purpose, we are told, than "to let everyone go home." As for *The Misanthrope*, it has long been regarded as an example of tragicomedy and a "true exception" to anything that one may say about comic endings. Thus, in *The Classical Moment* Martin Turnell feels compelled to defend his assertion that "*The Misanthrope* is pre-eminently a comedy; it is not a bourgeois tragedy."[10] Such confusion about the nature of these plays almost inevitably results in relegating the question of their meaning to a position of secondary importance at best, and at worst it leads to serious misinterpretation.

The plot of *Tartuffe* is closely integrated; and like the main plot of *Much Ado About Nothing*, it involves two distinct but interlocking errors. In *Much Ado* Claudio is tricked into making a mistake of identity (Margaret for Hero), which leads him into a mistake of judgment (Hero for harlot). In *Tartuffe* the mistakes are made by two different people—Orgon is badly mistaken in judging Tartuffe; and Tartuffe acts constantly upon a badly mistaken attitude toward other people. (In Molière attitudes are mistaken to whatever extent they are antisocial.) The two mistakes are reciprocal and mutually sustaining through most of the play. Tartuffe himself is the classic example of the "con man," and one cannot represent a con man in action without someone's being conned. Orgon is therefore essential to the play, but it is hardly reasonable to regard him as the "comic protagonist."

If the title and subtitle (*Tartuffe, or the Impostor*) are not sufficient evidence that we are to regard Tartuffe as the protagonist, we should recall Henry Fielding's observation in the Author's Preface to *Joseph Andrews*. The ridiculous, says Fielding, arises from affectation, which in turn has two sources: vanity and hypocrisy. In comedy, he continues, the ridiculous "always strikes the reader with surprise and pleasure; and that in a higher and stronger degree when the affectation arises from hypocrisy, than when from vanity; for to discover any one to be the exact reverse of what he affects, is more surprising, and consequently more ridiculous, than to find him a little deficient in the quality he desires the reputation of."[11] Molière's Orgon is a model of vanity; his motive is ostentation and he desires to be associated with piety without really taking the trouble to be pious. Tartuffe is of course a magnificent hypocrite and his motive is deception. To combine Fielding's terminology with ours, we may say that Tartuffe's mistake is more serious than Orgon's, and to that extent he is more ridiculous than his victim—provided always, of course, that the consequences of his error are controlled by the playwright.

Farcical form requires that the consequences of errors be controlled; but the crucial question, when the pattern is expanded into serious comedy, is whether or not the author's manner of controlling them corresponds satisfactorily to something real—that is, to something outside the context of the play. Farcical form merely reflects a deeper requirement of comedy, perhaps most succinctly stated by Aristotle. "The Ludicrous," he says in the *Poetics,* "consists in some defect or ugliness which is not painful or destructive."[12] This assertion echoes the position that Socrates takes in Plato's *Philebus:* "Those who are both deluded and weak, unable to avenge themselves when laughed at, may rightly be described as 'ridiculous'; but those who can retaliate might more properly be called 'formidable' and 'hateful.'"[13] In short, the difference between the ridiculous person and the formidable or hateful one is simply power. In any realistically represented situation (an empirical pattern) Tartuffe is more powerful than Orgon, his natural prey. But within the context of a well-ordered and efficiently administered society (a moral pattern), the "deluded" Tartuffe is reduced to a level at which he is as helpless to avenge himself upon the law as Orgon has been all along to avenge himself upon Tartuffe. It is the purpose of law to avenge those wrongs which the victim is either unwilling or unable to avenge. Putting Tartuffe in his place by some dextrous manipulation of the plot would imply that society deals with the impostor by outwitting him. Molière understood that when and if the law works, it does so not by being cleverer than the criminal but by being more powerful. The literary audacity of Molière's comic ending is an objective correlative for the political power that sustains society despite the energy and cleverness of those who would corrupt it.

The royal messenger's speech contains the play's only reference to the possibility of mistaken identity.

> The King soon recognized Tartuffe as one
> Notorious by another name, who'd done
> So many vicious crimes that one could fill
> Ten volumes with them, and be writing still.

Molière preferred not to exploit this possibility, however. No other character in the play had known Tartuffe by his other name (whatever it was), nor had anyone ever mistaken him for some other person. Unlike the main plot of *Much Ado,* which is built upon interlocking mistakes of identity and judgment, the plot of *Tartuffe* rests upon interlocking mistakes of judgment and attitude. Moreover, unlike the plot of *Measure for Measure,* which exploits all three types of error, *Tartuffe* makes significant use of the second and third, with a nod in the direction of the first. Shakespeare represents the controller of consequences as a human agent (with overtones of "power divine") operating within the structure of the plot, intervening after the midpoint in *Much Ado* but present from the beginning in *Measure for Measure*. Molière, on the other hand, prefers to equate the controller with the unlimited power of the king, intervening at the last moment on behalf of the beleaguered citizen. It is of course understood that the citizen in question has "paid his dues" as a member of society. The messenger's speech continues:

> By these decrees, our Prince rewards you for
> Your loyal deeds in the late civil war,
> And shows how heartfelt is his satisfaction
> In recompensing any worthy action,
> How much he prizes merit, and how he makes
> More of men's virtues than of their mistakes.

Since Tartuffe has paid no dues and since his only merit is in the undeniably brilliant implementation of an antisocial attitude, he is appropriately packed off to jail. Orgon gets what he deserves as the respectable citizen of an enlightened state rather than as a hopelessly incompetent judge of human character, and, of course, the way is cleared for Valère to marry Orgon's daughter, whose hand Orgon had foolishly promised to Tartuffe.

The Misanthrope is no less fascinating than *Tartuffe*, and its structure has been no less puzzling to both audience and critic. Just as the characters in *Measure for Measure* combine features of two or more roles in *Much Ado*, Alceste embodies characteristics of both Orgon and Tartuffe. He is more authentically respectable and virtuous than Orgon, and he is at least as shrewd as Tartuffe—that is, he is both well intentioned and perceptive enough to see through the falsity of other men. Like Don Quixote, he believes that righteousness and virtue are invincible, even invulnerable; and when he discovers that they are not, he becomes disillusioned and cynical. Unlike the "ingenious gentleman," he never abandons his claim to superiority; he chooses instead to abandon society. From the standpoint of comic characterization, he represents the only other "pure" type worthy to stand at the same exalted level as the hypocrite—the snob. He needs no Orgon to practice his variety of antisocial behavior as specified in the play's title; he becomes his own dupe.

The structure of *The Misanthrope* is easily described by reference to the pattern elaborated from basic farce. A mistaken attitude (rejection of fellow humans on a gradually expanding scale) leads directly to certain consequences (alienation from society) and culminates in the most basic of farcical endings—the protagonist flees from his aroused opponents (withdraws to self-imposed exile). There is no manipulator or controller of consequences because none is needed; in this case the empirical pattern and the moral pattern coincide from beginning to end. The protagonist gets what he deserves, namely companions who are no less virtuous and sincere than he is himself. Since the society represented by the play provides no examples of such a person except the protagonist himself, he winds up choosing his friends from a "class that has no members." The confusion created among critics by the ending of *The Misanthrope* arises from the unwarranted assumption that if the virtuous get what they deserve, they will also get what they want. Such is not the case in this imperfect world, where the price of snobbery is isolation.

Alceste faces three tests—of law, of literary criticism, and of love—and he fails all three though his cause is just, his taste is impeccable, and his love is apparently genuine. He allows his lawsuit to stand or fall purely on its own merits at a time when "gifts" to the presiding judge are thought to be entirely proper; and he is surprised to discover that merit counts for little in the disposition of his case. He speaks his mind in judging the work of a bad poet, and the offended scribbler takes revenge upon him. He assumes that true love is reciprocal by definition, but he learns that love is no more rational in its operation than either law or literary criticism. This third test is the most important of the three since it is through love that the existential world makes its strongest claim upon the humorous or eccentric character in comedy. Those who put the abstract considerations of virtue and sincerity above the claims of human love obviously cannot be reconciled to their fellow humans in typically comic fashion. Those who insist upon their own superiority by that very insistence remove themselves from the society to which they claim to be superior.

This analysis of several plays makes possible some tentative conclusions about the relationship between pure farce and serious comedy. First of all, the world symbolized in pure farce is a fantasy world in which the mistakes people make are trivial and superficial, and they lead only to injuries and losses that are likewise trivial and superficial. Moreover, the farcical world is clearly moral in character—a mistake leads to injuries and misfortunes, but correcting the mistake is sufficient to remove the effects of injury or loss that it has caused. There is no irretrievable loss or irreparable damage in farce; and everyone is automatically rewarded according to the goodness of his intentions. That is to say, the doctrine of poetic justice is inherent in farce. In serious comedy, on the other hand, the world is far more realistically represented—people may commit errors which, if carried to their natural conclusion, produce absolutely devastating results. A benevolent manipulator, whose controlling activity is necessary in farce if the sequence is to have a happy ending, is retained in serious comedy whenever the empirical and the moral patterns do not coincide. Playwrights may exercise this power themselves after the fashion of pure farce, as Molière does when he brings in the king's messenger at the end of *Tartuffe;* or they may delegate it to one of the characters in the play, as Shakespeare does to the Duke in *Measure for Measure* and to Prospero in *The Tempest.* But in either case the manipulator must reflect a deeper knowledge of the real world than is necessary in pure farce.

This manipulator, whose influence is necessary to the happy ending, reveals one of the most significant characteristics of comic structure. In pure farce the manipulation is blatant; and since the audience understands that the world of pure farce is largely fantastic, the manipulation becomes in and of itself a source of delight. But the real world, which serious comedy must represent with some fidelity, is far less manipulable than the world of farce. Consequently, comic writers run a double risk—their work will appear to be naive if they imply that the real world may be controlled no less arbitrarily than the world of farce; or their work will seem cynical if they suggest that they are aware of the difference between the two worlds but simply do not care about bringing them into any significant relationship with each other. The manipulation in serious comedy must, therefore, be based upon some belief or conception that both author and audience regard as being effective when applied to human society in general. For Molière, this conception reflects a confidence in political power, vested in the king, to protect the well-intentioned and faithful citizen from the activities of those who are aggressively antisocial. If the antisocial person happens also to be virtuous, then no manipulation is necessary since the effects of such an attitude will be confined to that one person. For Shakespeare, the conception reflects both a confidence in the political power of the legitimate ruler and a faith in the social efficacy of repentance and forgiveness. Thus Shakespeare seems more "optimistic" in his comedies than does Molière, since he holds out considerable hope for reclaiming the antisocial person, though he allows some (such as Jaques in *As You Like It* and Malvolio in *Twelfth Night*) to go their misanthropic way.

The comic emotion differs from laughter just as the tragic emotion differs from weeping; and both emotions are generated by contemplating human life as represented within a basic pattern or form. Most of the confusion about serious comedy is rooted in two widely held but grossly misleading assumptions: (1) that the word *comic* is synonymous with *funny*; and (2) that any genuinely comic work will have a happy ending. The difficulty with these assumptions is not that they are wrong, but that they are too narrow. The comic includes the laughable, but it also includes some things which are not adequately described by the term *funny*. The very linking of the two assumptions implies that this is the case, since the happy ending itself is not necessarily funny though it is consistent with the mood which laughter helps to create. Moreover, the phrase "happy ending" usually means both wish-fulfilling and morally satisfying. But the comic conclusion need not be both, since either of these characteristics (wish fulfillment or "poetic justice") is sufficient to distinguish the comic pattern from the tragic. The decision as to whether or not a work is fundamentally comic should depend upon its relation to a pattern rather than upon how funny it is or how happy we judge its ending to be. Indeed, the most useful pattern in connection with comedy is that of basic farce.

APPENDIX 2

Comic Character
The Invented Self

WHEN Don Quixote, in the midst of other moralizing, tells Sancho Panza that "all affectation is bad," he provides an excellent though deeply ironic motto for literary comedy. A century and a quarter later Henry Fielding makes the relationship between affectation and the ridiculous explicit in the Author's Preface to *Joseph Andrews*, which according to the title page is "written in imitation of the manner of Cervantes, author of *Don Quixote*." He indicates that the ludicrous and the ridiculous are the stock-in-trade of the comic epic poem in prose, as he calls the form in which he is writing; and he asserts that "the only source of the true Ridiculous (as it appears to me) is affectation." In its turn, says Fielding, "affectation proceeds from one of these two causes, vanity or hypocrisy." He observes that these two are very closely related and even that "there is some difficulty in distinguishing them." It may be helpful to suggest, however, that vanity and hypocrisy are two forms of moral blindness—vain people occasionally stumble over things they do not see because they are nearsighted, while hypocrites only pretend to be blind as they scrutinize their victims from behind dark glasses.

But the meaning of Don Quixote's assertion that all affectation is bad is more complex than it appears at first to be, since it is impossible for human beings to avoid all forms of affectation; and consequently the implication that one should *try* to avoid them can only lead to (and spring from) some particular affectation. Don Quixote speaks from the vantage point of the wise counselor, the righter of wrongs and injustices, the believer in a chivalric code; and when he himself discards that particular affectation, his occupation is gone—there is nothing left for him to do but take to his bed and die. The comic mentality never shows itself more clearly than when it condemns certain things; and when it does so, it usually manifests the very things it condemns. Don Quixote frequently becomes involved in such contradictions, as does Fielding's Parson Adams, who lectures Joseph sternly on the foolishness of setting our affections on another person so completely that if the person were taken from us, we would not be able "peaceably, quietly, and contentedly" to resign ourselves to the loss. At that moment someone informs him (wrongly, as it turns out) that his youngest son has been drowned, whereupon the good parson "soon began to stamp about the room and deplore his loss with the bitterest agony." Likewise, Parson Adams is exceedingly vain about one of his own sermons—one "which he thought his masterpiece, against vanity."

The attitudes and behavior of Don Quixote and Parson Adams thus reflect a completely unconscious irony and would seem to justify Northrop Frye's observation that the function of comedy is "to ridicule a lack of self-knowledge." But both of those characters represent the kind of ridiculousness that originates in vanity, and Fielding indicates that affectation may proceed from hypocrisy no less than from vanity. Frye's conception of comic function rests on the assumption, articulated by Socrates and supported by Aristotle, that "to know the good is to do it." In cases of vanity both Frye's conception and the assumption on which it rests are apparently applicable—comic characters behave as they do because their vanity keeps them from seeing that their own behavior illustrates what they are condemning. Their behavior is therefore unconscious, and they may be said to be lacking in self-knowledge. But what about the hypocrite? It would be far more difficult to establish that Molière's Tartuffe, for instance, is lacking in self-knowledge. The play makes it perfectly clear that Tartuffe knows exactly what he is doing and that for a long time he does it very skillfully.

If we insist on the lack-of-self-knowledge view in connection with *Tartuffe*, we are forced to concede that it is Tartuffe's victim, Orgon, who is most frequently held up to ridicule for what may be described as a lack of self-knowledge and a consequent lack of perception and penetration. This procedure makes Orgon at least as important as Tartuffe in relation to the play's comic function; and such a view is at odds with several important aspects of the play—Orgon is vindicated at the end, and Tartuffe has the title all to himself. It also fails to square with Fielding's statements about the relative ridiculousness of the affectations arising from vanity on the one hand and from hypocrisy on the other:

> From the discovery of this affectation arises the Ridiculous, which always strikes the reader with surprise and pleasure; and that in a higher and stronger degree when the affectation arises from hypocrisy, than when from vanity; for to discover any one to be the exact reverse of what he affects, is more surprising, and consequently more ridiculous, than to find him a little deficient in the quality he desires the reputation of.

From this point of view, Orgon's vindication in Act V (however arbitrarily it may be brought about) and the title's designation of Tartuffe as the protagonist are entirely consistent with the work's comic function; and it follows that the words "to ridicule a lack of self-knowledge" do not adequately define that function.

Tragedy may be described as representing the process by which an individual achieves self-knowledge; and this process is painful because "justice so moves that those only learn who suffer." In tragedy the process involves *discovery*; and it is never represented as being ridiculous. In comedy, however, the self which is the center of interest and the basis for action is not discovered but *invented*. Comic characters create such a personality for themselves by the time of their first appearance; that is, they have had time to prepare a face to meet the faces that they meet. And the basic difference between the two principal kinds of comic character is that the hypocrite has *consciously* prepared a face, while the vain person has done so *unconsciously*. If Fielding is right, then paradoxically hypocrites are more ridiculous (and therefore presumably more comic) precisely because of greater self-knowledge coupled with a cynical determination to use that knowledge to their own advantage. Seen from this perspective, the function of comedy is not merely to ridicule a lack of self-knowledge, but rather to display the behavior of a character who tries persistently to project upon the world an invented self that is the product of either conscious or unconscious affectation.

Literary comedy is rooted in the disparity between the straight lines and carefully plotted curves of reason and morality on the one hand and the ragged edges of human existence on the other. The invented self seeks to give the appearance of conforming as closely as possible to the dictates of reason and morality (or of deviating as far as possible from them), while the existential or factual self remains bound by the needs and frailties of the flesh. And it is not merely a noncorrespondence or incongruity that is at issue; it is rather that people make themselves ridiculous in their continuous and sometimes valiant struggle to combine the two. There is nothing inherently comic about the fact that oil and water do not mix; but there may very well be something comic about a person, armed only with a swizzle stick and no particular knowledge of chemistry, who spends most of his life and all of his resources in trying to make them mix. Falstaff is little more than a stock character in his capacities as swashbuckler, and coward, and loyal servant to the Prince of Wales. But when he explains that he fled from the disguised prince at Gadshill because he would not kill the heir apparent and he was therefore "a coward on instinct," he achieves his full comic stature. He demonstrates with the clarity of a mathematician that his loyalty to the prince and his physical terror had dictated the same course of action.

The comic effect of the Gadshill incident in *Henry IV, Part 1* thus comes to a focus in Falstaff's explanation of his behavior after the fact. As Poins indicates to Hal while they are planning the episode, "The virtue of this jest will be the incomprehensible lies that this same fat rogue will tell us when we meet at supper"; and he is right—as far as he goes. Falstaff does indeed tell "how thirty, at least, he fought with; what wards, what blows, what extremities he endured." But Poins is wrong in thinking that "in the reproof of this lives the jest," because for the play's audience the jest lives primarily in the way Falstaff succeeds in evading even the reproof. His resourcefulness enables him, at least verbally, to mix the oil and water of his experience and to emerge intact from his encounter with those who would unmask him and expose the gulf that separates Falstaff the swashbuckler and hero from Falstaff the liar and coward. The scene is one of the funniest in the entire range of Shakespeare's comic writing; and we need to understand what makes it funny. But traditional theories of laughter, some of which are highly ingenious, fail as theories of comedy mainly because they concentrate upon the single episode or statement rather than upon the overall structure of a comic work. That is, they focus upon situations, anecdotes, or witty remarks, not upon the continuing activity of the comic character. Nevertheless, they do illuminate some aspects of comedy and should be taken into account in formulating any comic theory, since the latter can hardly be adequate unless it explains at least as much as they do.

Among laughter theories, the incongruity theory (also sometimes called the intellectual theory) has its origin in Kant's suggestion that laughter results from "the sudden transformation of a strained expectation into nothing." Perhaps the best illustration of this view would be one of Rube Goldberg's cartoons representing a hugely elaborate machine whose only purpose is to do some simple task that would be much more easily accomplished without the machine—a complex mechanism with perhaps fifty moving parts (any one of which could easily break down) that supposedly makes it possible to turn the light switch on or off without getting up from one's chair. In such cases there is an absurd incongruity between the insignificance of the thing achieved and the complexity of the means for achieving it.

The first step in moving from laughter theory to comic theory is made when we realize that from the standpoint of logic Kant's statement applies to all laughter-producing situations, but not to all situations that involve the transformation of a strained expectation into nothing. (That is, the subject term of a universal affirmative statement is distributed; the predicate term is not.) We may distinguish tentatively then between the terms *funny* and *comic* by saying that all situations that show the transformation of a strained expectation into nothing are basically comic whether or not they strike us as being funny, because they have essentially the same structure as laughter-producing situations.

Even in its simplest form this procedure helps to clarify matters in connection with literary works that the author has specifically labeled comedies, but that critics tend to classify as dramas or tragicomedies. The ultimate transformation into nothing is death; and if the strained expectation which precedes it is represented as being ridiculous, the collapse which follows does not become tragic merely by virtue of its being sad in terms of everyday experience. (By the same token, the birth of a child is ordinarily a joyous event; but when a child is born into pestilence and famine—as happens in *Oedipus the King*—the emotional impact of the event is radically changed.) Consequently, the suicide of Trepliov at the end of *The Seagull* and the abandonment of Feers at the end of *The Cherry Orchard* are not inconsistent with Chekhov's title-page designation of these plays as comedies; both conclusions represent the total transformation of an extremely strained expectation into absolutely nothing.

Expanding upon the incongruity theory, Schopenhauer reformulates it as follows: we laugh, he says, when we suddenly perceive "the incongruity of sensuous and abstract knowledge." Sensuous knowledge is the data we receive from the senses; it comes to us directly and needs no verification (Seeing is believing). Abstract knowledge, on the other hand, is the cluster of conceptions under which we classify the various objects and events that we encounter in our experience. Since the process of classifying is bound to group some things together that differ with respect to characteristics other than the one or more on which the classification is based, incongruity inevitably results on this secondary level, and sometimes even on the first one. When we perceive these incongruities, we find it amusing to see "this strict, untiring, troublesome governess, the reason, for once convicted of insufficiency."

In volume 2 of *The World As Will and Idea* Schopenhauer cites the exploits of Don Quixote as examples of this process, "for [Don Quixote] subsumes the realities he encounters under conceptions drawn from the romances of chivalry, from which they are very different." The main difficulty here, if we try to apply this explanation to the work as a whole, is that in everything other than chivalry Don Quixote is represented as being perfectly reasonable and intelligent. If, as Schopenhauer argues, the ridiculous is purely an intellectual matter, why does "the ingenious gentleman" consistently fail, in the face of so many humiliating reverses, to revise his abstract knowledge to correspond more satisfactorily with the realities he encounters? Clearly, something is at stake in the thousand pages of *Don Quixote* besides two kinds of knowledge, and Schopenhauer gives no hint as to what that might be.

Schopenhauer offers a more technical explanation of the ludicrous as traceable to a syllogism "with an undisputed *major* and an unexpected *minor*, which to a certain extent is only sophistically valid, in consequence of which connection the conclusion partakes of the quality of the ludicrous." This analysis is beautifully illustrated in one of Sholom Aleichem's stories, in which a man from the author's hometown in Russia pays a visit to Baron Rothschild in Paris, offering him the secret of eternal life in exchange for three hundred rubles. The baron willingly pays the money, and his visitor explains that in order to live forever he need only move to the little town from which the visitor had come, because the baron is a rich man and "since Kasrilevka has been a town, no rich man has ever died there."

But Schopenhauer's explanation covers more than brief anecdotes; it applies to the main structure of at least some comic works. For instance, Molière's play *The Misanthrope* may be analyzed in this fashion. The major premise is that all people who are insincere are people that Alceste rejects. The somewhat unexpected minor premise, which the play gradually establishes, is that all people in the society represented by the play are more or less insincere. And the inescapable conclusion is that all people in the society represented by the play are people that Alceste rejects. "Betrayed and wronged in everything." Alceste resolves to "flee this bitter world where vice is king." From the standpoint of comedy, which is incurably social and which shows a marked preference for endings that involve marriage and reconciliation, the ending of *The Misanthrope* is patently absurd; but it is a perfectly logical conclusion drawn from the premises set forth in the play.

The Misanthrope is a sophisticated variation on a pattern which, in its more traditional form, is both comic and funny. Ordinarily, the strained expectation created by the eccentric behavior of a "humorous" character collapses at or near the end of the story when he abandons that behavior in order to marry the girl he loves. Audience familiarity with such a pattern has, by the time of Molière, created a new expectation—namely, that the hero's vanity will collapse into nothing (or at least something negligible) and that he will marry the girl not in order to reform her but in order to love her. It is precisely this new expectation which collapses into nothing at the end of *The Misanthrope,* and it is no less comic than the more familiar pattern; but because it is no longer wish-fulfilling from the standpoint of the factual self, it becomes disconcerting rather than funny or even amusing.

Thus a second distinction between the comic and the funny emerges when we consider a plot whose outcome is governed not by the requirements of the comic character's factual self (the fulfillment of personal desires) but the "logic" which underlies the invented self. Logic of the sort that Schopenhauer describes is, after all, the structuring principle of the invented self. The comic character's prepared face is created consciously or unconsciously in order to achieve certain ends, and these ends are analogous to the conclusion of a syllogism. That conclusion "partakes of the quality of the ludicrous" when it also turns out quite reasonably to be the "collapse of a strained expectation into nothing." By itself, irony (in the form of reversed expectations) may be either comic or tragic; and the distinction between comic and tragic irony will depend on whether the end result may be appropriately described as a collapse into nothing and, to a lesser extent, on whether the final outcome involves confirming or shattering the invented self. Oedipus had hoped to discover the identity of Laius's murderer; he does so, and since he himself turns out to be the murderer, he must abandon his earlier conception of himself. Alceste had hoped to win the respect and admiration of his fellows by his virtuous pronouncements and behavior; instead, they understandably reject him, and he interprets this rejection as a confirmation of his invented superiority.

What happens to the factual self enters in, though not consistently and not in the fashion that one might suppose—tragic Oedipus survives his ordeal; comic Don Quixote does not, nor does Falstaff long survive his rejection by the transformed Hal. Tragic characters, like their comic counterparts, are divided against themselves. The fundamental difference is that the invented self of the tragic character is not eccentric or "humorous"; on the contrary, it has a high degree of social acceptance. Hence the tragic convention of the hero as king or prince. Such figures are fully licensed to think of themselves as superior to their fellow humans without incurring personal ridicule. With the dissolution of the invented self, tragic characters come into their own, as it were, while comic characters simply come apart at the seams. Comic characters find it very difficult to tolerate such a coming apart; they either die decently like Falstaff or Don Quixote or steal away into the shadows like Tartuffe. Only a consummate prig like Alceste or a hopeless Puritan like Malvolio stomps off convinced of his own righteousness.

A third distinction between the comic and the funny may be said to rest upon the emphasis that both Kant and Schopenhauer (as well as Hobbes) place on the word *sudden*. Situations and courses of action that involve radical incongruity, either between expectations and achievements or between reason and logic on the one hand and ordinary human behavior on the other, will be comic because their structure resembles that of many laughable anecdotes and events. They will not be funny, however, if they reveal themselves gradually rather than suddenly. It is partly for this reason that Falstaff's assertion that he was "a coward on instinct" is much funnier than all of the action and maneuvering that lead up to it. What suddenly collapses when Falstaff speaks his great line is the strained expectation that the fat knight will at last be exposed as nothing more than a liar and coward. The incongruity between Falstaff's invented self and his factual self is present from the beginning; but the suddenness with which he combines them in a single feat of verbal dexterity is missing until that moment. In *The Misanthrope* such a moment never arrives—the hero persists in keeping the incongruous elements apart by his refusal to behave as we would expect him to do.

Among other shrewd observations on the subject of the ludicrous, Schopenhauer makes at least two more remarks that should be noted. He classified pedantry as a form of folly and says that "the pedant, with his general maxims, almost always misses the mark in life, shows himself to be foolish, awkward, useless." Besides the obvious relevance of this remark to Alceste, in *The Misanthrope*, we should notice its bearing on comic characters in general and their irrepressible tendency to moralize. Polonius, though he operates within the framework of a tragedy, is a splendid comic character; and it is chiefly his moralizing that creates the impression we have of him. Hamlet's attitude is of course biased, but his judgment that Polonius "was in life a foolish prating knave" has an element of truth in it. Don Quixote's assertion that all affectation is bad springs from the same kind of pedantry; and Parson Adams is nothing if not a pedant. But it is hardly sufficient to say that there is a bit of the pedant in almost every comic character—the truth of the matter goes much deeper than that. Moralizing, or the coining of what Schopenhauer calls "general maxims," is simply the verbal form of the process by which the invented self defines and expresses itself.

Since moralizing consists mainly of classifying things as "good" or "bad," it is not difficult to see this process as one that leads almost inevitably to what Schopenhauer calls the incongruity of sensuous and abstract knowledge, and hence to the ridiculous and the laughable. The sensuous knowledge is our perception of human actions and attitudes (which we usually see more clearly in others than we do in ourselves), and the abstract knowledge is the group of conceptions under which we subsume those actions and attitudes. More than almost any other mental activity, moralizing leads toward incongruity for several reasons, not least of which is the fact that it usually takes the form of universal statements, such as "all affectation is bad." Obviously, universal statements gather so many things under a single heading that there is almost bound to be incongruity among the things brought together under that heading. In addition, our lack of self-knowledge usually enables us to conceal from ourselves that our own behavior manifests the things that we classify as "bad" and that it fails to reflect what we classify as "good," all of which colors our "general maxims" with comic irony. Moreover, we are for the most part powerless to change, either in ourselves or in others, the things we call bad, with the result that the moralizing process further augments our lack of self-knowledge by making us confident that having classified certain things as bad we have adequately disposed of them.

Thomas Hobbes indicates in *Leviathan* that "whatsoever is the object of any man's appetite or desire, that it is which he for his part calleth *good:* and the object of his hate and aversion, *evil.*" But the process is more complicated than Hobbes will allow, since we resort to it less often to identify straightforwardly what we desire or hate than to justify ourselves and to conceal our faults. To engage in such justification and concealment consciously is to practice hypocrisy. As Colonel Korn suggests in *Catch-22,* "You know, that might be the answer—to act boastfully about something we ought to be ashamed of. That's a trick that never seems to fail." To do so *unconsciously* is to embrace vanity enthusiastically. Molière's Alceste, thinking more highly of himself than of anyone else, traces "all the vices of these days" to the flattery of those who, even when they see it, cannot distinguish true merit—as embodied in himself, of course. But we find this kind of self-justification much funnier when it is more transparent, as it is when Falstaff asserts that purse-taking is his vocation and " 'tis no sin for a man to labor in his vocation." The process is essentially the same in all three cases (differing only in the degree of consciousness with which it is practiced); and the pedant with his general maxims is simply a caricature of the basic comic character, who strives constantly and sometimes successfully to justify and preserve an invented self against the onslaughts of reality.

Schopenhauer's second observation that we should notice has to do with the relationship between comedy and the human will. After a discussion of tragedy he makes the following statement: "If we now have found the tendency and ultimate intention of tragedy to be a turning to resignation, to the denial of the will to live, we shall easily recognize in its opposite, comedy, the incitement to the continued assertion of the will." It is by an effort of the will that the facts are finally made to fit the dream when that does happen in comedy; and it is for this reason that plot manipulation and coincidence figure so prominently in comic works. Indeed, comic structure depends upon the activity of a benevolent manipulator—either the author performs this function offstage (as in *The Comedy of Errors*), or one of the characters may do so in "realistic" fashion (as Rosalind does in *As You Like It*), or the author may delegate this manipulative role temporarily by investing one of the characters with "magical" powers (as with Prospero in *The Tempest*). In order for the final effect to be comic, however, the manipulator must be benevolent in the traditional sense. If not, the author must intervene, as Molière does at the end of *Tartuffe*, excercising a kind of veto on the ridiculous but threatening machinations of the main character.

This "continued assertion of the will" (frequently disguised as "fortune") is the comic counterpart of tragic fate. The word *fate* designates those things in tragedy over which protagonists have no control, whose onslaught they are finally unable to withstand. But comic characters, through the exertion of their own (or the author's) will are able to withstand or perhaps to avoid those onslaughts. Consequently, comic characters often create the impression that, if one is sufficiently tenacious, one can "beat the game" or at least maintain an invented self in successive encounters with reality, provided always that they are more or less benevolent or well intentioned. In naive comedy, the will is represented as being able to alter the facts so that they actually fit the dream. In cynical comedy, the will has free rein in ordering the dream, and the facts hardly matter. In mature, sophisticated comedy, the will is able to transform the facts (though not necessarily to alter them) so that they become acceptable to one who participates in the vision that reconciles facts and dreams. In tragedy, the price of this reconciling vision is immense human suffering; in comedy, the price is only the effort necessary to a continued assertion of the will. In its highest form (as, for instance, in the best of the Shakespeare comedies) this willpower expresses itself as the activity of the enabling imagination, culminating in Prospero's "magic."

Schopenhauer is able to account for a good deal of what happens in comedy with his formulation of the incongruity theory; but he sees the moralizing tendency as simply one form of folly (pedantry), and he makes no connection between incongruity itself and the "incitement to the continued assertion of the will" which he finds in comedy generally. An alternative view is provided by Hobbes, some of whose remarks in *Leviathan* have become the basis for what is usually called the moral or superiority theory of laughter. According to Hobbes, laughter is a kind of "sudden glory," and the glory is clearly a self-glory, a sudden inflation of the ego caused by our perception of other people's failures or our own unexpected achievements. In actual experience we tend to encounter far more examples of other people's failures than of our own unexpected successes, with the result that Hobbes accounts primarily for derisive laughter, or laughter at other people's expense. Such laughter inevitably involves a kind of degradation, and Hobbes is led to conclude that laughter is unworthy of the philosopher.

What Hobbes says about laughter in *Leviathan* would seem to be a rather narrow foundation for a full-fledged laughter theory; but it has the enormous advantage of accounting satisfactorily for an element of literary comedy that the incongruity theory seems not to explain at all. We posed the question earlier in connection with *Don Quixote*—why does the mournful knight, after so many humiliating encounters with reality, refuse to modify his abstract knowledge so that it corresponds more closely with the realities he encounters? And since he does refuse, how is it that we do not lose interest in this apparently endless series of foolish exploits? Hobbes provides the basis for an answer: Don Quixote cannot change his view of the world without surrendering his conception of himself as morally superior to all of those people with whom he comes into contact. This moral superiority is the only thing that qualifies him to be a righter of wrongs and injustices; he could hardly play the role he does if he did not regard himself as more righteous and more just than those who commit the wrongs and injustices he finds everywhere he turns. He is sober and mournful precisely because his conviction of superiority is so constant and unshakable; that is to say, he is never surprised to discover that other people are inferior to him, and consequently he never experiences a "sudden glory" in his observation of anyone else.

But we the readers, who observe Don Quixote from a safe distance, are less confident of our own superiority, less impervious to humiliation than he is, with the result that each catastrophe he undergoes furnishes new proof of our superiority *to him*; and consequently each new disaster becomes the occasion for our experiencing a kind of "sudden glory" in relation to this poor fellow whose vision is so much less penetrating than ours. Intuitively we recognize that he cannot surrender his claim to superiority any more than we can, and we therefore identify with him at least partially. But the part of us which remains aloof watches the blows that rain down on him, and our seeing this evidence of his failure inflates our egos—a process of which we never tire. This may not be a flattering commentary on our interest in comedy, but we should bear in mind that we use the words *ridicule* and *ridiculous* as a matter of course in connection with comedy, and *derision* is very close to *ridicule*. In this way, the superiority theory provides a far more cogent explanation of Don Quixote's ability to hold our attention through countless misfortunes than does anything that the incongruity theory states or even implies.

It also seems clear that Don Quixote's claim to moral superiority can only be sustained by a continued assertion of the will. And just as Don Quixote's conviction of his own superiority is more constant than ours, so his will is proportionately stronger and more inflexible. It finally collapses, of course; but the collapse is hardly sudden. The ending of *Don Quixote* may be accurately described as comic since it involves the "transformation of a strained expectation into nothing," though it is certainly not funny because (among other things) the element of suddenness is missing and because it is sad in terms of ordinary experience. In some respects this ending is similar to that of *The Misanthrope*, which comes about not because Alceste's will collapses, but because the final assertion of that will actually removes him from the society represented by the play; and if the play were to go on, it would have to do so without him.

The incongruity and superiority theories of laughter, which are usually regarded as alternative explanations, both seem essential to the understanding of comic character as revealed in the course of a literary work. Schopenhauer's analysis calls attention to the intellectual side of the comic character's situation; and Hobbes's view furnishes insight into his motives and our relation to him. The conception of the invented self unifies the two and incorporates some features of comedy that are not satisfactorily explained by either Schopenhauer or Hobbes. This view regards the comic character as projecting upon the world an invented self that results from the character's own conscious or unconscious affectation, that defines and expresses itself verbally through rationalizing and moralizing statements, and that sustains itself only by a considerable effort of the will. The invented self stands always in opposition to an existential or factual self which, for reasons basic to the human condition, its possessor finds unacceptable or unsatisfactory as a public personality.

Hobbes acknowledges a split between "self" and "other" when he distinguishes between other people's failures and our own unexpected successes as two sources of the personal gratification (sudden glory) that he associates with laughter. He apparently assumes that each personality is unified and therefore identifies itself wholly with any particular success or failure. But in fact such identification is often ambivalent and variable. If it were not, we would *always* be pleased by other people's failures; and this is not consistently true in human experience. The split between invented self and factual self is at least as important to comedy as that between Hobbes's self and other. It is for this reason that the most gratifying of all comic situations comes about when the comic character is able to convert a failure by the factual self into a triumph for the invented self, as Falstaff does when he accounts for his behavior at Gadshill by saying, "I was now a coward on instinct." He does so by substituting a characteristic associated with his invented self (deference to the true prince) for one rooted in his factual self (uncontrollable fear) as the deepest motive for his action.

Falstaff's achievement in this case is only verbal; the comic effect is even richer when the character's ability to transform failure into success is reflected in the movement of the plot. Tartuffe engineers such a triumph when, denounced as a lecher by Orgon's son, he uses the occasion to ingratiate himself even further with Orgon, who forthwith adopts him as son and heir. Molière's impostor seizes the opportunity to indulge in an orgy of self-deprecation, an exercise that his patron associates with sainthood, and thereby heightens the latter's esteem for him. The richness of the comic situation depends here upon the ambivalence of our attitude toward the "hero"—at one and the same time we despise his affectation of holiness ("all affectation is bad") and yet we admire his apparently unlimited resourcefulness (such cleverness is surely admirable, or "good"). We experience a kind of sudden glory in contemplating both the failure of the factual Tartuffe to seduce a virtuous wife and the nearly simultaneous success of the invented Tartuffe in gulling her husband.

This analysis of comic character provides insight into aspects of comedy other than characterization. A great many comedies incorporate some form of utopia, though the function of such a utopia may vary widely from one comic work to another. It may be a vehicle for satire as in Aristophanes' Cloudcuckooland; it may represent a serious proposal as in Rabelais's Abbey of Theleme; it may serve as a place (or a means) for the transformation of attitudes as in Shakespeare's Forest of Arden; or it may simply stand for an unattainable ideal as in Voltaire's Eldorado. It may be described in considerable detail as it is in Rabelais; or it may be only vaguely glimpsed as it is in Molière's *Misanthrope*—a desert place where "one may be free to live as honour bids." But in any case the utopia stands in approximately the same relation to contemporary society as does the invented self to the factual self. The contrast between the two societies, however, is probably less stark than that between the two selves for the simple reason that any functioning society is to a large extent already the creation or invention of the people who live in it, reflecting their ideals and aspirations. The factual self on the other hand is a rather primitive thing which embodies little more than a continuing need for food, drink, clothing, shelter, and sex.

Another feature of comedy that the conception of the invented self helps to illuminate is snobbery as manifested in Restoration comedy or Oscar Wilde. Snobbery is simply a specialized form of moralism—whereas the moralist deals in abstractions (good and evil, right and wrong), the snob deals in particular persons and things ("these are fashionable; those are not"). The mental process is the same in each case—it consists of dividing everyone and everything into two categories, one of which is acceptable and the other of which is not. The criterion in both cases is the categorizers' idealized conceptions of themselves, since moralists certainly conceive of themselves as embodying the good (Molière's Alceste) and snobs are nothing if not fashionable (Wilde's Algernon). Because the division is so basic, incongruity will abound; and the process will lead to unlimited examples of the ridiculous regardless of whether it is conducted consciously (by the hypocrite or snob) or unconsciously (by the vain person or moralist).

These observations do not mean, however, that comic writers are necessarily either moralists or snobs. They may or may not be. Fielding was surely a moralist in the best sense of the word, though Shakespeare was probably not. One often senses while reading Fielding that characters are being judged at least implicitly by the author and found wanting. In Shakespeare one has this feeling less frequently; even the villains have a magnetism that prompts us to something other than judgment—fascination or at least interest. When a comic character in Shakespeare speaks in a fashion that seems consistent with the meaning of the play as a whole, the tone is antimoralistic rather than moralistic. That is, the speaker calls to account those who would judge harshly, urging them to consider their own frailties before condemning the same faults in others.

At bottom literary comedy rests upon a paradox that no human being can either solve or avoid: *in ridiculing we become ridiculous*. The inescapability of this fact is probably what caused Thomas Hobbes to conclude that laughter was unworthy of a philosopher. But the best literary comedies acknowledge the paradox freely, and such acknowledgment is what redeems them from cruelty and cynicism. One of the problems presented to Sancho Panza as governor will serve to illustrate both the paradox and the genuinely comic attitude toward it. A foreigner arrives in Sancho's domain and tells him that over a particular river was a bridge, and at the end of the bridge stood a gallows where four judges sat to enforce a law decreed by their lord. The law was this: "Anyone who crosses this river shall first take oath as to whither he is bound and why. If he swears to the truth, he shall be permitted to pass; but if he tells a falsehood, he shall die without hope of pardon on the gallows that has been set up there." All went well for some time; many came along who told the truth and were allowed to pass. Then one day a certain man appeared who "swore and affirmed that his destination was to die upon the gallows which they had erected and that he had no other purpose in view."

Predictably, the judges were perplexed. They had only two categories at their disposal; and here was a case which fit neither and both. The invented self proposes a meaningful destiny and undertakes to fulfill it; the factual self knows deep down that its destiny is simply to die. Judgment is based upon our separateness from the invented self of another person; but mercy (or "indulgence") springs from what we have in common with the other person's factual self. When someone else presents his deepest factual self to us, our judgment is confounded. At any rate, the four judges realized that if they allowed the man to pass, he would have perjured himself and should be put to death. And if they hanged him, then he would have spoken the truth and should be allowed to pass. After reviewing the facts of the case several times, Sancho makes the following "hard-line" comic decision: "That part of the man that swore to the truth should be permitted to pass and that part of him that lied should be hanged, and thus the letter of the law will be carried out."

The foreigner replies that it is impossible to divide the man in this fashion without killing him, and in such a case "the law would in no wise be fulfilled." At this point Sancho is compelled to abandon his hard-line position and to suggest that "since there is as much reason for acquitting as for condemning him, they ought to let him go free, as it is always more praiseworthy to do good than to do harm." He acknowledges that in offering this decision he is only recalling "one of the many pieces of advice which my master Don Quixote gave me the night before I came here to be governor of this island." He sums up the situation by saying, "When justice was in doubt, he said, I was to lean to the side of mercy; and I thank God that I happened to recollect it just now, for it fits this case as if made for it." Appropriately, the episode is concluded when the order is given that "my Lord Governor be served a meal that is very much to his taste." Sancho knows intuitively that when the needs of the factual self are well supplied, the invented self (Sancho as governor) will prosper; and he issues this final command: "See to it that I eat, and then let it rain cases and problems and I'll make quick work of them."

The relationship between the invented self and the factual self is extremely intricate. The present analysis tends to suggest that they are separate and distinct, when in fact they are not. They cannot be isolated from each other any more than could the two parts of the man who swore that his destiny was to be hanged upon the gallows at the end of the bridge. They are, in a sense, like the poles of a magnet—opposite to each other but inseparable, creating a field of force that is invisible but easily demonstrable. The invented self is that part of the human personality which is subject to affectation but which, at the same time, is so lacking in perspective that it may confidently assert that "all affectation is bad." The only thing which limits its inconsistencies and extravagances is the factual self, the animal side of human nature which makes it necessary for us—in Don Quixote's restrained language—to do that which nobody else can do for us. This is why there is so much emphasis upon the physical element in comedy; for if the activity of the invented self were completely unchecked, it would lead not to comedy or to tragedy, but only to cynicism and tyranny. Even the benevolent Prospero must surrender his magical power in order to return to human society, apart from which comedy has no interest or meaning.

NOTES

Chapter 1. Introduction

1. Ralph Berry asserts that "the difficulties of synthesizing some 15 to 16 comedies into a single comic structure are very great" and that the various comedies "belong, in effect, to separate species." Berry, *Shakespeare's Comedies: Explorations in Form* (Princeton: Princeton University Press, 1972), 3. More recently Kenneth Muir has said flatly, "There is no such thing as Shakespearian Comedy; there are only Shakespearian comedies." Muir, *Shakespeare's Comic Sequence* (Liverpool: Liverpool University Press, 1979), 1.

2. C. L. Barber, *Shakespeare's Festive Comedy* (Princeton: Princeton University Press, 1959), and Robert G. Hunter, *Shakespeare and the Comedy of Forgiveness* (New York: Columbia University Press, 1965).

3. Hunter, *Shakespeare and the Comedy of Forgiveness*, 8.

4. Alfred Harbage, ed., *William Shakespeare: The Complete Works* (Baltimore: Penguin Books, 1969), 54.

5. Kenneth Muir, ed., *Shakespeare: The Comedies* (Englewood Cliffs, N.J.: Prentice-Hall, 1965), 2.

6. Ludwig Wittgenstein, *Philosophical Investigations*, trans. G. E. M. Anscombe (Oxford: Basil Blackwell, 1963), 32e.

7. Aristotle, *Poetics*, trans. Ingram Bywater, in *The Basic Works of Aristotle*, ed. Richard McKeon (New York: Random House, 1941), 1469. Unless otherwise indicated, all Aristotle quotations are from this edition, referred to hereafter simply as Aristotle.

8. Q. *Horatius Flaccus, His Art of Poetry Englished by Ben Jonson* (London, 1640). A facsimile is reprinted in the English Experience Series, no. 670 (Amsterdam: Walter J. Johnson, 1974), 8.

9. Horace, *Ars poetica*, trans. Alexander Falconer Murison, in *Latin Literature in Translation*, ed. Kevin Guinagh and Alfred P. Dorjahn (New York: Longmans, 1942), 492.

10. Marvin Herrick, *Comic Theory in the Sixteenth Century* (Urbana: University of Illinois Press, 1964), 145.

11. *Shr.* I.i.31–33. Harbage, ed., *William Shakespeare*, 87. All Shakespeare quotations are from this edition, referred to hereafter as the *Pelican Shakespeare*.

12. Hardin Craig and David Bevington, eds., *The Complete Works of Shakespeare*, rev. ed. (Glenview, Ill.: Scott, Foresman, 1973), 160n.

13. James O. Halliwell, ed., *The Works of William Shakespeare* (London, 1856; facsimile rpt., New York: AMS Press, 1970), 6: 351.

14. J. A. K. Thomson, *Shakespeare and the Classics* (London: George Allen and Unwin, 1952), 42. Thomson lists various classical references in the narrative poems and says that they are all "commonplaces of Renaissance poetry, and all, as it happens, to be found in the *Metamorphoses*, whence comes nine-tenths of Shakespeare's classical mythology."

15. Aristotle, 1463–65.
16. Aristotle, 1465–66. Bywater uses the words *discovery* and *peripety*.
17. In his introduction to *Love's Labor's Lost* in the *Pelican Shakespeare*, Alfred Harbage mentions a 1631 printing of the play in quarto form and says that "for centuries thereafter critics considered it not only Shakespeare's first but his worst play, and actors preferred to ignore it" (177).
18. I confess that I am unable to explain why Shakespeare should have returned, in just one play written near the middle of his career, to a twin-plot and to the satiric mode. That he did so, however, is plain from even a cursory examination of *Twelfth Night*. Whatever the reasons may have been, they were perhaps similar to those which induced him to return to the farcical vein with *The Merry Wives of Windsor* at about the same time.
19. Barber, *Shakespeare's Festive Comedy*, 135.
20. Wittgenstein, *Philosophical Investigations*, esp. 193e ff.
21. Marcus B. Hester, "Metaphor and Aspect Seeing," *Journal of Aesthetics and Art Criticism* 25, no. 2 (1966): 205–12, and Virgil C. Aldrich, "Visual Metaphor," *The Journal of Aesthetic Education* 2, no. 1 (1968): 73–86. See also Marcus B. Hester, *The Meaning of Poetic Metaphor* (The Hague: Mouton, 1967), esp. 169–92.
22. Wittgenstein, *Philosophical Investigations*, 213e.
23. Larry Champion, *The Evolution of Shakespeare's Comedy* (Cambridge: Harvard University Press, 1970), 40; M. A. Shaaber, introduction to *Henry IV, Part 1, Pelican Shakespeare*, 668; Brents Stirling, introduction to *The Merchant of Venice, Pelican Shakespeare*, 212, as a paraphrase of an objection modern readers often make to the play's denouement.
24. Shaaber, introduction to *Henry IV, Part 1, Pelican Shakespeare*, 668.
25. Aristotle, 1467.
26. I wholeheartedly agree with Leo Salingar, who takes Frye to task for assuming that Shakespeare makes use of wish fulfillment simply for its own sake. According to Salingar, "the grip of convention can be strong. No doubt, in comedy much of its strength comes from wish fulfilment, as Northrop Frye has argued. But to hold, as Frye appears to do, that Shakespeare's romantic comedies are composed of nothing more nor less than wish fulfilment is surely to reduce them all to a flat level of sentimentality; plays which were transparently wish fulfilment might please many, but not long. Something else is needed, within the sphere of convention itself, if only to make the convention portable. . . . Even for convention, he needs a substratum of belief. And Shakespeare's comic and romantic improbabilities do imply a belief, a general attitude towards the world." Salingar, *Shakespeare and the Traditions of Comedy* (Cambridge: Cambridge University Press, 1974), 21–22.
27. Northrop Frye, "The Argument of Comedy," rpt. in *Theories of Comedy*, ed. Paul Lauter (Garden City, N.Y.: Anchor-Doubleday, 1964), 452. The essay first appeared, of course, in *English Institute Essays, 1948*.
28. Ibid., 460. Likewise reprinted in Lauter, ed., *Theories of Comedy*, is an excerpt based on the Jowett translation of Plato, *Philebus* (5–8).
29. Three book-length studies deal with transformation in Shakespearean comedy: Harry E. Curtis, Jr., "The Parted Vision: Metamorphosis as the Central Rite of Shakespearean Comedy," Ph.D. diss., Pennsylvania State University, 1976; Ruth Nevo, *Comic Transformations in Shakespeare* (New York: Methuen, 1980); and Wil-

liam C. Carroll, *The Metamorphoses of Shakespearean Comedy* (Princeton: Princeton University Press, 1985). My own emphasis upon metaphor is different from Curtis's upon metamorphosis as "a basic dramatic device that is analogous in some respects to the peripety or reversal of fortune that the protagonists in a comedy must undergo to achieve success at play's end" (vi). My emphasis upon metaphor is likewise different from Nevo's conception of Shakespearean comic form as "the function of two inconstant variables: the Donatan formula for comic plots . . . and the battle of the sexes" (1). Finally, because Carroll focuses "more on the fact of metamorphosis than on the genre to which it may be assigned" (39), he is less concerned than I am to discover and to trace family resemblances among the comedies as verbal structures.

Chapter 2. Metamorphosis and Other Transformations

1. *The Oxford Classical Dictionary*, 2d ed., S. V. "metamorphosis."
2. *Ovid's Metamorphoses: The Garth Translation into English Verse* (New York: Heritage Press, 1961), 3. Referred to hereafter as *Garth's Ovid*.
3. Homer, *The Iliad*, trans. Richmond Lattimore (Chicago: University of Chicago Press, 1951), 84–85.
4. *Paradise Lost* 1.17–22. Merritt Y. Hughes, ed., *John Milton: Complete Poems and Major Prose* (New York: Odyssey Press, 1957), 212.
5. Gilbert Highet, *The Classical Tradition* (Oxford: Oxford University Press, 1949), 205.
6. G. Karl Galinsky, *Ovid's "Metamorphoses": An Introduction to the Basic Aspects* (Berkeley: University of California Press, 1975), 45.
7. *Garth's Ovid*, 24.
8. Galinsky, *Ovid's "Metamorphoses,"* 48.
9. L. P. Wilkinson, *Ovid Recalled* (Cambridge: Cambridge University Press, 1955), 192; John M. Fyler, *Chaucer and Ovid* (New Haven: Yale University Press, 1979), 4.
10. F. N. Robinson, ed., *The Works of Geoffrey Chaucer*, 2d ed. (Boston: Houghton Mifflin, 1957), 200. All Chaucer quotations are from this edition.
11. *Garth's Ovid*, 82.
12. Wilkinson, *Ovid Recalled*, 191.
13. Ibid., 191–92.
14. Ibid., 161.
15. Galinsky, *Ovid's "Metamorphoses,"* 48–49.
16. For a recent application of the Echo motif to literary theory, see Jonathan Goldberg, *Voice Terminal Echo* (New York: Methuen, 1986). Chapter 4 deals primarily with *The Two Gentlemen of Verona* and, incidentally, with *Hamlet*.
17. Peter G. Phialas, *Shakespeare's Romantic Comedies* (Chapel Hill: University of North Carolina Press, 1966), xiv.
18. See Susanne Howe, *Wilhelm Meister and his English Kinsmen: Apprentices to Life* (New York: Columbia University Press, 1930), and G. B. Tennyson, "The Bildungsroman in Nineteenth-Century English Literature," *University of Southern California Studies in Comparative Literature* 1 (1968): 135–46.
19. Lauter, ed., *Theories of Comedy*, 5–8.
20. Champion, *Evolution of Shakespeare's Comedy*, 39–40.

Chapter 3. Character-Change as Time-Lapse Metaphor

1. See Mark Johnson, ed., *Philosophical Perspectives on Metaphor* (Minneapolis: University of Minnesota Press, 1981), 3–44.

2. See two review-essays in *Texas Studies in Literature and Language*: Robert Merrill, "The Generic Approach in Recent Criticism of Shakespeare's Comedies and Romances: A Review-Essay," *TSLL* 20 (1978): 474–87, and Wayne A. Rebhorn, "After Frye: A Review-Article on the Interpretation of Shakespearean Comedy and Romance," *TSLL* 21 (1979): 553–82. Rebhorn regards 1957, when both Frye's *Anatomy of Criticism* and John Russell Brown's *Shakespeare and His Comedies* appeared, as the beginning of the critical deluge on the Shakespeare comedies.

3. Johnson, *Philosophical Perspectives on Metaphor*, 4.

4. Alfred Harbage, *William Shakespeare: A Reader's Guide* (New York: Farrar, Straus and Giroux, 1963), 26, 33, 23.

5. Aristotle, 1479, 1464.

6. Quoted in Johnson, *Philosophical Perspectives on Metaphor*, 7. This passage is omitted from the McKeon edition—see p. 1436. For the Greek text, see *The Rhetoric of Aristotle*, with a commentary by E. M. Cope (1877; rpt., New York: Arno Press, 1973), 3: 48.

7. I flatly disagree with Goodman and others who follow Aristotle in claiming that "the difference between simile and metaphor is negligible." Nelson Goodman, *Languages of Art* (Indianapolis: Bobbs-Merrill Co., 1968), 77–78. Consider for instance the play title *The Domestication of the Woman Who Was Like a Shrew*. Shakespeare's title is twice metaphoric—the word *taming* is borrowed from animal training, and the comparison with a shrew does not involve the word *like* or *as*.

8. Max Black reaches the same conclusion in his later essay, "More About Metaphor": "And just as there is no infallible test for resolving ambiguity, so there is none to be expected in discriminating the metaphorical from the literal." *Dialectica* 31, nos. 3–4 (1977): 450.

9. Paul Edwards, ed., *The Encyclopedia of Philosophy* (New York: Macmillan, 1967), 8: 330. Ludwig Wittgenstein, *Tractatus Logico-Philosophicus*, trans. D. F. Pears and B. F. McGuiness (London: Routledge and Kegan Paul, 1961), 37, 39; the German text appears on facing pages throughout the book. *Encyclopedia of Philosophy* 8: 333, 330.

10. According to Mark Johnson, the phrase "twice-true metaphor" was coined by Ted Cohen (*Philosophical Perspectives on Metaphor*, 22).

11. *Encyclopedia of Philosophy* 8: 330.

12. Ibid., 1: 105, 107.

13. See Lisë Pederson, "Shakespeare's *The Taming of the Shrew* vs. *Pygmalion*: Male Chauvinism vs. Women's Lib?" in *Fabian Feminist: George Bernard Shaw and Woman*, ed. Rodelle Weintraub (University Park: Pennsylvania State University Press, 1977), 14–22, and Dorothea Kehler, "Echoes of the Induction in *The Taming of the Shrew*," in *Renaissance Papers, 1986*, ed. Dale B. J. Randall and Joseph A. Porter (Southeastern Renaissance Conference, 1986), 31–42. For a much more sympathetic feminist response to *The Taming of the Shrew*, see Martha Andresen-Thom, "Shrew-taming and other rituals of aggression: Baiting and bonding on stage and in the wild," *Women's Studies* 9, no. 2 (1982): 121–43. According to Andresen-Thom, the last scene of the

play, including Kate's long and problematic final speech, is "a 'triumph ceremony' of successful courtship" (139).

14. For an interesting historical example of progressively literal-metaphoric understanding of a cryptic, supernatural communication, consider the story associated with St. Francis of Assisi's conversion, or vocation: "The summons of Christ to take up the cross and follow him included the specific instruction to 'go and repair my house [the church], which is in total disrepair.' At first Francis interpreted this command in a literal sense, undertaking to repair several church buildings in the vicinity that needed restoring. But gradually it dawned on him that the church to whose rebuilding Christ had called him was not merely this sanctuary or that parish church, but nothing less than the very church of Christ on earth." Jaroslav Pelikan, *Jesus Through the Centuries: His Place in the History of Culture* (New Haven: Yale University Press, 1985), 134.

15. Elizabeth A. Livingstone ed., *The Concise Oxford Dictionary of the Christian Church* (Oxford: Oxford University Press, 1977), S.V. "Incarnation."

16. Consider the Johannine formulation: "And the Word became flesh and dwelt among us, full of grace and truth" (John 1.14, RSV). The KJV makes use of a passive-voice construction, "And the Word was made flesh"; but the transformation is crucial to the meaning in either case. This historical manifestation of the Incarnation, expressed in the past tense ("And the Word *became* flesh"), becomes in turn the basis for its continuing manifestation, expressed in the present tense (The bread and wine *become* the Body and Blood of Christ). Church liturgy reminds the worshiper repeatedly, by means of the word *mystery,* that these sentences are something other than literal statements: "We most heartily thank thee for that thou dost feed us, in these holy mysteries"; "Because in the mystery of the Word made flesh"; "Therefore we proclaim the mystery of faith," and the like. *The Book of Common Prayer* (New York: Oxford University Press, 1979), 339, 346, 363, et passim. The same liturgy also recognizes and emphasizes the subjectivity of this continuing manifestation when it directs the worshiper to pray that God will "bless and sanctify these gifts of bread and wine, that they may be unto us the Body and Blood" (342). The subjectivity is implicit in both the subjunctive form of the verb ("that they may be") and the insertion of the personal pronoun ("unto us").

We should observe too that the doctrine of Transubstantiation involves what might be called an "inverted metamorphosis." With metamorphosis, according to Galinsky, "the physical characteristics . . . are subject to change, but their quintessential substance lives on" (*Ovid's "Metamorphoses,"* 45). Transubstantiation, on the other hand, involves "the conversion of the whole substance of the bread and wine into the whole substance of the Body and Blood of Christ, only the accidents (i.e., the appearance of the bread and wine) remaining" (*Concise Oxford Dictionary of the Christian Church,* 520). In brief, metamorphosis entails changed appearance and preserved substance, whereas transubstantiation involves changed substance and preserved appearance.

17. *Concise Oxford Dictionary of the Christian Church,* S.V. "parables."

18. Compare St. Paul's metaphoric explanation to the church at Corinth: "I fed you with milk, not solid food; for you were not ready for it; and even yet you are not ready, for you are still of the flesh" (1 Cor. 3.2–3).

19. The picture, which appeared in *Puck* in 1915, is by W. E. Hill, and its full title is "My Wife and My Mother-In-Law. They are both in this picture—find them." It is

often reprinted in psychology textbooks. The Jastrow duck-rabbit sketch appears in Wittgenstein, *Philosophical Investigations*, 194e.

20. Shaaber, introduction to *Henry IV, Part 1*, Pelican Shakespeare, 668.

21. One cannot help wondering whether Dr. Johnson ever seriously pondered the fact that the Christian Church, including the Church of England, came into existence with the utterance of a pun: "And I tell you, you are Peter [Rock], and on this rock I will build my church" (Matt. 16.18). See Northrop Frye, *The Great Code: The Bible and Literature* (New York: Harvest-Harcourt Brace, 1982), 53. Dr. Johnson might say, I suppose, that the name Peter is metaphoric and that Christ was exploiting a metaphor rather than making a pun. But in this case, as in many others, it is difficult to know at what point metaphor ends and pun begins.

Chapter 4. Farce and Beyond

1. G. Blakemore Evans, "Chronology and Sources," in *The Riverside Shakespeare* (Boston: Houghton Mifflin, 1974), 50.

2. I do not mean to underestimate the play's dependence on ancient sources, both Christian and classical—especially Plautus's *Menaechmi* and *Amphitruo*. See, for instance, Geoffrey Bullough, ed., *Narrative and Dramatic Sources of Shakespeare* (London: Routledge and Kegan Paul; New York: Columbia University Press, 1957–75), 1: 3–54, and Catherine M. Shaw, "The Conscious Art of *The Comedy of Errors*," in *Shakespearean Comedy*, ed. Maurice Charney (New York: New York Literary Forum, 1980), 17–28. Nevertheless, almost everything in the play depends finally upon the twins' similarity and their concomitant separateness.

3. Northrop Frye, *A Natural Perspective* (New York: Harcourt, Brace and World, 1965), 106; Carroll, *Metamorphoses of Shakespearean Comedy*, 65, 72–73.

4. Champion, *Evolution of Shakespeare's Comedy*, 40.

5. In his introduction to the Oxford edition of *The Taming of the Shrew* (Oxford: Clarendon Press, 1982), H. J. Oliver summarizes the problems and theories in connection with the Induction (34–43), saying among other things that "it has become orthodoxy to claim to find in the Induction the same 'theme' as is to be found in both the Bianca and the Katherine-Petruchio plots of the main play and to take it for granted that identity of theme is a merit and 'justifies' the introduction of Sly" (37).

6. Goldberg, *Voice Terminal Echo*, 68, 71, 69.

7. Homer, *Odyssey*, trans. Richmond Lattimore (New York: Harper-Colophon, 1975), 77; book 4, ll. 454–59.

8. W. H. D. Rouse, Litt.D., ed., *Shakespeare's Ovid: Being Arthur Golding's Translation of the "Metamorphoses"* (Carbondale, Ill.: Southern Illinois University Press, n.d.), 177–78; book 8, ll. 910–23.

9. Berners A. W. Jackson, introduction to *The Two Gentlemen of Verona*, Pelican Shakespeare, 116.

10. Hunter, *Shakespeare and the Comedy of Forgiveness*, 85–87. Hunter treats the matter only briefly in connection with *The Two Gentlemen of Verona*, but he elaborates it in his commentaries on the six comedies of forgiveness.

11. See D. H. Monro, *Argument of Laughter* (Notre Dame, Ind.: University of Notre Dame Press, 1963), 83–90, 147.

Chapter 5. Romantic Comedy

1. Norman Rabkin, *Shakespeare and the Problem of Meaning* (Chicago: University of Chicago Press, 1981), chap. 2.

2. Marjorie Garber, *Dream in Shakespeare: From Metaphor to Metamorphosis* (New Haven: Yale University Press, 1974), 72.

3. Carroll, *Metamorphoses of Shakespearean Comedy*, 152.

4. Ibid., 142. See also David Young, *Something of Great Constancy* (New Haven: Yale University Press, 1966), 157.

5. For unsavory details (inferred by the critic) of Lavinia's rape in *Titus Andonicus*, written at about the same time as *A Midsummer Night's Dream*, see S. Clark Hulse, "Wresting the Alphabet: Oratory and Action in *Titus Andronicus*," *Criticism* 21 (1979): 106–18, and Mary L. Fawcett, "Arms/Words/Tears: Language and the Body in *Titus Andronicus*," *Journal of English Literary History* 50 (1983): 261–77.

6. Evans, "Chronology and Sources," *Riverside Shakespeare*, 51.

7. Phialas, *Shakespeare's Romantic Comedies*, 107.

8. C. T. Onions lists both definitions in *A Shakespeare Glossary*, 2d ed. (Oxford: Clarendon Press, 1953), 44; but he makes no reference to *A Midsummer Night's Dream* under either definition. Compare, however, the lines Bottom speaks (as Pyramus) in the play within the play, "Come, tears, confound, / Out, sword, and wound / The pap of Pyramus" (V.i.288–90), with Lysander's line earlier in the play, "So quick bright things come to confusion" (I.i.149). The two meanings blend in Puck's assertion that "fate o'errules, that, one man holding troth, / A million fail, confounding oath on oath" (III.ii.92–93).

9. Alternative explanations for the disappearance of the mulberry at the end of the Pyramus and Thisbe episode are essentially negative in emphasis, suggesting that the metamorphosis is simply discarded or else that it is deliberately suppressed. According to J. A. K. Thomson, the story "is followed with remarkable fidelity in Peter Quince's production; the lion, the wall, the tomb of Ninus—everything is there except the mulberry tree, which is important only for Ovid" (*Shakespeare and the Classics*, 78). William Carroll ventures somewhat further: "In his most openly Ovidian play, then, Shakespeare halts his equally Ovidian play-within-the-play just before representing a second Ovidian metamorphosis. The point is that that kind of representation will no longer succeed *on the stage*. It pretends to a kind of verisimilitude which Lion and Moonshine have already comically discredited" (*Metamorphoses of Shakespearean Comedy*, 166–67).

10. J. Dennis Huston, *Shakespeare's Comedies of Play* (New York: Columbia University Press, 1981), 94–121; see esp. 95–111.

11. See Walter F. Staton, Jr., "Ovidian Elements in *A Midsummer Night's Dream*," *Huntington Library Quarterly* 26 (1963): 165–78.

12. Hallett Smith, *Elizabethan Poetry* (Cambridge: Harvard University Press, 1952), 93; Carroll, *Metamorphoses of Shakespearean Comedy*, 148.

13. See Carroll, *Metamorphoses of Shakespearean Comedy*, 166, 277 n. 14.

14. Modern editors, following Rowe's emendation, place the comma after the word *in*. But the First Folio and both of the quartos indicate that the comma originally stood *before* the word *in*, which suggests that *in* should function not as an adverb with *come*, but as a preposition with *man* and *lion*. My only point is that

Bottom likewise represents "two noble beasts"—a man and an ass. Unlike Snug, however, he is perfectly comfortable in that double role. Snug is a counterfeit and he knows it; but Bottom is "the real thing," and he never doubts it.

15. Phialas, *Shakespeare's Romantic Comedies*, 111.
16. Young, *Something of Great Constancy*, 161.
17. Alexander Leggatt, *Shakespeare's Comedy of Love* (London: Methuen, 1974), 137.
18. Ibid., 121 n. 13.
19. Onions, *Shakespeare Glossary*.
20. Champion, *Evolution of Shakespeare's Comedy*, 65.
21. Harley Granville-Barker, *Prefaces to Shakespeare*, vol. 1 (Princeton: Princeton University Press, 1952), 335.
22. Lynda Boose, "The Father and the Bride in Shakespeare," *PMLA* 97 (1982): 335–36.
23. Information in this paragraph is taken from the *New Encyclopedia Britannica* (1974), the *Encyclopedia of Philosophy*, and Ernst F. Winter, ed. and trans., *Erasmus-Luther: Discourse on Free Will* (New York: Ungar, 1961). In *Erasmus-Luther*, see esp. v–xi, 3–5 (inc. nn. 1–4), 20 (definition of free will), 44–45 (Luther's Article 36, quoted by Erasmus), and 119–22 (Luther's refutation of Erasmus's definition). The *Britannica* article on Henry VIII is by Geoffrey R. Elton.
24. Champion, *Evolution of Shakespeare's Comedy*, 65.
25. Leggatt, *Shakespeare's Comedy of Love*, 208.
26. Carroll, *Metamorphoses of Shakespearean Comedy*, 127.
27. Robert Meyer, "Chaucer's Tandem Romances: A Generic Approach to the *Wife of Bath's Tale* as Palinode," *Chaucer Review* 18 (1984): 235.

Chapter 6. History as Personal Reformation

1. Rabkin, *Shakespeare and the Problem of Meaning*, 34.
2. Karl P. Wentersdorf, "The Conspiracy of Silence in *Henry V*," *Shakespeare Quarterly* 27 (1976): 265. Wentersdorf lists representatives of both groups, with bibliographical information (266 nn. 3 and 4). Among those who see Henry as "ideal monarch" are J. Dover Wilson, J. H. Walter, G. W. Keeton, and F. P. Wilson. Among those "who believe that Shakespeare presents Henry V and his foreign policy in an unfavorable light" are Mark Van Doren, J. Palmer, R. Battenhouse, and H. M. Richmond.
3. E. H. Gombrich, *Art and Illusion: A Study of the Psychology of Pictorial Representation* (New York: Pantheon Books, 1960), esp. 5–6.
4. Rabkin, *Shakespeare and the Problem of Meaning*, 43–44.
5. Ibid., 34.
6. In *The Drama of Speech Acts: Shakespeare's Lancastrian Tetralogy* (Berkeley: University of California Press, 1979), Joseph A. Porter accounts for "the epic-antiepic tension" in *Henry V* as a result of "the disparity between the audience's and Shakespeare's attitude toward nationalistic militarism" (136, 136n). According to Porter, "the battle of Agincourt for the audience would have been an example of glorious heroism worthy of epic, and their view would have been too strong to be denied directly in the play. But Shakespeare, with his customary skepticism and lack of sympathy for military exploits, goes a long way toward countering and modifying

that view." I would argue, however, that such an assertion is simply another example of the kind of interpretation that would explicate Shakespeare's puns by denying that they *are* puns. In this case the interpreter is claiming in effect that the author knows that the audience will seize upon the obvious (and "wrong") meaning of the word in question, but he in fact "intends" the subtler, more modern meaning of the word. I would say on the contrary that the writer is deliberately exploiting and playing upon two word meanings—or, in this case, two attitudes toward the heroic tradition. He is not "playing down" to the audience or "throwing a sop to the groundlings" while attempting to educate them. He is instead exulting—as he does at every opportunity—in the multiple possibilities contained in word meanings, human attitudes, and human personalities.

7. Rabkin, *Shakespeare and the Problem of Meaning*, 44.

8. Christopher Hibbert, *Agincourt* (New York: Dorset Press, 1978), 121.

9. Mark Van Doren, *Shakespeare* (New York: Henry Holt, 1939), 170.

10. L. J. Potts, *Comedy* (London: Hutchinson's University Library, 1948), 130.

11. Paul A. Jorgensen, "'Redeeming Time' in *Henry IV*," in *Redeeming Shakespeare's Words* (Berkeley: University of California Press, 1962), 59, 68.

12. *The Geneva Bible: A Facsimile of the 1560 Edition*, with an introduction by Lloyd E. Berry (Madison: University of Wisconsin Press, 1969), NT, p. 91r.

13. See Joseph T. Shipley, *The Origins of English Words: A Discursive Dictionary of Indo-European Roots* (Baltimore: Johns Hopkins University Press, 1984), 95–96, 330.

14. Dover Wilson is quite right, I think, in associating Vernon's description of "Young Harry" with Spenser's narration of the Red Cross Knight's fire-baptism and subsequent immersion in the Well of Life (which in turn owes something to Psalm 103.5): "So new this new-borne knight to battell new did rise." As a result, his enemy "the old dragon" is somewhat bewildered: "No wonder if he wondered at the sight, / And doubted whether his late enemy / It were, or other new suppliéd knight" (*The Faerie Queene* 1.11.34.2–9, 35.2–4). Shakespeare's description is less explicit than Spenser's allegory, but the idea of "renewal" or "reform" seems equally clear in the two passages. According to Wilson, "that Shakespeare in penning these lines, turned for inspiration to Spenser's description of the Red Cross Knight rising lusty as an eagle from the Well of Life shows . . . that in evoking this vision he had specially in mind the notion of regeneration." Dover Wilson, *The Fortunes of Falstaff* (Cambridge: Cambridge University Press, 1961), 65.

15. Aristotle, 1469.

16. Barber, *Shakespeare's Festive Comedy*, 198.

17. In an article entitled "Thematic Contraries and the Dramaturgy of *Henry V*," Brownell Salomon says, in a way that echoes or anticipates Joanne Altieri, Ann Barton, and others, "When one considers the important question of genre, then, necessarily a side issue in the present essay, the cumulative structural and stylistic evidence makes it clear that *Henry V* is as much a festive comedy or a heroic romance as a history play." *Shakespeare Quarterly* 31 (1980): 355.

18. Samuel Johnson, ed., *The Plays of William Shakespeare* (London: 1765), 4: 479.

19. J. H. Walter, introduction to the New Arden edition of *King Henry V* (1954; rpt. London: Methuen; Cambridge: Harvard University Press, 1961), xxxi.

20. Lionel Giles, trans., *The Analects of Confucius* (Norwalk, Conn.: Heritage Press, 1970), 8.

21. Somewhat surprisingly, in *The Drama of Speech Acts* Porter deals with Hal's

rejection speech only within the context of the relationship between Falstaff and the Lord Chief Justice (102-10, 120-21). He thus passes up, I think, the opportunity to deal with these twenty-five lines as one of Hal's most important "illocutionary acts."

22. Barber, *Shakespeare's Festive Comedy*, 213-19.

23. Hugh Dickinson, "The Reformation of Prince Hal," *Shakespeare Quarterly* 12 (1961): 43.

24. Barber, *Shakespeare's Festive Comedy*, 217.

25. See Plato's *Philebus*, excerpted in Lauter, ed., *Theories of Comedy*, 5-8. "Those who are both deluded and weak," says Socrates, "unable to avenge themselves when laughed at, may rightly be described as 'ridiculous'; but those who can retaliate might more properly be called 'formidable' and 'hateful.' For ignorance in the strong is hateful and ugly, because mischievous to all around—both in reality and in stage copies. But ignorance in the weak may be reckoned, in truth is, ridiculous" (7).

26. *The Interpreter's Bible* (New York: Abingdon, 1952-57), 2: 984.

27. Ibid., 982.

28. Van Doren, *Shakespeare*, 172.

29. Ibid.

30. Ibid., 171.

31. Ibid., 175.

32. Ibid., 174; E. K. Chambers, *Shakespeare: A Survey* (London: Sidgwick & Jackson, 1925), 143.

33. Van Doren, *Shakespeare*, 174.

Chapter 7. Transformation in Problem Comedy and Romance

1. Hunter, *Shakespeare and the Comedy of Forgiveness*, chap. 4. See also appendix 1, below, for analysis of *Much Ado* in relation to farcical structure.

2. Eileen Z. Cohen, who regards the bed trick as a form of disguise, argues that Shakespeare elevates the bed trick far above its lowly origins in farce: "If the healing and loving are wondrous, then the bed-*trick* is a misnomer and is the bed-*miracle*, instead, just as the King's recovery apparently is." Cohen, "'Virtue is Bold': The Bed-Trick and Characterization in *All's Well That Ends Well* and *Measure for Measure*," *Philological Quarterly* 65 (1986): 176.

3. According to Leonard Barkin, in *The Winter's Tale* "Shakespeare's denouement also involves him in some very high levels of improbability—even for the world of romance.... He piles one extreme improbability on top of another." Barkin, "'Living Sculptures': Ovid, Michelangelo, and *The Winter's Tale*," *Journal of English Literary History* 48 (1981): 640, 641.

4. Frye, "Argument of Comedy," in Lauter, ed., *Theories of Comedy*, 450-51.

5. Anne Barton, introduction to *All's Well That Ends Well*, *Riverside Shakespeare*, 500.

6. Hunter, *Shakespeare and the Comedy of Forgiveness*, 112.

7. Giovanni Boccaccio, *Decameron, Filocolo, Ameto, Fiametta*, ed. Bianchi, Salinari, and Sapegno (Milan: Riccardo Ricciardi, n.d.), 257. (Vol. 8 in the series La Letteratura Italiana: Storia e Testi.) The translation is my own.

8. Lisa Jardine describes the relationship between Helena's special powers and

the play's plot: "The plot of *All's Well That Ends Well* hinges on Helena's specialist knowledge, and on the power that knowledge gives her." Jardine, "Cultural Confusion and Shakespeare's Learned Heroines: 'These are old paradoxes,'" *Shakespeare Quarterly* 38 (1987): 7.

9. Jonas Barish, introduction to *All's Well That Ends Well*, Pelican Shakespeare, 368.

10. See, for instance, Gerard J. Gross, "The Conclusion to *All's Well That Ends Well*," *Studies in English Literature* 23 (1983): 257–76; David Scott Kastan, "*All's Well That Ends Well* and the Limits of Comedy," *Journal of English Literary History* 52 (1985): 575–89; and Maurice Hunt, "*All's Well That Ends Well* and the Triumph of the Word," *Texas Studies in Literature and Language* 30 (1988): 388–411.

11. Kastan, "Limits of Comedy," 580.

12. See appendix 2, below, for a discussion of Schopenhauerian incongruity.

13. Hunt, "Triumph of the Word," 390.

14. Richard A. Levin, "*All's Well That Ends Well* and 'All Seems Well,'" *Shakespeare Studies* 13 (1980): 139.

15. Barton, introduction to *All's Well That Ends Well*, Riverside Shakespeare, 501.

16. If the reference is to Balaam's ass, this would be consistent with other Old Testament tall-tale references in *All's Well*, such as the speech in which Helena refers, in rapid succession, to several such stories (II.i.134–44). According to the *Riverside* editor, in the lines "great floods have flown / From simple sources" (139–40) Shakespeare is "perhaps alluding to Moses' smiting of the rock in Horeb (Exodus 17:1–7)"; and he asserts that "the great'st" by whom "miracles . . . have been denied" is Egyptian Pharaoh. But the playwright could equally well be referring to another version of the same story in Numbers 20.7–11, in which case "the great'st" would be, not Pharaoh, but Moses and Aaron (v. 12). The marginal note to Numbers 20.11 in the Geneva Bible reads, "The punishment, which followed hereof, declared that Moses & Aaron beleued not the Lords promes, as appeareth in vers 12." Within the biblical framework, it is far more significant that Moses and Aaron should fail to believe in the Lord's power to perform miracles than that Pharaoh should do so. The story of Balaam's ass comes only three pages after this example of a "great flood from a simple source"; and the Balaam story seems particularly relevant to Parolles. The marginal note to Numbers 22.32 moralizes the Lord's message to Balaam as follows: "Bothe thy heart is corrupt and thine entreprise wicked."

17. *The Book of Common Prayer, 1559: The Elizabethan Prayer Book*, ed. John E. Booty (Charlottesville: University Press of Virginia, 1976), 291, 292.

18. Barton, introduction to *All's Well That Ends Well*, Riverside Shakespeare, 548.

19. J. H. Walter makes the same point in connection with *Henry V*; but he is attempting to justify the content of almost the entire fifth act on that basis (introduction to the New Arden ed. of *King Henry V*). Here, the point is closely related to the subject matter of the play (the social significance of sex and marriage); and the question of the Duke's marriage, which is only one of four in this case, comes in as "the icing on the cake," rather than as the principal business of the play's final act. In *Shakespeare's Development and the Problem Comedies: Turn and Counter-Turn* (Berkeley: University of California Press, 1981), Richard P. Wheeler takes quite a different view of the marriages, however, including this fourth one: "The proposed marriage of Vincentio to Isabella, the ghostly father and the aspiring nun, is the appropriately barren culmination of the play's moralized comic design" (153).

20. See Alexander Leggatt, "Substitution in *Measure for Measure*," *Shakespeare Quarterly* 39 (1988): 342–59.

21. Russ McDonald, "Poetry and Plot in *The Winter's Tale*," *Shakespeare Quarterly* 36 (1985): 315–29.

22. Stanton B. Garner, Jr., "Time and Presence in *The Winter's Tale*," *Modern Language Quarterly* 46 (1985): 348, 349.

23. Baldwin Maxwell, introduction to *The Winter's Tale*, Pelican Shakespeare, 1334.

24. Ibid.

25. See Barkin, "Living Sculptures," 641.

26. C. G. Jung, *Analytical Psychology: Its Theory and Practice* (New York: Vintage–Random House, 1968), 3–25, esp. 13.

Chapter 8. Conclusion

1. Muir, *Shakespeare's Comic Sequence*, 1.

2. Ibid., 2.

3. Alice Rayner, *Comic Persuasion: Moral Structure in British Comedy From Shakespeare to Stoppard* (Berkeley: University of California Press, 1987), 22.

4. For Schopenhauer's suggestion that the ridiculous is analogous to a syllogism "with an undisputed *major* [premise] and an unexpected *minor*," see appendix 2, below.

5. Conversely, comic resurrection has its secular and farcical side, as we see in *Henry IV* (Falstaff at Shrewsbury) and more recently in Synge's *Playboy of the Western World* (the return of Christy's "Da"). It can even turn a story of multiple murders into a sparkling comedy—in *Kind Hearts and Coronets* (1949), Alec Guinness undergoes repeated reincarnation as various members of the D'Ascoyne family, all of whom serial killer Dennis Price dispatches both because he wants revenge upon the entire family and because each of them stands between him and the title Duke of Chalfont.

6. Nevill Coghill, "The Basis of Shakespearian Comedy: A Study in Medieval Affinities," *Essays and Studies*, n.s., 3 (1950): 9.

7. See Phialas, *Shakespeare's Romantic Comedies*, xiv. Quoted more fully above, in chap. 2.

8. *Encyclopedia of Philosophy* 8: 129.

9. Harbage, *Reader's Guide*, 80.

10. See the opening lines of *1H4* I.ii. In response to Falstaff's question, "Now Hal, what time of day is it, lad?" Hal speaks ten lines of humorous banter but provides no information whatever of the sort requested.

11. Leggatt, *Shakespeare's Comedy of Love*, 208–10.

12. Garner, "Time and Presence," 347.

Appendix 1. Comic Structure

1. L. J. Potts, *Comedy*, 151.

2. Elder Olson, *The Theory of Comedy* (Bloomington: Indiana University Press, 1968), 47.

3. Ibid., 88–89.

4. Ibid., 104, 106.
5. Potts, *Comedy*, 133.
6. *Aristotle's Poetics,* trans. S. H. Butcher, with an introduction by Francis Fergusson (New York: Hill and Wang, 1961), 77.
7. Quoted in Frederic T. Blanchard, *Fielding the Novelist* (New York: Russell and Russell, 1966), 320–21.
8. Walter Kerr, *Tragedy and Comedy* (New York: Simon and Schuster, 1967), 66.
9. Ibid., 69.
10. Martin Turnell, *The Classical Moment* (London: Hamish Hamilton, 1954), 96. I have put into English Turnell's term *tragédie bourgeoise*.
11. Henry Fielding, Author's Preface to *Joseph Andrews* (New York: Modern Library, 1950), xxxvi–xxxvii.
12. *Aristotle's Poetics,* trans. S. H. Butcher, 59.
13. Excerpted in Lauter, ed., *Theories of Comedy,* 7. The corresponding passage in the Jowett translation appears in *The Dialogues of Plato* (London: Oxford University Press, 1931), 4: 623.
14. Molière, *Tartuffe,* trans. Richard Wilbur (New York: Harvest Books, 1963), 162.

INDEX

Actaeon, 17
Addison, Joseph, 21
Aeneid (Virgil), 20, 41
Affectation, 165, 170–72, 176–77, 180–81, 183
Agenor, 61
Aldrich, Virgil C., 9
Aleichem, Sholom, 174
Alexander the Great, 100, 117
Allegory, 62, 193 (n. 14)
Allegorical interpretation, 133, 148
Ambiguity, 62, 68, 104, 130, 133
Andresen-Thom, Martha, 188–89 (n. 13)
Animal characters, 20
Antisocial behavior (in comedy), 13, 40, 167, 169
Apollo, 19, 74–75, 127, 138–39
Apuleius, 76
Aristophanes, 23, 181
Aristotle, 3–7, 13, 25, 27, 32–36, 40, 46–47, 107, 141, 145–46, 157, 161, 166, 171
Artistic economy, 151

Bacchus, 21
Barber, C. L., 1, 9, 31–32, 107, 113–14, 144
Barish, Jonas, 128
Barkin, Leonard, 194 (n. 3)
Barton, Anne, 126, 130, 133
Baucis, 63
Beast fable, 20
"Beauty and the Beast," 127
Bed trick, 80, 124–25, 129, 132, 135, 162, 164, 194 (n. 2)
Berry, Ralph, 185 (n. 1)
Bible, 25, 28–29, 44, 48, 79–80, 82–83, 93, 104–5, 111, 131, 134, 136, 140–41, 148, 195 (n. 16)
Bildungsroman, 25

Black, Max, 32, 188 (n. 8)
Boccaccio, Giovanni, 126–28
Book of Common Prayer, The, 131, 189 (n. 16)
Boose, Lynda, 84
Browne, Sir Thomas, 73
Browning, Robert, 73

Candide (Voltaire), 164
Caricature, 61, 177
Carroll, William C., 56, 72, 75, 92, 186–87 (n. 29), 191 (n. 9)
Catch-22 (Heller), 48, 177
Centaur, 74, 100
Cervantes, Miguel de, 170
Chambers, E. K., 118
Champion, Larry, 30, 83, 89
Change. *See* Character-change, Conversion, Metamorphosis
Chapman, George, 63
Character-change, 16, 26–27, 32–51, 71, 88–89, 91–97, 135, 146
Character consistency (in neoclassical drama), 3, 16, 46–47, 107
Charlton, H. B., 32
Chaucer, Geoffrey, 20, 24, 51, 67, 81, 85, 92–94, 100, 126–28, 148–49
Cherry Orchard, The (Chekhov), 157, 174
Christology, 44
Cinthio (Giovanni Battista Giraldi), 134
Circumcision, 29, 81–83, 85
Coghill, Nevill, 149
Cohen, Eileen Z., 194 (n. 2)
Coleridge, S. T., 157
Comedy of forgiveness, 1, 17, 123, 126
Comic distance, 20–21, 23
Comic form, 13, 130, 157
Confessional writings, 25, 28
Confucius, 112

199

Index

Confusion (vs. ambiguity), 68
Contrast and balance (of characters), 103, 107, 157
Conversion, 10, 26, 28, 79, 81, 83–85, 87, 92–95
Costume, 2; relation to character, 58–59
Curtis, Harry E., Jr., 186–87 (n. 29)

Daphne, 19, 61, 74–75
Darwin, Charles, 47
David, King of Israel, 82, 100–102, 110, 116–17
Definition, 38–40, 56
Devaluation (of persons), 123–24, 135, 139
Dickinson, Hugh, 113
Diction, 16, 34, 46–47, 112
Diphilus, 53
Disguise, 2, 11, 58, 60–61, 90–91, 93, 103, 114, 162
Distortion (comic), 60, 124
Don Quixote (Cervantes), 142, 158, 167, 170–71, 174, 176, 179–80, 182–83
Donne, John, 37–38, 57, 64
Double entendre. *See* Pun
Double vision, 71, 99, 138
Doubling (as comic device), 8–9, 74, 78, 116–17
Dramatic irony, 159
Drant, Thomas, 3
Duck-rabbit picture, 46, 98–99

Echo and Narcissus, 24, 78
Einstein, Albert, 36, 153
Elton, Geoffrey R., 85
Elyot, Sir Thomas, 65
Equivocation, 12, 65, 76, 87, 129, 133. *See also* Pun
Erasmus, Desiderius, 85
Errors. *See* Mistakes
Europa, 61
Exaggeration, 59, 61–62, 82, 115–17, 122, 155

Fantasy, 130
Farce, 11, 16, 40–41, 59, 74, 90, 121–24, 130, 145, 155–57, 160–62, 164, 166, 167–69
Festive comedy, 1, 31, 145
Fielding, Henry, 165–66, 170–72, 182
Fiorentino, Ser Giovanni, 81
First Folio (1623), 1, 4, 101, 108, 124, 136, 144–46, 191 (n. 14)
Folklore, 25, 79
Forgiveness, 16, 28, 52, 66–68, 122–23, 126, 135, 140–42, 160–61, 163–64, 169
Framing device, 52, 58
Francis of Assisi, Saint, 97, 189 (n. 14)
Fränkel, H., 22–23
Freedom of the will, 84–87
Frye, Northrop, 14–15, 26, 31–32, 56, 125–27, 133, 149, 171, 186 (n. 26)
Fyler, John M., 20

Galinsky, G. Carl, 19, 23–24, 189 (n. 16)
Games analogy, 11, 157
Ganymede (mythological figure), 90
Garber, Marjorie, 71
Garner, Stanton B., Jr., 137–38, 153
Gide, André, 23
Gods, 17–18, 20–23, 28. *See also* Apollo, Bacchus, Janus, Juno, Jupiter, Mercury, Pan, Phoebe
Goldberg, Jonathan, 62–63, 187 (n. 16)
Goldberg, Rube, 173
Golding, Arthur, 5, 63, 73–75, 78
Gombrich, E. H., 98
Goodman, Nelson, 188 (n. 7)
Grace, 28, 47, 133, 137
Granville-Barker, Harley, 83–84, 120
Green world (pastoral setting), 68–71, 151
Greene, Robert, 138
Griffon, 74–76, 100. *See also* Hybridization
Guinness, Alec, 196 (n. 5)

Hakluyt: *Voyages*, 42
Happy ending, 2, 13, 27, 31, 47, 95, 103, 132, 136, 141, 146, 156, 159–60, 163–64, 168–69
Harbage, Alfred, 2, 186 (n. 17)

Helen of Troy, 61
Heller, Joseph, 48
Henry VIII, 85
Heraclitus, 19
Herrick, Marvin, 3
Hester, Marcus B., 9
Hibbert, Christopher, 101
Highet, Gilbert, 18, 24
Hill, W. E., 189 (n. 19)
History plays (as a genre), 108–9, 136; history vs. story, 120
Hobbes, Thomas, 14, 67, 152, 176–80, 182
Homer: *Iliad*, 17, 90; *Odyssey*, 63
Horace, 3, 25, 27, 46, 100
Hunt, Maurice, 130
Hunter, Robert G., 1, 31, 67, 123, 126, 136, 144, 161, 190 (n. 10)
Huston, J. Dennis, 75
Hybridization, 74–78, 100, 131, 150
Hypocrisy, 30, 165–66, 170–72, 181

Ideology, 41
Iliad (Homer), 17, 90
Imagery, 28, 32, 43
Imagination, 96, 98, 112, 142, 147, 149, 178
Importance of Being Ernest, The (Wilde), 161
Incarnation, 44, 189 (n. 16)
Incongruity, 130, 133, 141–42, 172–73, 176–78, 181
Incongruity theory (of laughter), 67–68, 130, 141–42, 173–74, 177–80
Interpreter's Bible, The, 116
Intuition, 142
Invented self, 11, 170–83
Io, 18, 61
Iphis and Ianthe, 8, 18
Irony, 12, 30, 59, 61–62, 80, 86–87, 98, 113, 170, 175, 177

Jackson, Berners A. W., 64
Janus, 100
Jardine, Lisa, 194–95 (n. 8)
Jastrow, Joseph, 9, 46, 190 (n. 19)
John, Saint, 44–45, 148, 189 (n. 16)
Johnson, Mark, 33, 36

Johnson, Samuel, 10, 38, 46, 51, 109, 119, 128, 190 (n. 21)
Jonson, Ben, 3, 14, 26, 78, 130, 149
Jorgensen, Paul A., 104
Joseph Andrews (Fielding), 165, 170
Jung, C. G., 142
Juno, 18, 20, 24, 90
Jupiter, 18, 20–21, 24, 61, 90

Kalchas, 17
Kant, Immanuel, 39–40, 68, 152, 173, 176
Kastan, David Scott, 129
Keats, John, 72
Kerr, Walter, 158

La Faye, G., 22
Laughter, 146–47, 169
Laughter theories, 152, 173, 179–80
Laurel and Hardy, 156
Leda, 61
Leggatt, Alexander, 81, 90, 152
Literal statement, 33, 35–41, 49–50, 55, 57, 77, 117, 189 (n. 14)
Loathly Lady story, 61, 126–27, 132, 138, 140, 148
Lodge, Thomas, 90
Love at first sight, 25, 51, 60, 68, 76, 93, 109, 124
Luke, Saint, 29
Luther, Martin, 85
Lyly, John, 76

McDonald, Russ, 137
Manipulator (comic device), 14, 48, 70–71, 86, 95, 97, 102–3, 124, 135, 141, 161–62, 167–69, 178
Marriage, 72–73, 90, 109–10, 126–27, 131–35, 158, 160–61, 164, 167, 175
Marx Brothers, 156
Matthew, Saint, 29, 45, 93
Medieval drama, 28, 126
Melodrama, 155
Menander, 27, 126
Menelaus, 63
Mercury, 105
Mercy, 28, 123, 164, 182–83

202 Index

Metamorphoses (Ovid), 2–5, 17–20, 22–24, 61, 63, 73, 90, 140, 148, 185 (n. 14), 191 (n. 9)

Metamorphosis (Ovidian), 16–27, 29–30, 74–75, 186–87 (n. 29), 191 (n. 9)

Metaphor, 6, 9–10, 15, 32–46, 48–55, 57–60, 68, 71, 76–77, 84, 99, 102, 119–20, 125, 130, 133, 145, 148; relation to literal statement, 33, 35–40; how metaphor generates metaphor, 33, 44–46, 53, 56–57; relation to simile, 33–36, 54; "pure metaphor," 37, 39; chain metaphor, 64, 69. *See also* Time-lapse metaphor

Metaphysical conceit, 7

Meyer, Robert, 93

Midas, 19, 24

Milton, John, 18, 85

Miracle, 23, 29, 60–61, 79, 92–93, 124–25, 127–28, 131, 138, 140, 142

Misanthrope, The (Molière), 156–57, 165, 167–68, 175–77, 180–81

Mistakes (as comic device), 53, 55, 74, 78, 123, 158–69

Molière, 5, 14, 26, 156–60, 165–69, 171, 175, 177–78, 181

Mona Lisa's legs, 73

Montemayor, 65

Moral appropriateness. *See* Poetic justice

Moral change (in a character), 16, 24–28, 30

Moral pattern of comedy, 158–60, 166–68

More, Sir Thomas, 85

Muir, Kenneth, 2, 144–45, 185 (n. 1)

Narcissus. *See* Echo and Narcissus

Necessity (determinism), 85

Nevo, Ruth, 186–87 (n. 29)

New Comedy, 30, 83, 107, 125–27, 131–35, 138

Newton, Sir Isaac, 149

Novel (as a genre), 25

"Nun's Priest's Tale, The" (Chaucer), 20, 85

Occult, 105

Odyssey (Homer), 63

Oedipus, 125, 175–76

Oedipus the King (Sophocles), 174

Offstage (conjectures about what may happen there), 72–73

Oliver, H. J., 190 (n. 5)

Olivier's film version of *Henry V,* 98, 100–101, 116

Olson, Elder, 155–56

Onions, C. T., 81, 191 (n. 8)

Ovid, 2–5, 8–9, 16–25, 27, 61, 63, 73–76, 78–79, 128, 131, 140, 148–49, 191 (n. 9)

Pan, 19

Parables, 45

Parody, 61, 69, 78, 117, 145, 157

Pastoral romance, 95

Paul, Saint, 28–29, 83, 93, 134, 189 (n. 18)

Pedantry (comic), 176–78

Pegasus, 105

Pelikan, Jaroslav, 189 (n. 14)

Peter, Saint, 28–29, 190 (n. 21)

Phialas, Peter G., 25, 73

Philemon (Greek playwright), 53

Phoebe, 72–73

Physics, 13, 47

Pinocchio, 20

Plato, 15, 26, 46–47, 194 (n. 25)

Plautus, 53, 134

Play within the play. *See* Reflexive structure

Plot, 41, 53–54, 60, 65, 70, 73, 77–78, 80, 89–91, 116, 122, 126–28, 132–34, 136–37, 139–40, 143, 165, 167, 175, 181; as context for character-change, 9, 16, 89, 95; metaphoric nature of, 34, 48–51, 57–58, 68–69, 71, 84, 124; as basis for distinction between comedy and tragedy, 108, 136. *See also* Transformation comic plot

Poetic justice (moral appropriateness), 11, 13–14, 16, 47–48, 94, 128, 130, 135, 141, 145–46, 158, 161, 167–69

Poetry, 33, 69, 71, 78, 137–38, 143
Porter, Joseph A., 192–93 (n. 6), 193–94 (n. 21)
Posodonius, 19
Potency as a heroic virtue, 110–11
Potts, L. J., 103, 155–58
Power, 114, 166
Price, Dennis, 196 (n. 5)
Prism analogy, 13
Proteus (mythological figure), 63–65, 67
Proust, Marcel, 104
Pun, 7, 9–10, 46–48, 51, 75, 99, 115, 130–31, 133, 146, 190 (n. 21). *See also* Equivocation
Pygmalion, 140
Pyramus and Thisbe, 17–18, 73, 78, 95–96, 191 (n. 9)
Pythagoreans, 19

Quine, Willard, 40

Rabelais, 23, 181
Rabkin, Norman, 71, 98–100
Rationalization, 65–66, 114, 163, 180
Rayner, Alice, 146–47
Realism, 51, 65, 78, 91–93, 99–100, 121–22, 124, 147
Reality (in physics), 46–47
Rebhorn, Wayne A., 188 (n. 2)
Recognition and reversal (Aristotelian), 6–7, 15, 125
Reconciliation, 5, 149, 160, 164, 175, 178
Reflexive structure (envelope, parallelism, play within play, story within story), 23–24, 29–30, 52, 69, 91–92, 106, 124, 149
Relativity theory, 150–51, 153
Religious awakening, 16, 25, 27–30
Repentance, 10, 28, 30, 52, 66–68, 122, 135, 139, 160–64, 169
Restoration comedy, 181
Resurrection, 44, 125, 196 (n. 5)
Revenge, 14, 82, 88, 95, 104, 123, 160, 164, 168
Reversal (as comic device), 74–75, 78

Richards, I. A., 32
Ridicule, ridiculous, 14–15, 26–27, 68, 116–17, 136, 149, 155, 165–66, 170–73, 176–79, 181–82
Rings (as plot device), 87–89, 125, 129
Role reversal (or exchange), 52, 57–58, 60
Romance(s), 1, 11, 17, 52, 56, 61, 94–95, 121, 123–25, 132, 145, 174
Romantic comedy, 1, 11, 16–17, 65, 121–22, 126, 145, 159, 186 (n. 26)
Romantic love, 25, 28, 68

Salingar, Leo, 186 (n. 26)
Salomon, Brownell, 193 (n. 17)
Satire, 14, 98–102, 157
Saul, King of Israel, 82, 101, 116
Schopenhauer, Arthur, 130, 141–42, 174–80, 196 (n. 4)
Seagull, The (Chekhov), 174
"Seeing-as," 9, 91
Self-justification, 177
Self-knowledge, 27, 80, 83, 90–91, 134, 162, 177; lack of, as subject matter for comedy, 14, 16, 133, 149, 171–72; attainment of, 14–16, 26, 48, 136, 151; Socrates on, 15, 26, 47
Semele, 21
Senex (New Comedy), 125–27
Settings, contrasted, 69–71, 78, 103, 124, 149
Sexual element in metamorphosis, 18, 22–23
Shaaber, M. A., 108
Shakespeare, William
PLAYS
—*All's Well That Ends Well*, 7, 17, 26–27, 31, 40, 46, 89, 123–32, 134–35, 138–39, 142, 194–95 (n. 8)
—*Antony and Cleopatra*, 9
—*As You Like It*, 5, 7, 14, 17, 24, 26–27, 31, 48, 63, 68, 70–71, 89–95, 100, 112, 151–53, 156, 169, 178
—*Comedy of Errors, The*, 7–9, 30–31, 51–56, 62, 69–70, 74, 109, 116, 121, 131, 136, 144–45, 150, 159–60, 162, 178

Index

—*Cymbeline*, 1, 7, 108, 136, 139, 146
—*Hamlet*, 6–8, 24, 48, 85, 139, 161, 176
—*Henry IV, Part 1*, 1, 5, 7, 10, 31, 48, 50, 96, 98, 100, 103–21, 129, 144, 146, 172–73, 176–77, 180, 196 (nn. 5, 10)
—*Henry IV, Part 2*, 1, 7, 10, 31, 98, 104, 107–9, 111–13, 125, 129, 146, 176
—*Henry V*, 7, 31, 50, 71, 96–121, 126, 146, 153, 192–93 (n. 6), 193 (n. 17)
—*Julius Caesar*, 109
—*King John*, 7, 120, 146
—*King Lear*, 2, 24, 33, 37, 108, 117–18, 123–24
—*Love's Labor's Lost*, 7–9, 31, 109, 131, 136, 155, 186 (n. 17)
—*Macbeth*, 109–11, 125, 139
—*Measure for Measure*, 7, 17, 31, 124–25, 131–36, 141–42, 148, 161–64, 166–68, 194 (n. 2)
—*Merchant of Venice, The*, 7, 10, 17, 47–48, 53, 70–71, 78–90, 92, 94–95, 100, 107, 116, 119
—*Merry Wives of Windsor, The*, 7, 17, 54, 120, 122, 186 (n. 17)
—*Midsummer Night's Dream, A*, 7–8, 17, 24–25, 31, 43, 54, 64, 69–78, 89–91, 95, 99–100, 116–19, 128, 135, 140, 142–43, 149–50, 152, 155–56, 191 (nn. 8, 9), 191–92 (n. 14)
—*Much Ado About Nothing*, 7, 17, 28, 122–23, 156, 159–67, 194 (n. 1)
—*Othello*, 81, 124
—*Pericles*, 136
—*Richard II*, 105, 109, 120
—*Romeo and Juliet*, 117–18, 145
—*Taming of the Shrew, The*, 3–5, 7, 10, 17, 24, 27, 30–31, 40–41, 47–53, 56–62, 64–66, 69, 79, 83, 89–90, 92, 119–21, 124, 136, 142, 145, 148, 150, 152–53, 190 (n. 5)
—*Tempest, The*, 1, 5, 7, 12, 14–15, 17, 28, 30–31, 41–47, 49–51, 71, 118, 124–25, 136, 138–43, 145, 148, 150, 152–53, 168, 178, 183
—*Titus Andronicus*, 5, 191 (n. 5)
—*Troilus and Cressida*, 5, 123, 126, 136, 145
—*Twelfth Night*, 7–8, 14, 25, 27, 31, 56, 78, 90, 109, 122, 131, 136, 145, 147, 149, 152, 169, 186 (n. 18)
—*Two Gentlemen of Verona, The*, 7, 10, 17, 25, 27, 30, 52, 62–69, 77, 79, 90, 92, 142, 145, 148, 152
—*Two Noble Kinsmen, The*, 136
—*Winter's Tale, The*, 1, 7, 17, 30–31, 40, 124–25, 136–40, 142, 152–53, 194 (n. 3)

Shakespearean comedy, 30, 86, 141–42, 147, 151, 160, 188 (n. 2); as meaningful term, 1, 144–46; distinguished from traditional comedy, 2–3, 149–50; self-knowledge in, 14, 26–27, 47–49, 90–91, 133, 136, 151, 162; overall tone of, 14–15, 149; stages of development, 16–17; structural features of, 52, 68–69, 97, 103, 124–25, 146

Shaw, George Bernard, 41

She Stoops to Conquer (Goldsmith), 158

Simile, 34–36, 45–46, 52–55, 57, 69, 145; contradicts corresponding metaphor, 34, 54; grammatical distinction (in English) from metaphor, 35, 46; as eviscerated metaphor, 35, 46; as basis for plot, 52; relation to time, 55

Smith, Hallett, 75

Snobbery, 121, 124, 127, 167–68, 181–82

Social emphasis of comedy, 129, 135, 147, 150, 175, 183

Socrates, 15, 26, 47, 150, 166, 171, 194 (n. 25)

Solomon, King of Israel, 100, 110

Speech act theory, 130

Spenser, Edmund, 193 (n. 14)

Spurgeon, Carolyn, 32

Statement. *See* Literal statement

Stein, Gertrude, 34, 38
Stephen, Saint, 28
Subplot, 49, 53, 56–58, 60–61, 77–78, 145, 160
Substitution, 27, 136, 162
Suddenness (in comedy), 67–68, 152, 176, 179–81
Superiority theory (of laughter), 67, 179–80
Syllogism, 38–39, 114, 174
Synge, John Millington, 196 (n. 5)
Synthesis, 39, 54, 56, 69, 72, 75, 102, 105, 112, 115, 119, 126, 129, 134, 140
Syrinx, 18

Tartuffe (Molière), 14, 156, 158–59, 165–68, 171–72, 176, 178, 181
Tautology, 34, 38, 55, 68
Telemachus, 63
Tennyson, Alfred Lord, 41
Terence, 15, 27, 134
Thomson, J. A. K., 185 (n. 14), 191 (n. 9)
Time, 11, 40–44, 50, 55–56, 103–7, 115, 119–20, 124, 137–38, 147–53; time dilation, 151–52
Time-lapse metaphor, 33, 69, 75, 149–53; defined and analyzed, 10, 40–46, 120; relation to transformation plot, 15, 48–53, 109, 132, 137–38, 140, 143, 145; pre-Shakespearean examples, 45, 148–49; relation to characterization, 46, 77, 96, 140; relation to meaningful ambiguity, 62, 68
Tiresias, 18, 24, 90
Tolstoy, Leo, 10, 88
Tom Jones (Fielding), 157–58
Tragedy, 155, 172, 178
Transformation comic plot, 9, 11, 52, 61, 70, 96, 103, 118, 121, 130; as distinguishing feature of Shakespearean comedy, 2–3, 140–41, 146–48, 153; relation to characterization, 13–14, 71, 78, 107, 111–12, 142–43; relation to time-lapse metaphor, 15, 33, 48–51, 109, 132, 137–38, 140, 143, 145, 153; superimposed upon historical events, 96–97, 102, 115, 119–20
Transubstantiation, 44, 189 (n. 16)
Turnell, Martin, 165
Twice-true statements, 37, 39, 77, 131
Twins (as basis for plot), 52–56, 145. *See also* Simile

Unities, the, 55
Utopias, 181

Van Doren, Mark, 98, 102–3, 117–19, 126
Vanity, 165–66, 170–71, 175, 177, 181–82
Virgil, 41
Voltaire, 164, 181

Walter, J. H., 109, 195 (n. 19)
Wentersdorf, Karl P., 98, 192 (n. 2)
Wheeler, Richard P., 195 (n. 19)
Whetstone, George, 134
"Wife of Bath's Tale, The" (Chaucer), 24, 51, 67, 92–93, 126–27, 129, 132, 140, 148–49
Wilde, Oscar, 181
Wilhelm Meisters Lehrjahre (Goethe), 25
Wilkinson, L. P., 20–23
Will-power, 142, 178, 180
Wilson, John Dover, 109, 193 (n. 14)
Wish fulfillment, 14, 47, 126–27, 130, 132, 146–48, 158, 169, 175, 186 (n. 26)
Wittgenstein, Ludwig, 2, 9–10, 36–39, 46, 77, 91, 96, 98, 138, 147, 153
World As Will and Idea, The (Schopenhauer), 174
Worth (intrinsic) vs. value (estimated), 123–24, 126, 128, 134, 138–39

Yeats, William Butler, 76–77
Young, David, 73

www.ingramcontent.com/pod-product-compliance
Lightning Source LLC
Chambersburg PA
CBHW011743220426
43666CB00017B/2886